Contributing to Educational Change

THE NATIONAL SOCIETY
FOR THE STUDY OF EDUCATION

Series on Contemporary Educational Issues
Kenneth J. Rehage, Series Editor

The 1988 Titles
Contributing to Educational Change: Perspectives on Research and Practice,
   Philip W. Jackson, editor
Leaders for America's Schools: The Report and Papers of the
   National Commission on Excellence in Educational Administration,
   Daniel E. Griffiths, Robert T. Stout, and Patrick B. Forsyth, editors

The National Society for the Study of Education also publishes Yearbooks which are distributed by the University of Chicago Press. Inquiries regarding all publications of the Society, as well as inquiries about membership in the Society, may be addressed to the Secretary-Treasurer, 5835 Kimbark Avenue, Chicago, IL 60637. Membership in the Society is open to any who are interested in promoting the investigation and discussion of educational programs.

Contributing to Educational Change

PERSPECTIVES ON RESEARCH AND PRACTICE

Edited by

Phillip W. Jackson

University of Chicago

.

McCutchan Publishing Corporation

P.O. Box 774
Berkeley, California 94701

Contents

Contributors

Geraldine Jonçich Clifford, Department of Education, University of California, Berkeley

David K. Cohen, School of Education, Michigan State University, East Lansing, Michigan

Larry Cuban, School of Education, Stanford University, Stanford, California

Samuel Messick, Educational Testing Service, Princeton, New Jersey

James R. Squire, Ginn and Company, Lexington, Massachusetts

Ralph W. Tyler, Director Emeritus, Center for the Study of Behavioral Sciences, Palo Alto, California

John I. Goodlad, Center for Educational Renewal, University of Washington, Seattle, Washington

Gordon Ambach, Executive Officer, Council of Chief State School Officers, Washington, D.C.

Marilyn Rauth, American Federation of Teachers, Washington, D.C.

P. Michael Timpane, President, Teachers College, Columbia University, New York, New York

Foreword

On May 15 and 16, 1987, the Benton Center for Curriculum and Instruction of the University of Chicago held an inaugural conference at the university to celebrate the center's first year of operation. Beyond being a celebration, the purpose of the conference was to bring together a group of researchers, practitioners, and producers of educational materials to discuss issues of common concern. This book is the outgrowth of those discussions.

As background to the planning that went into the conference, which in turn will help explain both the structure and the title of this volume, a few words about the center itself are in order.

The Benton Center for Curriculum and Instruction pursues a research agenda that is divided into three distinct, though overlapping, programs. The first, called "Instructional Methods and Materials," focuses on curricular and instructional issues as they arise within the context of teaching specific school subjects. The second program, called "Secondary Analysis and Research Synthesis," also looks at substantive issues having to do with curriculum and instruction, but it does so chiefly by reanalyzing large data sets from national surveys and by combining research results from prior investigations. The third program, "Historical and Conceptual Studies," examines the historical and philosophical underpinnings of past and present educational practices.

Given this broad spectrum of research interests within the center, we naturally sought to invite as speakers and presenters at our inaugural conference a group of distinguished educators who share many of our own interests and whose range of expertise is correspondingly broad. We wished, however, to give our participants as free a rein as possible in addressing our common concerns. Therefore, we assigned them very broad topics to consider, such as "teachers and educational change" or "how tests have helped to shape our schools," and placed no further constraints on what they might choose to say.

Responses to our invitations were more than gratifying; they were overwhelming. We succeeded in attracting every person we approached, which must be something of a record for such efforts. Our good fortune not only assured the success of our conference; it also yielded a set of papers and talks well worth sharing with a larger audience.

In some ways, the presentations are even more rewarding to encounter in print than they were to listen to for the first time. Readers have the obvious advantages of being able to reflect on passages that arrest their attention and of returning to them if they so wish, neither of which we who attended the conference were able to do at the time. And much within these pages merits reflection and continued study, as will soon be apparent to the reader.

To maximize the continuity created by the authors' references to each other's remarks and to the conference as a whole, the original order of the presentations has been preserved. Geraldine Clifford's chapter, which was the opening address at the conference, comes first, followed by the four chapters by Cohen, Cuban, Messick, and Squire, which were presented in separate sessions immediately thereafter. The chapters by Tyler and Goodlad were originally delivered as luncheon and dinner remarks during the first day of the conference. The last chapter, a panel report by Ambach, Rauth, and Timpane on the relationship between research and practice, is an edited version of the conference's closing session, held on the morning of the second day.

Though the book as a whole treats a variety of topics, making it nearly impossible to summarize effectively, two recurring themes contribute to its unity. The first, which is introduced by Clifford and strongly echoed by Tyler, as well as by all three of the panelists in the final chapter, treats the importance and the difficulty of developing close and effective ties between the educational research community on the one hand and the community of educational practitioners on the other. The second theme, which comes up again and again in the four chapters by Cohen, Cuban, Messick, and Squire, as well as in Goodlad's presentation, focuses on the many conditions that stand in the way of educational change, the bulk of which appear to have little or nothing to do with whether or not the change in question has the backing of research.

Both of these are familiar themes to educators. We have all heard on innumerable occasions the sad lament about the gap between research and practice, a gap made wider, we are told, by differences in outlook and perhaps even psychological makeup between researchers and practitioners. We also are well aware that educational change is difficult to bring about, with or without the help of research. It occurs very slowly, when it occurs at all. That too is not news.

What we have not yet heard, at least not sufficiently, and what we are not yet fully aware of is how these recurring themes, shopworn though they may be, are given shape and substance within the context of today's schools and under today's changing social and cultural conditions. That is what the present volume does for us. By helping to bring us up to date on a variety of educational topics, while sounding themes that by now have become perennial, it serves to restore our determination to narrow the gap between research and practice and to press for educational change, no matter how difficult or slow the process may be.

Clifford traces the history of the relationship between the worlds of educational research and practice as it has been worked out in the design and operation of professional schools of education. Her story is not terribly encouraging, I must say, particularly for those of us who continue to work in research-oriented schools and colleges of education. But it is one to which we must listen and from which we must learn. Clifford calls for renewed attempts on the part of the research community to join with practitioners in attacking the wide range of problems now facing our schools.

Tyler's message is similar, though a bit more optimistic. His capsule depictions of the Eight Year Study and of more recent research on the education of the disadvantaged not only show that a close tie between research and practice is possible; they highlight some of the conditions that may be necessary for it to happen. All three contributors to the final chapter also call for a renewed effort to bring the communities of researchers and practitioners closer together. Ambach goes at the problem from the perspective of a state school officer. He identifies three major issues that call for immediate attention and asks researchers to tackle them. Rauth, speaking as a representative of a major teachers' organization, outlines the difficulties that stand in the way of teachers' use of research and goes on to describe recent attempts to overcome those difficulties. Timpane, drawing on his experience as a former director of the National Institute of Education, points to past errors made by social scientists in the name of educational improvement and cautions against making them again.

The forces that stand in the way of educational change, leaving aside the notoriously strained relationship between researchers and practitioners, are spelled out in considerable detail in the central chapters of the book. Both Cohen and Cuban look at those forces as they relate to how teachers teach, though each does so in a different way. Cohen seeks to understand why teachers do not adopt the kinds of teaching methods advocated by Dewey and other reformers. He skillfully enumerates the various constraints that contribute to their inability and unwillingness to do so. He shows that many of the problems facing teachers are shared by other occupations that have human improvement as their goal. Cuban also looks at why teachers do not change. He brings to our attention "the power of organizational settings, cultural norms, and the individual teacher's beliefs in shaping classroom behavior." He proposes we scale down our ambitions for change while seeking to better understand the inherent contradictions within our system of schooling.

Messick is sensitive to both the benefits and the difficulties occasioned by the introduction of tests into the schools. On balance, he sees the testing movement as beneficial and as open to continual improvement, though he is mindful of the many criticisms that have been directed at tests, and he is responsive to them.

In Messick's view, much more would be lost than gained by eliminating tests from our schools.

Squire's well-documented review of research on the textbooks shows just how complicated the analysis of teaching materials can be. It also reveals how research on those materials, specifically textbooks, has at times yielded answers that, if not wrong, were at least unacceptable to practitioners. Here again we encounter yet another way in which the gap between research and practice may be inadvertently enlarged.

Goodlad recounts his own experience of being sidetracked and frustrated by curricular arrangements and responsibilities that stood in the way of innovative teaching. His colorful examples point to problems with which many teachers are familiar. He ends by encouraging us to reconsider those sources of integration that he, following Tyler, calls "organizing centers." These preserve a lesson's unity, giving meaning and focus to what would otherwise be a fragmented and ultimately worthless endeavor.

These brief remarks do not do justice to the intellectual richness of what you are about to read. They are meant only to orient those who may wonder how this volume came into being and why it bears the title it does. We at the Benton Center are proud to have played a part in its creation.

Finally, I wish to thank Diane Bowers for her invaluable aid in arranging the center's inaugural conference and in overseeing the preparation of its proceedings for publication. Kenneth Rehage edited the entire manuscript with scrupulous care, for which I am also very grateful.

Philip W. Jackson

Director, Benton Center for

Curriculum and Instruction

September 1987

1

The Professional School and Its Publics

Geraldine Jonçich Clifford

The institution that sponsors this conference on "Teachers, Curricula, and Schools" represents a class of professional schools the first of which appeared in Iowa a century ago: the university professorship, school, college, or department of pedagogy. The University of Chicago has operated an entity under at least one of these rubrics since 1892. In the course of their histories, schools of education have taken various steps to do what the heirs of Senator William Benton wished, in 1970, to see done at Hyde Park: "Study the acquisition and dissemination of knowledge and . . . ways in which new techniques and methods can be applied to the improvement of teaching and learning, especially at the elementary and secondary levels." In this chapter, I employ elements of their collective history to explain why schools of education have disappointed themselves or others in the achievement of these objectives, especially those specifying the *application* of knowledge of teaching and learning.

The Many Publics of the Professional School of Education

Whether housed in public or private universities, any professional school is, I would argue, a peculiarly *public* institution. This status comes from its intrinsic connection to those occupations that have exchanged a measure of their autonomy for a greater or lesser degree of privilege and protection from government. Compared to other professional schools, education schools appear subject to more sustained and oftentimes more conflicting views from those in or speaking for "the public"; they have, in fact, multiple "publics." Two reasons for this come quickly to mind. One is that the majority of learners and teachers—consistently around 90 percent over the past century—are found in publicly financed and publicly governed schools. When the national library was raised in Washington, D.C., one of the lofty sentiments inscribed on its walls was "Give instruction to those who cannot procure it for themselves." The public schools did that, while *also* coming to enroll most of those able to go elsewhere. This comingling of publics is related to a second fact: that schooling has been heavily invested with *public purpose*, including the objective of creating and sustaining a common culture and a shared loyalty. Belief in the secular religion of education has been, and remains, widespread in this pluralistic society. A typical example is this statement:

> No profounder duty confronts a state than the necessity of constructing sane and serviceable citizens out of the material of childhood. No higher privilege awaits the individual in this land of opportunity than the privilege of contributing to such an end. . . . Manifestly nothing can more profitably engage the time and thought of statesmen and sages than the perfecting of these processes [of education]. . . . The interest of the commonwealth in the result is transcendent.[1]

The author of these words, Anna J. Cooper, was the daughter of slaves and was a prominent Negro rights advocate. She was also a teacher—representing another of the *publics* of the school of education.

In what follows, I discuss what may be considered a range of the publics of our professional schools of education. At one end of this continuum is *The public*, sometimes denoted as "society." Its will *may* be expressed by governmental actions, and it includes such disparate interest groups as school patrons, employers, taxpayers, and, perhaps, students. (Whether students are the "ultimate consumers" of schooling is, to me, in doubt.) Next, in the middle range, are such other publics implicated in the past, present, and future of education schools as philanthropic foundations and teachers' organizations. At the far end are educational institutions themselves, represented by their trustees, faculties, and administrations. For the education school, the three most important sets of publics here are (1) the universities (including their critical organizational units of departments and faculty senates and committees), (2) school administrators of various grades, and (3) teachers.

Although in my own research I have examined in depth only the relations of leading education schools to their universities and school publics, I will offer some reflections on all three publics, informed by general historical study and historical perspective. In the spirit of consumer protectionism, first I offer this warning label: The ingredients include much selectivity, jumping around in the past, the telescopic fallacy (i.e., "making a long story short" or "putting big questions to little tests"), and a dash of hyperbole, special pleading, and pointing a moral. I do not subscribe, however, to what David Hackett Fischer describes as that school of thought that says, "The real question is not whether historians can be objective, but which cause they will be subjective to."[2]

The Public

The most difficult of the publics of the professional school to speak of with clarity, cogency, and conviction is *The* public. Is it even aware of schools of education, and does it accord them significance? In opening his 1985–1986 "President's Report" to the board of overseers, Harvard's Derek Bok noted the curious omission of references to education schools in the plethora of books, articles, and commission studies that articulate the current school reform movement. Moreover, he writes, "members of their faculties have played only a small part in the commissions," and "the surging interest in the schools has likewise failed to lift the stature of education faculties on campus."[3]

In beginning to think about this question historically, we may find it useful to recall that teacher preparation, the initial mission of the university education school, is owed to genuine nineteenth-century public demand for common schools. Wisconsin was one of several states where local citizens, newspaper editors, and some public officials opposed state universities, wishing to see their funding go to common schools. To establish a university normal department associated the institution with public preferences and moderated charges of elitism. In this spirit, the new normal department of the University of Wisconsin was characterized as "the nursery of the educators of the popular mind . . . the *school of the schoolmaster.*"[4] Writing in 1909 of Wisconsin and similar institutions, Helen Olin related the growing numbers of students to the needs of the public school system: "The demand for these teachers is making its influence felt in an increased appreciation of a university education on the part of those who would supply the demand."[5]

We also know that some citizens wanted normal schools only in order to secure for themselves more general education before public high schools were widely available or to increase local property values and commerce. But we do not yet know how the public thought about pedagogical training and whether pedagogues were responsive to that opinion. Probably *other publics*, especially academics and government officials, merely claimed to speak for a perpetually unprepared, inchoate public opinion. For their part, education professors entered into alliances with local and state school administrators to capitalize upon professed public concern about economy, efficiency, and accountability; the educational research movement and university courses in school administration, supervision, and testing profited from this appeal to public "wants." Other examples can probably be found.

It is far easier to demonstrate government as a constituency of education schools than to make the connections with something as amorphous as "the public." Education schools worked with government to effect something of a professional monopoly in training and certifying education professionals. It was *government* that certified schools of education as the preferred and most practicable route of entry into school careers. Although we lack evidence that the public wanted and was willing to pay for better educated teachers, the desire to qualify more easily or to secure more attractive teaching positions sent thousands of young men and women to normal schools and their successor institutions. In the early years of this century, as many as 85 percent of women students enrolled at Berkeley planned to teach. Nationally, in the peak years of teacher production (the decade before 1972), over one-third of all college graduates were education "majors" or the equivalent. Early on, envious university professors expressed the opinion that educationists had acquired power by colluding with the public's representatives. Thus, in 1916, an academic stated:

> In many of our state universities, even in some endowed institutions, the professional pedagogue is feared as one of the powers behind the throne. This is due to the tyranny of school boards and town councils acting . . . [upon] regents and president.[6]

Another wrote that inserting pedagogical courses necessary for the teacher's certificate into baccalaureate requirements demonstrated political influence "exercised, not in the meetings of the faculty— here the professor of pedagogy prefers, as a rule, to remain discreetly silent—but in the president's office and in the lobby of the legislature."[7]

This complaint reminds one of Arthur Bestor's 1953 identification, in *Educational Wastelands*, of the "interlocking directorate." America's lamentable pedagogy was the product, Bestor argued, of a national network of professors of education, state and big-city school superintendents, federal and NEA functionaries, and textbook publishing company officials. No doubt a few major schools of education figured prominently in building and maintaining a personal and professional interest group that was already speaking for public education in the United States before World War I. If most educational practitioners really do identify more closely with local schools than with the profession, the gulf between practitioners and pace-setting education schools, all of which are regional or national in orientation, is further explained.[8] It might be revealing to examine the educational views and interests of the teachers who sat in state legislatures in this century—there were many of them, especially representing rural areas—and compare them with the views of the education "establishment."

The Foundations

In contrast to schools of medicine, law, and business, Derek Bok describes education schools as programmatically unstable, unable to resist the "changing desires of presidents, foundations, and government agencies."[9] Like their host institutions, education deans sought support from the philanthropic foundations that played a large role in the late nineteenth-century transition from college to university norms and in the reform of American medical education. Endowment from the General Education Board was crucial at Chicago and Harvard. At Harvard, it permitted the Graduate School of Education to open in 1920, relieving the intense criticism of pedagogy coming from the arts and sciences faculties. The announcement of the gift stated:

> [The school] will train school and college teachers, school superintendents and normal school teachers; will conduct researches in education, and will have its own library, laboratory and model school, and a clinic for the study of children, their growth and work.[10]

It is unclear whether it was because of insufficient funds or academic opposition to the applied work and the influx of women it would bring to Harvard, but the proposed laboratory and model school did not open.

Education received more academic support for its appeals to foundations for research. Also getting more academic favor were the master of arts in teaching programs launched in the 1930s by President Conant at Harvard. Under Ford Foundation sponsorship, these spread to some other campuses, including Chicago, after 1950. Aimed at attracting into teaching bright students from prestigious liberal arts colleges, too sophisticated to put up with the usual curriculum of "dull education courses," such programs awarded scholarships and paid internship year stipends. But they seldom outlasted the withdrawal of foundation funding, altered the standard teacher preparation program of the institution, or created permanent ties of common interest between academics and educationists on the same campus.[11]

Despite this evidence of education schools' vulnerability to the changing priorities of foundations, their relations with philanthropy have not, I think, been broadly addressed. The influence, if any, of deans and professors of education upon foundation priorities and programs is, to me, unknown.

Teachers' Organizations

The relation between education schools and teachers' organizations is more fully understood. The success of state and big-city school superintendents in wresting control of the National Education Association from university presidents and academics, including the role played by militant women teachers, like Kate Kennedy, has been recounted. Their triumph in 1910 in electing Chicago Superintendent Ella Flagg Young to the presidency of the NEA finally convinced university elites, like Nicholas Murrary Butler of Columbia University, that public schooling had fallen to that "small but dangerous element of educational politicians and anarchists that has crept into the Association as it has grown larger."[12] The teachers' triumph was short-lived, however: NEA leadership passed to male administrators and their allies and mentors among university professors of education.

Following World War I, the combination of an intense teacher shortage and a war-connected sense of personal freedom—and, perhaps, the women's suffrage movement—produced a restive teaching population. "The war has quickened the social consciousness" and "new ambitions have been awakened in the breasts of many hitherto content with humble stations," wrote Professor James Hosic of the Chicago Normal School, a nationally known figure in the reform of the high school.[13]

Reporting on the 1920 meeting of the NEA's Department of Superintendence, Professor Michael O'Shea of the University of Wisconsin wrote,

> No one who kept his ears open at Cleveland could fail to note that there is some discontent among classroom teachers on account of what they consider to be the undemocratic management of the schools. They feel they have not been given a prominent enough place in the administration of the schools, and they intend now to assert their rights and their power. . . . In order to accomplish their aims, they propose to join hands with the Federation of Labor, and in this way they expect to acquire power to carry through their plans[14]

Realization of these teachers' expectations waited for decades.

Without making a systematic study of the teachers' union as one of the publics of the education school, it appears that, except for John Dewey, George Counts, and a handful of others, there were few points of either personal or ideological contact between the two institutions. For their part, union leaders and members paid little evident heed to education schools. In examining several years' run during the 1930s of the journal of the American Federation of Teachers, the *American Teacher*, I recall no references to education schools. That neglect may have been influenced by the more pressing economic concerns of the depression, but there are probably other factors also operating. In the case of the lighthouse schools of education, this is not surprising, given their prominent association with preparing school administrators and conducting a particularly socially myopic species of educational research. Would the story be different if we looked at local teachers colleges in cities where there were active AFT locals, even during the dark years?

In 1926, Otis Caldwell of Teachers College thought that, as teachers "improved in subject scholarship and in professional understanding," they were equipping themselves to share, at the least, with academic specialists and educational philosophers the design of fundamental curricular changes.[15] Between 1935 and 1955, the percentages of college graduates among elementary school teachers rose from 10 percent to 70 percent and among high school teachers from 85 percent to 97 percent.[16] Subsequent changes in the age and experience levels of teachers, like improvements in their educational qualifications, have not, however, been accompanied by significant alterations in the structures of their workplaces.

In reacting to a replication of his study of teachers' attitudes in Dade County, Florida, Dan Lortie wondered in 1986 if "strains are emerging in the system of internal governance of school districts—a system that continues to work in ways that mature, experienced, and highly prepared teachers do not consider appropriate. . . ." He went on to note that "changing the status of teachers significantly will require protracted consideration of alternative approaches; extensive and demanding negotiations, both formal and informal; and sustained commitment to that goal on the part of teachers and those who share their concerns."[17] In that statement, there is clearly a role for unions, and they did profit enormously from earlier strains in school governance and school-community relations and alterations in teacher welfare and status in the 1960s and 1970s. Nowhere in Lortie's statement is there reference to a role for education schools, unless we include them among those who "share the concerns" of teachers.

The relationship of education schools to teachers' unions seemingly moved from nonexistent before 1950 to distant and troubled thereafter. The explicit opposition that the American Federation of Teachers eventually expressed to the hegemony of professional schools in teacher education has been fueled by the perception that the premier education schools gave teacher education a low priority, when they did not evade it altogether. The word went out from unions that preservice and in-service teacher education should be field based and controlled by organized teachers. Unions presumably supported the newly enacted laws in Texas and California that required university teacher educators to secure field experience in schools at stated intervals, an action likely to widen the distance between "regular" professors of education and teacher education. The AFT tried to influence federal funding of educational research, in opposition to the research "establishment" dominated by education schools. Although this adversarial posture has been moderated lately by fears of the alternative, "warm body" programs being pursued in New Jersey and Los Angeles, the conditions set forth by unions are that teachers must dominate state licensing bodies and that education schools take teacher education more seriously.

If the appointment of a law professional, Shirley Hufstedler, as the first United States secretary of education was viewed as a rebuff to the teachers' organizations that did the political work that brought the department into being, education schools could take small comfort in that action. President Carter's advisors showed no regard for the professional school of education and its own long-stated claim to be creating the *leadership* for American education.[18] It might be propitious for teachers' organizations to become recognized as an important public of schools of education, with all that this implies in the way of reciprocity.

The Colleges and Universities

As education schools labored to bring the field within the orbit of the professions (as distinct from the trades or crafts connoted by union membership), the academic departments in their own institutions were becoming quasi-professional schools of their respective disciplines. Lewis Mayhew has observed that this means they were organizing their courses and cultures "to conform to their own professional goals," reducing "the possibility of a seamless education program for professional work" in law, education, business, or whatever.[19] Early on, the pedagogues asked academic departments preparing teachers to "professionalize" their subject matter (i.e., to teach it in ways that exposed issues of teaching and learning). But that ran counter to many academics' beliefs about what teachers need and to such other goals as maintaining traditional ideas about liberal culture or preparing future scholars for graduate school.

Along with the general inability to shape the character of pre-professional education to serve professional ends, education schools suffered what Bernard Gifford calls "congenital status deprivation" on their campuses.[20] However successful they were in securing the acquiesence of trustees, presidents, and legislators in founding and enlarging departments of education, they could not convince the academic community that they possessed a unique discipline or even a transmissible skill. The problem of massive indifference to the preparation of teachers among college faculty impelled Horace Mann to help create the first public normal schools in the 1830s; it persisted. In the later twentieth century, however, it was not a competition between different institutions—the normal school and the college—for the battle was joined on the university campus. In the intense competition for student "headcount" and resources, the faculties, administrators, and students of education schools paid a high price for their victories—a price exacted in minimal resources (especially for teacher education), isolation, ridicule, lowered self-esteem, chronic defensiveness, and understandable reluctance to devote themselves to the full implications of being a professional school of education.[21]

Given the low status of pedagogy, one may wonder why it was ever admitted. One answer was given earlier: Education programs were a sop to public officials or progressive sentiments about widening opportunity and public service. Additionally, in an era when under 5 percent of the age group pursued traditional higher education and aspiring colleges were attempting the very expensive conversion to university status, a large part of the bill could be paid by cheaply run, large-enrollment programs attractive to an under-served clientele: young women who aspired to become teachers. The investment need not be large because high school teachers particularly could be served mainly by the existing and undersub-scribed liberal arts and science departments. When women became half the enrollment of the ten-year-old University of Chicago, an economics professor explained this alarming, but also profitable, development: "The undergraduate courses are practically used by women as an advanced normal school to prepare for teaching, the one profession easiest to enter by them. At present, this part of the university is the main part."[22] The women who would be teachers became so numerous at young Stanford University by 1900 that Jane Stanford imposed a five-hundred-woman quota that lasted until the Great Depression reawakened interest in female tuition dollars.

The very universality of American schooling means that America's teachers, the student body of education schools, can embody neither an intellectual nor a socioeconomic elite. Attracting women and lower-status men to college bears a complicated relationship to the position of education schools on university campuses. These groups do generate operating income that may be important in times when economic or demographic factors find institutions with overbuilt capacity and underemployed faculty. But they do not bring social prestige or the promise of affluent alumni donors. Hence, the education school is a kind of *attractive nuisance* and a whipping boy in various circumstances.

When higher education boomed in the 1950s (enrollments went from 3.9 percent of the age group in 1900 to 39 percent in 1960), education schools were less necessary to the solvency of the institution than they had ever been before. Was it coincidental that this was also a period when they were under unremitting, pre-Sputnik attack from academics and university presidents? During the 1970s, they were made vulnerable anew by the collapse in the market for teachers; even academic bureaucrats, who cannot afford to act on the basis of simple academic prejudice, saw the sharply reduced education schools as targets of opportunity in the search for alternative sources of enrollments. The fivefold increase in enrollments caused by the baby boom finds many institutions today with severe excess capacity that a modest demand for new teachers will not fill.

Additional stress came with the radically altered relationship between the college and the public high school. In 1917, James Hosic wrote, "the chief problem of articulation is not *how* to connect the high school and the college but *now* to connect the high school with the elementary school."[23] Harold Rugg of Teachers College spoke of the conservatism of universities and their "retarding influences" on school curriculum and teaching.[24] But for his part, a professor of Amherst College wrote with feeling, in 1916,

> This huge and wriggling arm of the school octopus, reaching up to the college and sucking it steadily downwards, I would hack at with every sharp instrument in my grasp; and if I should succeed in cutting it off, the schools themselves, being forced then to follow the higher institutions instead of trying to lead, would be benefited as much as the college.[25]

Disciplinary professors could see themselves as antidotes to the technocratic and pragmatic thrusts of American culture, triumphant already in school keeping and edging into the academy—most notably through the education school.

Thus, the education school stood, caught, between two cultures: that of the professions of teaching and school management and that of the academy. Milton Schwebel, former dean of the Graduate School of Education at Rutgers University, characterizes the differences in the socially prescribed missions of the university and of the school: the one aiming "to reproduce the elite leadership of the nation and to produce new knowledge in the interests of government and the economy; the other "to reproduce the mass of workers and the unemployed."[26] If one is put off by such intimations of class warfare and exploitation, the concept of cultural clash is framed differently by Burton Clark:

> [T]he high school is biased against excellence in preparing students for the university. . . . Indeed, given its structure and agenda, the high school must set its face against serving effectively as a feeder unit for the university. [T]he university in turn is biased against serving effectively in the selection and training of teachers for the high school. These institutional biases are a distinctively American problem.[27]

So far I have suggested the attitude of the academic community, especially in prestigious institutions, toward education schools and the profession they purportedly represent. What of the posture of educationists toward academics? Failing to find acceptance and goodwill on their campuses did *not* provoke professors of education to turn gratefully to others of their publics. In fact, I would argue the opposite: that leading schools of education have consistently made the academic community their *most important* public, however unappreciative it was. The signs are everywhere. They show in the abandonment of teacher education, its subcontracting to the university's apathetic academic departments, or its relegation to the margins of the education school. They appear in the accommodations made to an academic culture that is suspicious of practice and applied research (*even* when they are lucrative); unaccepting of women as students or faculty; distrustful of part-time study, the value of experience, and mature students; and scornful of off-campus programs of professional development. Perhaps most ironic of all is the rejection of one's own doctoral products— preferring to recruit social and behavioral science graduates for the professoriate, so as to earn arts and sciences approbation and, perhaps, that dearest token of all: *a joint appointment.*

Such tendencies toward "academicizing" the professional school are neither new nor unique to education schools. The nineteenth-century normal schools showed the tendency because their students were too unprepared academically or because their faculties were uncertain about *how* to bridge the gap between the normal school classroom (the school of theory) and the schools of practice.[28] Placing increasing emphasis upon the high status, abstract, and academic parts of the syllabus is reported in virtually every other professional school, even those with high political and economic power and self-confidence. (It takes such forms as renaming engineering schools "schools of applied science," eliminating undergraduate professional programs, and passing over for promotion medical doctors engaged in clinical research and teaching in favor of life scientists.[29]) I doubt, however, that engineering, medicine, agriculture, theology, and their like will be as undermined as I believe teaching has been by the widespread perception—in *the field* and in *university circles*—that notable segments of leading schools of education evade the preparation of professionals, especially novices, and conduct their academic studies in isolation from clinical applications.[30] (Incidentally, a sophisticated member of one top-

ranked education faculty told James Guthrie and me that he
thought a desirable balance might be eight to twelve social and
behavioral scientists to "keep up the ratings" and pacify the
university administration and forty to build and travel the bridges
to the field.)

School Administrators

To propose to close an education school has not invariably
aroused appreciable opposition from professionals. This seems
strange given the efforts of education schools to professionalize
school administration. As early as 1916, an academic who claimed
to know pedagogues and their students wrote of the typical school
superintendent that he "represents a race of politicians which is
peculiarly the product of pedagogy. . . . The school superintendent
is becoming ever less a graduate of experience in teaching and ever
more, like the professor of pedagogy, a product of the abstract
science of education."[31] In addition, the superintendent is bound to
the pedagogy professor as the certifier of his graduate courses and
the controller of jobs in school administration.

In 1919, Professor J.L.V. Morris of Northwest State College
in Oklahoma began an exchange in *School and Society* with the boast
that the very best schools of education hope to "turn out graduates
who as superintendents, supervisors, principals and specialists will
raise the teaching profession to the high rank now accorded in
international circles to our engineers." To this a critic of education
schools retorted, "Why call such an institution a college for
teachers?"[32] Why indeed! It is quite clear from the historical record
that prominent educationists concluded that the prospects for
effective education lay first—and perhaps last—with the professionalization of school management. As Stanford's Ellwood Cub-
berley stated early, training of leaders for the "executive direction"
of the schools and study of their organization, administration, and
supervision were more important services than was preparing
teachers. The expanding and diversifying school systems created
positions that prompted education schools to offer advanced degrees in school administration by 1905 and certificate programs as
quickly as the states were persuaded to require them for school
managers. As Arthur Powell has frequently noted, preferment,

prestige, and patronage were given to those who were leaving the classroom. The status gradient affected even the principalship. Between 1918 and 1944, the elite High School of the University of Chicago lost eight principals.[33]

Nonetheless, troubling signs arose in the relations of education schools to their school administration public. School systems undertook elaborate curriculum projects without the involvement of local universities.[34] Like teachers, administrators blamed education schools for teachers unprepared for school realities. They might be saying, implicitly at least, the same thing about their own training. Is there a degree of alienation in that relationship that came to a head with the employment of social scientists without school experience in many university school administration programs and in their devotion to context-free organizational theory? Were the student complaints that Powell reported about Harvard in the 1930s and Mayhew found at Stanford in the 1960s muttered elsewhere?[35] Had administrators unconsciously noticed what J. W. Getzels verified when he contrasted the 1946 and 1964 *Yearbooks* on school administration by the National Society for the Study of Education—the first having a slight majority of practitioner authors, the second having none?[36]

Or consider the conclusions from recent surveys of the research field. The same study that reports that more doctorates are awarded in educational administration than any other academic field, except possibly chemistry, concluded that most of the research conducted to secure those degrees represented "intellectually random events"—trivial, without theoretical or practical relevance, the dubious skills acquired in the research process having little bearing on the practitioner's future professional work. The chief consolation was that the studies produced were unlikely to find publishers.[37] Another survey claimed that this research field is badly fragmented, "the doctoral candidate is the producer of volume in inquiry in educational administration," and that research in educational administration appears infrequently in the chief scholarly journal, *Administrative Science Quarterly*. The chief good news in this study was of the several-sided challenges to the traditional paradigm.[38]

Teachers

In contrast to the proposition that salvation resided in more expert school management, the secretary of the Wisconsin State Board of Education recalled the old maxim, "As the teacher so the schools." He granted that "[s]omething, of course, depends upon supervisors and administrators, but unless these officers can actually translate their ideals and practices into attitudes, appreciation and habits of the classroom teacher, their leadership is in vain."[39]

In 1921, Ohio State's education dean acknowledged that the state's teachers subjected the university's work in education to "caustic comment."[40] The teachers of Ohio were evidently as unimpressed by the professors of education as Wisconsin's lawyers were with the "narrow legal logic" that the University of Wisconsin Law School dispensed or preachers laboring over their Sunday sermons were with the archeological and philological musings of the Harvard Divinity School faculty. Some teachers may also have concluded that education schools supported the ideologies of bureaucratic management and "teacher-proof" curricula at the same time that they protected themselves from the image of being "mere normal schools" within the university by hiding from teachers.

Undoubtedly, certain professors of education did not despair of the eventual professionalization of *teaching*. Consider Harold Rugg, who taught at the University of Chicago and at Teachers College, Columbia University. On the first page of the 1927 NSSE volume on curriculum making (albeit in a footnote), he wrote

> If we had 750,000 teachers (or even, say, 300,000) who, like William Rainey Harper, "could teach Hebrew as though it were a series of hair-breadth escapes," the *curriculum* itself would stand merely as a subordinate element in the educational scheme. The teacher would occupy the important place of guidance we have given to the materials of instruction. But under the current hampering conditions . . . of inadequately trained teachers of large and numerous classes, heavy teaching programs, insufficient facilities and lack of educational perspective—I fear we tend to reverse the process and teach hair-breadth escapes as though they were Hebrew. Hence my allegiance to the curriculum rather than to the teacher as the effective educational intermediary between child and society.[41]

Unable themselves to remedy the other conditions Rugg described, teachers were acquiring progressively more training and "educational perspective." But schools' new managers claimed specialized, technical, and theoretical knowledge—including that of the science of curriculum making dispensed at the University of Chicago by Franklin Bobbitt. Thus, teachers encountered the problem later faced by nurses and social workers: each group struggling after the same university-dispensed knowledge that was in the more secure possession of the physician, school, hospital, or welfare agency administrator. At the same time, their fields were repudiating the vestiges of such alternative claims to professional autonomy as came from natural aptitude, womanly mission, religious drive, or altruism.[42]

The paradoxical contrast between the high regard for education and the low esteem of teachers antedated education schools by centuries. But some administrators and faculty apparently shared the disdain for teaching evident in the social classes from which many professors came. Yale's Henry Seidel Canby wrote of the opinion of Wilmington, Delaware, in the 1880s and 1890s that

> Teaching as a profession was regarded by my friends and family as a last resort for those who could not do anything else. . . . There seems to have been an idea . . . that the teacher . . . did his work in a childish world from which adult men and women had escaped by taking up the really important tasks of life.[43]

And given prevailing views of the moral superiority but intellectual inferiority and passivity of women, teaching could be dismissed because of its prominent feminine cast. Women inhabit a "gender world which is ascriptive, diffusely defined, particularistic, collectivity-oriented, and affective," Jesse Bernhard has noted. Such qualities contrast with the "achievement-oriented, contractual, specifically defined, universalistic, and affectively neutral" Parsonian variables claimed for the professional realm.[44] Cynthia Fuchs Epstein concludes, "the female and professional role configurations are painted by this society as mutually exclusive rather than overlapping or concurrent."[45]

Educational sciences other than sociology appeared to confirm popular stereotypes. When Columbia's Ben Wood tested college students in the 1920s and 1930s, he found that prospective teachers' averages were often below those of most college groups. As developer of the National Teacher Examinations, Wood aimed to see the NTE establish a "certain minimum in intelligence, culture, and professional knowledge."[46] Stanford's Lewis Terman classified some teachers as "congenital ninth graders." Arguably, such expert testimony confirmed the wish of many education school faculty members to dissociate themselves from teacher training, even if popular opinion was more favorable toward teachers than was academic sentiment. Although professors might think teachers' work unchallenging, if they thought about professors' work at all, teachers might have concluded that educational scientists failed to distinguish between the accuracy of something and its importance.[47]

Over time, a growing proportion of education faculty lost contact with teachers and a personal sense of the world they inhabit. University laboratory schools failed to get or keep the interest of faculty researchers. At Chicago, the early studies of Walter Dearborn and William Gray in reading and Frank Freeman in handwriting were the exception that proved the rule of disassociation. Laboratory schools functioned, for the few professors, staff, and graduate students who used them, like the freshman psychology class: a place of captive subjects, mostly for testing.[48] Elsewhere I have demonstrated extensively the relative devaluation of teaching experience in the qualifications of students and faculty in leading education schools.[49] By the 1930s, a federal study of the education of teachers nationwide uncovered the fact that, except in normal schools and teachers colleges, the significant majority of education faculty had no professional experience in elementary schools—as teachers, school principal, or supervisor. A slight majority even lacked any secondary school experience.[50]

To advance the many reasons for the chasm created between the influential education schools and teachers is not to condone it. Ineffective or disgruntled teachers *do* reflect badly upon education schools, even if they acquired the majority of their preparation in academic departments, and even if administrative action and school board policies inhibit the growth of teacher competence and self-esteem. Education schools are also vulnerable in that organized teachers can throw their political weight around in directions that further undermine the professional school's legitimacy in political circles, including those acting in and upon their own campuses.

Conclusion

In December 1937, the incoming chairman of the Department of Education, Ralph Tyler, wrote to University of Chicago President Robert M. Hutchins about some of his intentions. He wrote, in part, that the study of education should consider normative as well as instrumental and administrative issues. He advanced the wish for "a reduction in the tendency to glorify research which has no significance to mankind, and an increase in the zest for the study of questions that bear upon the improvement of educational programs in both school and college." Tyler advocated bringing the university into alliance with other community agencies concerned with education.[51] Harold Wechsler's analysis of the *School Review* during Tyler's chairmanship found that practicing high school teachers became authors in almost every issue. Given other pressures, these emphases may not have survived Tyler's incumbency intact. But I am hard put to improve upon them as a set of recommendations. What I *will* do here is to elaborate a little on what this might mean in the context of the late twentieth century—which includes, I believe, a disposition to acknowledge, and even revel in educational research as "soft science" in support of a still-to-be-codified craft knowledge of teaching and learning.

Through most of this century, the major schools of education, I have argued, made academics their *chief* public. The goal of a significant cadre of their leaders and faculties was the acquisition of what Mark Ginsburg calls "academic capital."[52] Today, however, most universities are enmeshed in the mean politics of "steady state" or retrenchment economics, confront the demographics of a declining youth population except among some restive ethnic groups, face challenges directed at the tawdry confusion of the undergraduate curriculum, and are unable to claim an end to the prolonged depression facing many arts and sciences graduate students. We read that "methodological turmoil" characterizes the social sciences and those professions that build upon them.[53] However, the American public and many politicians have concluded that public education is recoverable, now that the specter of school busing does not overshadow the entire enterprise. There is some reduction of the popular sport of "teacher bashing," although many teachers feel that the current school reform movement impinges on what little professional discretion they have. This combination of events offers a "window of opportunity" through which even cautious professors of education may climb. It leads to creative collaborative possibilities with schools and teachers—unprecedentedly hopeful, I think, in both spirit and form.

In 1958, scientist and philosopher Michael Polanyi attacked what he called the absurd ideal of strict objectivism, disregarded by the exact sciences but a destructive influence on the social sciences.[54] He began in *Personal Knowledge* an explication of the workings of tacit knowing. Influenced by this and related work in existentialism and phenomenology, at a 1971 conference, Van Cleve Morris spoke about the "phenomenological crises" confronting professional schools, given the challenges posed by the distinctive outlooks of ethnic subcultures. The teacher educator, Morris said, admitted to the faculty club on the basis of a claim that education is a science, "like any other science" that can be studied and taught about, is burdened with a "kitful of psychological, sociological, and biological concepts which are no longer relevant to his work, not because they are not true . . . but because they are scientific and his professional task is not."[55] Professional education needs a new view of personal knowledge, recognizing that connoisseurship in any field is "as much an art of doing as it is an art of knowing."[56]

Epistemological challenges confront teaching and researching within professional schools. To extend Morris's point, the black experience and the female experience now assert that "social science, phenomenologically speaking, is *either* white or black, male or female, and *not* the disinterested, objective, value-free 'quest for truth' it has always been advertised to be."[57] There is, of course, a strong inbred disposition to dispute contentions that the "as yet unmanageable requirements of idiosyncratic or at least subcultural phenomenology," the awarenesses and outlooks "learned in the street," do represent a form of knowledge with which universities must deal. Yet, some disciplines and professional schools *are* showing high interest in problem-based research. The September 1985 *Chronicle of Higher Education* reported a survey of research trends in twenty-two fields. Business schools reported more business researchers working inside business, with experience-rich researchers doing the work on the cutting edge. Realism and openness were reported in economics, political science, and law, among others. The conclusion of the survey was that, overall, "The work of a new kind of scholar-practitioner has lent vitality to research."[58]

As there are fresh ways to look at things, there are new ways for us to work with our publics. The phenomenologies of teachers, for example, are already being used by the National Writing Project and in the Institute for Research on Teaching at Michigan State University, where teacher collaborators usually teach in the morning and pursue research at the IRT in the afternoon.[59] It is also noteworthy that *all* the foundations faculty at Michigan State University—historians, philosophers, sociologists—are now housed in the Department of Teacher Education; the effects, if any, on its teaching and research are worth watching. With foundation and public funds, university-school partnerships are flourishing. *Are they partnerships?* When the monies cease, will they founder, *as happened before*, for failure to have sunk roots in either the universities or the schools?

With the Holmes Group's proposal for professional development centers, it is time to look anew at the lessons offered by the laboratory schools' history; perhaps some of our conclusions will be different. Informed by the situation at Chicago and in the spirit of positivism, Harold Rugg and George Counts wrote in 1927:

> [A]fter thirty years of curriculum-making in laboratory schools, one of the most regrettable wastes lies in the lack of definite scientific information concerning the results of these fine dynamic places of education. . . . [T]here are almost no measured records of the output of these schools. . . . [S]uch accounts as we have of learning and teaching processes in these schools are casual and retrospective—not systematic and objective.[60]

Another "fine dynamic place" was the University Elementary School of UCLA. Its education faculty was sure that it had much to teach the staff but little to learn in return about research questions or professional training.[61] But attitudes may be changing. Through dissemination and historical studies, we have learned something of the futility of curricular imposition in the face of the strong craft culture of the schools. More positively, what John Burgoyne says of management education may be true of our field: The problem is less one of relating theory to practice than of recognizing that there is theory in all practice.[62] Finally, in the first volume of *School Review*

(1893), Britain's J. J. Findlay described the master teacher as one impelled to develop his methods constantly and to impart his ideas to his colleagues, "to submit his discoveries, his judgment, to their criticism."

> Your successful teacher is almost always a missionary. For him, then, training means a discipline which shall keep his isolated efforts from running astray; . . . a set of principles by which he can check his plans, and can fit them into their place in the whole pedagogic scheme.[63]

Heretofore, such a teacher has gone off to the university to find a niche to do this. Why not in the Benton Center? Why not, with its help, *in the schools*? Failing this, another conference will be convened a few years hence, and, with Casey Stengel, we can all say, "It's *déja vu* all over again!"

Notes

1. Anna Julia Cooper, "On Education" (typescript in the Anna J. Cooper Papers, Moorland-Spingarn Research Center, Howard University).

2. David Hackett Fischer, *Historians' Fallacies: Toward a Logic of Historical Thought* (New York: Harper & Row, 1970), p. 147.

3. Derek Bok, "The President's Report, 1985–86" (Cambridge, MA: Harvard University, April 1987), p. 2.

4. Quoted in William R. Johnson, *Schooled Lawyers: A Study in the Clash of Professional Cultures* (New York: New York University Press, 1978), p. 151.

5. Helen Olin, *Women of a State University* (New York: Putnam's, 1909), p. 167.

6. Anonymous, "If I Were a College President," *Unpopular Review* 5 (January–March 1916): 64.

7. Anonymous, "The Professor of Pedagogy—Once More," *Unpopular Review* 6 (July–September 1916): 64.

8. Robert E. Roemer and Marian L. Martinelo, "Divisions in the Education Professioriate and the Future of Professional Education," *Educational Studies* 13 (Summer 1982): 203–223, esp. 217.

9. Bok, "The President's Report," p. 3.

10. "The Harvard Graduate School of Education," *School and Society* 11, no. 267 (February 7, 1920): 166–167, esp. 167. The "postponement" of the school for children was announced in the April 17, 1920, issue of *School and Society*, p. 467.

11. Richard J. Coley and Margaret E. Thorpe, "A Look at the MAT Model of Teacher Education and Its Graduates: Lessons for Today," Final Report (Princeton, NJ: Educational Testing Service, December 1985).

12. Butler published this complaint first in September 1987, in *Educational Review*, which he edited.

13. James Fleming Hosic, "The Democratization of Supervision," *School and Society* 11, no. 273 (March 20, 1920): 332.

14. Michael V. O'Shea, "Dominant Educational Interests at the Cleveland Meeting," *School and Society* 11, no. 274 (March 27, 1920): 384.

15. Otis W. Caldwell, "The Lincoln Experimental School," in *Curriculum-Making: Past and Present*, ed. Guy M. Whipple, Twenty-sixth Yearbook of the National Society for the Study of Education, Part I (Bloomington, IL: Public School Publishing, 1927), pp. 271–289, esp. p. 271.

16. Michael Sedlak and Steven Schlossman, *Who Will Teach? Historical Perspectives on the Changing Appeal of Teaching as a Profession* (Santa Monica, CA: Rand Corporation, 1986), p. 36.

17. Dan C. Lortie, "Teacher Status in Dade County: A Case of Structural Strain?" *Phi Delta Kappan* 67 (April 1986): 568–575, esp. 571, 572.

18. Roemer and Martinello, "Divisions in the Education Professoriate," p. 218.

19. Lewis B. Mayhew, *Changing Practices in Education for the Professions* (Atlanta: Southern Regional Education Board, 1971), pp. 23–24. In *College: The Undergraduate Experience in America* (New York: Harper & Row, 1986), Ernest L. Boyer writes of the loss of coherence in undergraduate education, the confusion of mission, and the operation of the marketplace mentality in the actions of some institutions as well as many students.

20. Philip Jackson observes that even the "disciplinists" in schools of education enjoy relatively low status in the academic community. See his "Divided We Stand: The Internal Organization of the Education Professoriate," in *The Professor of Education: An Assessment of Conditions*, ed. Ayres Bagley (Minneapolis: College of Education, University of Minnesota, 1975), pp. 61–70, esp. p. 67.

21. Geraldine Jonçich Clifford and James W. Guthrie, *Ed School: A Brief for Professional Education* (Chicago: University of Chicago Press, 1988).

22. J. Lawrence Laughlin, letter of July 25, 1902. Quoted in Rosalind Rosenberg, "The Academic Prism," in *Women of America, A History*, ed. Carol Ruth Berkin and and Mary Beth Norton (Boston: Houghton Mifflin, 1979), p. 321.

23. James Fleming Hosic, comp., *Reorganization of English in Secondary Schools*, Bulletin 1917, no. 2 (Washington, DC: United States Bureau of Education, 1917), p. 11.

24. Harold Rugg and George S. Counts, "A Critical Appraisal of Current Methods of Curriculum-Making," in *Curriculum-Making: Past and Present*, ed. Whipple, pp. 425–447, esp. p. 430.

25. Anonymous, "If I Were a College President," p. 65. It is the use of internal evidence that leads to the supposition that it was an Amherst faculty member who wrote this article.

26. Milton Schwebel, "The Clash of Cultures in Academe: The University and the Education Faculty," *Journal of Teacher Education* 36 (July–August 1985): 2–7, esp. 2.

27. Burton R. Clark, "The High School and the University: What Went Wrong in America, Part I," *Phi Delta Kappan* 66 (February 1985): 391–397, esp. 391–392. Clark attributes this situation to such factors as the extent to which the American system has achieved universal participation; the fact that high schools

are typically comprehensive and serving "both as the only mass system of terminal education and as the only mass system of preparation for higher education"; their being coupled with the elementary schools in curriculums, administration, and ideology; the deprofessionalization of teaching as a result of local control; and the monopolistic position of most public high schools in their communities.

28. A preliminary study of these problems is William R. Johnson, "Teacher Training in Maryland, 1850–1915" (paper presented at the annual meeting of the American Educational Research Association, Washington, DC, April 1987).

29. Mayhew, *Changing Practices in Education for the Professions*, esp. p. 20. See also the examples in David Warren Piper, "Sources and Types of Reform," in *Education for the Professions: Quis cutrodiet . . . ?*, ed. Sinclair Goodlad (Guildford, Surrey, England: Society for Research into Higher Education/NFER-Nelson, 1984), pp. 233–248, esp. pp. 237–238.

30. Roemer and Martinello, "Divisions in the Education Professoriate," esp. p. 220. On the distinction between academic professions (which value "enlightenment" and "truth") and applied professions and technologies (which value "success" and "reliability"), see also Talcott Parsons, "Professions," in *International Encyclopedia of the Social Sciences*, vol. 12, ed. David Sills (New York: Macmillan-Free Press, 1968), pp. 536–546.

31. Anonymous, "The Professor of Pedagogy—Once More," p. 65.

32. Harris Hancock, "Colleges for Teachers," *School and Society* 11, no. 266 (January 31, 1920): 139–143. Morris's article was published in the November 1, 1919, issue of *School and Society*.

33. Ida B. DePencier, "The History of the Laboratory Schools, the University of Chicago" (typescript, 1957), pp. 149–150.

34. The only mention of university involvement in one city's effort was the use of the library facilities at Washington University. See Walter D. Cocking, "The St. Louis Program of Curriculum-Revision," in *Curriculum-Making: Past and Present*, ed. Whipple, pp. 241–248, esp. p. 247.

35. Arthur G. Powell, *The Uncertain Profession: Harvard and the Search for Educational Authority* (Cambridge, MA: Harvard University Press, 1980), pp. 139, 152; Lewis B. Mayhew and the Committee on Administration and Policy Analysis, Stanford University, *Educational Leadership and Declining Enrollments* (Berkeley, CA: McCutchan, 1974), esp. p. 25.

36. Jacob W. Getzels, "Paradigm and Practice: On the Impact of Basic Research in Education," in *Impact of Research on Education: Some Case Studies*, ed. Patrick Suppes (Washington, DC: National Academy of Education, 1978), p. 498.

37. Edwin M. Bridges, "Research on the School Administrator: The State of the Art, 1967–1980," *Educational Administration Quarterly* 18 (Summer 1982): 12–33.

38. Normal J. Boyan, "Administration of Educational Institutions," in *Encyclopedia of Educational Research*, 5th ed., ed. Harold E. Mitzel (New York: Free Press, 1982), pp. 22–49, esp. p. 23.

39. Edward A. Fitzpatrick, "Problems Before the Normal Schools of Wisconsin," *School and Society* 11, no. 270 (February 29, 1920): 246–251, esp. 246.

40. H. G. Good, *The Rise of the College of Education of the Ohio State University* (Columbus: Ohio State University, 1960), p. 110.

41. Harold Rugg, "The School Curriculum and the Drama of American Life," in *Curriculum-Making: Past and Present*, ed. Whipple, pp. 3–16, esp. p. 3. Other comments in the same vein concluded that "the greatest hope for improvement in our generation lies in the construction of a curriculum which shall . . . overcome the handicaps of the present school situation" of large classes, "relatively uninformed teachers," the early elimination of pupils, and so forth (p. 6); "Lacking a half-million dynamic teachers, are we not forced to put into our schools a dynamic curriculum?" (p. 7); "The policy of delegating entirely to teachers the making of curricula would be as fallacious as was the policy of leaving the teachers entirely out of this process, and would likewise fail to take account of the indispensable contribution that must be made by research and by specialists who, by devoting their lives to the study of teaching in particular subjects, become authorities in their fields" (p. 240); "Growing teachers, better materials, and more effective methods of instruction necessitate constant revisions of the curriculum" (p. 256).

42. See Barbara Melosh, *"The Physician's Hand": Work Culture and Conflict in American Nursing* (Philadelphia: Temple University Press, 1982).

43. Henry Seidel Canby, *Alma Mater: The Gothic Age of the American College* (New York: Farrar and Rinehart, 1936), p. 151.

44. As discussed in Patricia N. Feulner, *Women in the Professions: A Social-Psychological Study* (Palo Alto, CA: R & E Research Associates, 1979), p. 2 and passim.

45. Cynthia Fuchs Epstein, *Women's Place: Options and Limits in Professional Careers* (Berkeley, CA: University of California Press, 1970), p. 23.

46. Quoted in Ann Jarvella Wilson, "Knowledge for Teachers: The Origin of the National Teacher Examinations Program" (paper presented at the annual meeting of the American Educational Research Association, Chicago, April 1985).

47. "Scientists must be able to recognize what is manifestly trivial, just as what is manifestly false. . . . The accuracy of an observation does not in itself make it valuable to science"—or to practice. Michael Polanyi, *Personal Knowledge: Towards a Post-Critical Philosophy* (London: Routledge & Kegan Paul, 1958, New York: Harper 1964, p. 136).

48. DePencier, "The History of the Laboratory Schools," pp. 61–63 and passim.

49. Geraldine Jonçich Clifford, "The Formative Years of Schools of Education in America: A Five-Institution Analysis," *American Journal of Education* 94 (August 1986): 472–500; Clifford and Guthrie, *Ed School*, esp. chap. 3.

50. The probability of having such experience was lowest in the class of universities (state and land-grant public universities and private, nondenominational institutions) in which the most influential education schools were located. See *National Survey of the Education of Teachers*, Bulletin 1933, no. 10 (Washington, DC: U.S. Office of Education, 1935), vol. 2, p. 120.

51. Tyler to Hutchins, as reported in Harold S. Wechsler, "From Practice to Theory: A History of *School Review*, Part II," *American Journal of Education* 88 (February 1980): 216–244, esp. 225, 228.

52. Mark B. Ginsburg, "On Developing a Critical Sociology of Teacher Education" (paper presented at the annual meeting of the American Educational Research Association, Washington, DC, April 1987), p. 14.

53. John Burgoyne, "Curricula and Teaching Methods in Management Education," in *Education for the Professions*, ed. Goodlad, pp. 141–147, esp. p. 146.

54. Polanyi, *Personal Knowledge*, p. xiii.

55. Van Cleve Morris, "Who Knows What's Really Going On? The Phenomenological Crisis in Teacher Education," in *Responding to the Power Crisis in Teacher Education*. Papers presented at the 1971 conference of the Society of Professors of Education, Chicago. (Washington, DC: Society of Professors of Education, 1971), pp. 64–74, esp. pp. 65, 68, 70, 72.

56. Polanyi, *Personal Knowledge*, p. 54.

57. See, for example, Jill McCalla Vickers, "Memoirs of an Ontological Exile: The Methodological Rebellions of Feminist Research," in *Feminism in Canada*, ed. Geraldine Finn and Angela Miles (Montreal: Black Rose Books, 1982).

58. "Major Trends in Research: 22 Leading Scholars Report on Their Fields," *Chronicle of Higer Education* 31 (September 4, 1985): 12–14, 18.

59. The claim is that "faculty ask better research questions, use more externally valid research methods, and interpret their findings more fully than when they do not collaborate with teachers. Teachers more fully understand and appreciate the strengths and limitations of their own practice and they become more receptive to new ideas and more analytic about applications of those ideas than when they do not collaborate with faculty on research." *IRT Communication Quarterly* (Michigan State University) 9 (Fall 1986): 1.

60. Harold Rugg and George S. Counts, "A Critical Appraisal of Current Methods of Curriculum-Making," in *Curriculum-Making: Past and Present*, ed. Whipple, 425–447, esp. p. 438.

61. Dan Lortie makes the point that such courses as "torts" or "internal medicine" have their origins in the problems of practice, not in the experiments of researchers. Teaching has not produced such codified, cumulative professional knowledge because it has failed to capture practitioner knowledge. Dan C. Lortie, "The Robinson Crusoe Model of Teacher Work Socialization" (paper prepared for the New York conference of the National Commission on Teacher Education and Professional Standards, National Education Association, 1965).

62. Burgoyne, "Curricula and Teaching Methods in Management Education," p. 147.

63. J. J. Findlay, "The Problem of Professional Training: Recent Movements in Germany and England," *School Review* 1 (May 1893): 281–290, esp. 283.

2

Teaching Practice: Plus Que Ça Change . . .

David K. Cohen

Americans always have been hopeful about education. But they also have been deeply divided about how best to promote it. Horace Mann, Catherine Beecher, and legions of other nineteenth-century school boosters were convinced that education would flourish in state-maintained schools. They believed that such schools could turn a rough and divided collection of peoples into a self-governing political community. Among other things, they worried about urban crime, Irish immigrants, delinquent children, uneducated teachers, and how to teach the political knowledge required if a popular democracy were to work. Some of these school boosters wrote in a sunny, hopeful voice; others were mean and fretful. Few paid much attention to teaching and learning: They assumed a simple pedagogy and that children would learn what they were taught. Partly because of this last assumption, they saw schools as a powerful creative force. They believed that compulsory public schools could make over an ignorant and unruly people and thereby redeem a threatened democracy.[1]

But many other Americans had a radically different vision of education. J. F. Cooper, Mark Twain, and other Romantics saw

27

education as a do-it-yourself proposition, carried out alone or with a few friends. They depicted education as an adventure, a collision between untamed impulses and real experience. More often than not, these adventures were played out in tough and lonely struggles to learn the wild country. But if the Romantics attended closely to learning, their conception of teaching was modest. In fact, the only real teachers in this tradition were the learners themselves, as they struggled with an unforgiving nature of unyielding masters. In Twain's lovely story of learning to become a Mississippi riverboat pilot, he notes that, although he learned from master pilots, he had no teachers.[2]

Because they saw education as a solitary adventure, these Romantic writers were great school haters. They saw the nation's spreading public schools as the antithesis of education because schools replaced compelling adventures with boring, formal instruction. Schools shifted the locale of learning from the wild country to slates and books. Learning from oneself, from those who knew the country, and from the country itself was giving way to learning from people who hardly knew anything—teachers, many of them women. The promise of schooling was of formal and rigid "sivilization," sure to stifle that wild spirit that the Romantics celebrated in America.[3] None of the great school haters ever took up a crusade against formal education; they much preferred to celebrate innocent learning rather than to denounce arid institutions. But if we believe such contemporary accounts as Edward Eggleston's, the literary objections to schools that I have sketched had broad popular roots.[4]

These two educational traditions remained more or less distinct during most of the nineteenth century. They still have lives of their own today. One is visible in the persistent "boosterish" belief that formal education can patch any gash in the social fabric. The other is evident in a still popular romanticism of real experience, and in a lively contempt for those who know only books and can only teach. But late in the last century, John Dewey changed everything for American education when he joined these two divergent faiths. He announced that the innocent education, which the Romantics had celebrated, could occur in the schools that they had damned. He argued that public schools, boosted for their power to put a common stamp on rebellious outsiders and rancorous strangers, could nurture the risky, adventurous, quirky learning that Twain had found on the river.

This was Dewey's most astonishing idea: that education (in the Romantic sense) was possible in schools. It was not his alone, but he was easily its greatest apostle, and it may have been his greatest contribution. He drew on a stream of passionate school hating for his conception of learning and education, and like the other Romantics, Dewey was a good school hater. But unlike them, he hated only the schools that happened to exist. Unlike them, he was a tireless evangelist for the idea that existing schools could be redeemed, that schools could foster adventure and build on idiosyncracy. And unlike the earlier school haters, who had believed that the education they cherished would wither in the mere vicinity of formal instruction, Dewey insisted that it could flourish in schools. Indeed, he argued that education would be perfectly natural in schools, perhaps even easy. He devoted little attention to explaining why it had never happened before, but he seems to have thought that it was only because people had not decided that it should happen, and had not devoted themselves to the task.[5]

Dewey's synthesis of these two traditions offered Americans a new vision of what schools could do. They could harmonize real experience and academic learning. They could break down the walls between schools and communities. They could replace the arid regime of drill and practice with spontaneous discovery and excited learning. This vision implied an extraordinary new conception of teaching. Teachers would have to be knowledgeable about experience, academic knowledge, and learning, knowing these territories as well as mountain guides knew theirs. Teachers would then be able to devise ways for children to "adventure" their way to real knowledge: to rediscover science and technology for themselves, to reenact the essential history of the race, and to re-solve the great problems of human thought and history. Teachers would have to become a species of mental mountaineer, finding bridges between innocent curiosity and the great store of human knowledge and leading children in the great adventures from one to the other. Such teachers could make schools into places in which everyone would learn and love it. And, good small-town New England boy that he was, Dewey firmly believed that everyone could learn the same essential lessons in schools, even though they would pursue somewhat different paths. Teachers would thus help turn Americans into a single people, competent and thoughtful, independent and cooperative.

This was an astonishing vision. It remarkably expanded the aims of schooling. It greatly broadened the schools' embrace to include the most contrary Americans: cowboys and Indians, children and scientists, haters of school and lovers of education. And it therefore radically reimagined the nature of teaching. Dewey's vision helped create a new faith in schools as innocent institutions, which may be one of our most distinctive inventions. His vision also gave a real boost to the still youthful tradition of innovative teaching on which he had drawn so heavily. The decades in which Dewey produced so much of his educational writing (1890–1910) also saw the flowering of many efforts to invent new instructional practices, to build the new education of which he wrote so often.

Despite that early flowering, the legacy of Dewey and his early allies has been oddly mixed. Many studies during this century have claimed that the innovations they championed have had slow and heavy going. Capping this line of work recently, Larry Cuban concluded that Progressive ideas about instruction have made only modest headway in practice, at best.[6] But if Dewey's new vision did not affect American schools as profoundly as many had hoped, it did have a great impact on Americans' view of schools and on ideas about how to evaluate them. When Mark Twain wrote *The Adventures of Huckleberry Finn*, the best that any good school hater could do was to write about the evils of schools and the virtues of stealing away from them into the woods or down to the river. But John Dewey taught that we could change schools, that we could bring our woods-and-rivers adventures into the classrooms, and enrich both in the process.[7] By fusing American traditions of hating and boosting schools, Dewey helped to set new standards for judging formal education. He helped to make it legitimate to expect intellectual adventure as a regular part of any neighborhood school.

Dewey's synthesis thus gave Americans something new and different to hate about schools: not just their sterility compared to woods and streams, but their failure to produce intellectual adventure in standard classrooms. His vision therefore gave new and potent content to America's old habit of school hating. Not surprisingly, this change in our ideas about what schools could do had its effects on educators. School hating soon became a staple in the educational mainstream: Dewey's ideas helped teachers, administrators, and school reformers become articulate critics of schools' formality and traditionalism and their lack of adventure and excitement.

Another way to put all this is that Dewey helped create a new social problem: schools that refused to change or failed to change, schools that stuck to the bad old ways in spite of the good new education. This could not have been a problem for most of the nineteenth century because the chief changes that Americans desired from schools then was their expansion, and that occurred with great speed. But the lack of innovation began to become a problem at the end of the century, when Dewey and his allies helped convince Americans that schools could do things that had rarely been imagined for them.

These new ideas about what to expect from schools revised our views about what needed to be explained about them. For Twain and other school haters, what had needed to be explained was simple: How could such strange institutions exist in this wild and innocent land? How would they spoil it, and how quickly? But after Dewey, something new needed to be explained: Why did schools remain in their hated old condition? Given the new light, why did they not change?

Explaining Failure

I explore the answers offered thus far, in part because I doubt their adequacy and in part because I question the way the issues have been posed. Although there have been many efforts to change instruction, I restrict myself to a broad tradition of efforts to make teaching more adventurous, a tradition that embraces Dewey's progressivism, discovery learning, Jerome Bruner's ideas about learning, and most of the curriculum reforms of the 1950s. This tradition is not marked by doctrinal coherence or consistency, and adherents have fought with each other more than a few times. But considered against the broader background of American education, the tradition is distinguished by several crucial common beliefs: that school instruction can be exciting, and must be if children are to learn; that instruction also should be intellectually challenging, that it must be attuned to children's ways of thinking, to their experience, and to their own efforts to make sense of experience, in order to be either challenging or exciting, and that some of the greatest intellectual adventures are to be found in the structure and content of academic knowledge. This is a tradition to which Dewey has made fundamental contributions. It is the tradition whose modest acceptance in schools many reformers have bemoaned. It is the tradition whose disappointing track record several researchers have tried to explain, and to which many other theories of innovative failure might apply.[8] I synthesize many explanations under four broad headings.

School Organization

One line of work has focused on school organization. Researchers have argued that America's decentralized system of educational government and our loosely jointed organization of schools give teachers enormous autonomy, even if their formal authority seems quite limited. When innovations launched elsewhere seem inconsistent with teachers' views of instruction, they have plenty of room to ignore, turn aside, pervert, or otherwise frustrate the innovations' intent and effect.[9] This line of argument is appealing; among other things, it paints a persuasive picture of schools' political and organizational situation. But it does not explain why teaching seems equally resistant to change in much smaller, more centralized, and tidy school systems, such as those of Australia, Singapore, or Great Britain. Nor does it explain why teaching appears to be very difficult to change in private schools and small colleges, whose organization and scale bear little resemblance to American public schools. So even if we find the argument from organization attractive, it seems inadequate to explain the relative immobility of teaching practice.

The Conditions of Teaching

A second explanation points to the circumstances in which teachers labor. Larry Cuban and others have noted that most schoolteachers must work with a curriculum that they did not devise, and often with materials they do not like, as a matter of local practice, state policy, or both. This restricts their opportunities to do things differently. They must accept a schedule that contains little flexibility for dealing with subjects and students and little time to prepare new lessons or reconsider old ones. These conditions further restrict their opportunities to change or improve their teaching. And their workloads are ordinarily quite heavy: Either they must offer instruction in a great range of subjects, or they must teach the same subject to many students. Many must additionally supervise extracurricular activities; monitor lunchrooms, hallways, and playgrounds; and fill out a small blizzard of forms. Most teachers simply do not have the opportunities or energy to try something new, especially if it is a demanding something. Finally, although their jobs are difficult and increasingly demanding, they usually are poorly paid and held in low esteem. This does not enhance teachers' inclination to take on the demanding new assignments that much innovation entails.[10]

Finally, many innovations ignore these conditions, from either ignorance or principled objection. Larry Cuban has argued, for instance, that most educational technology has not been widely adopted because it has been quite inflexible. Most schools had only one or two television sets, radios, movie projectors, or computer terminals. In the days before the Sony Walkman or the microcomputer, either everyone in a class used these technologies or no one did. Such rigidity meant that radio, TV, and films could not easily be adapted to classrooms in which there was any internal variation in students' work.[11] And studies of other innovations, like the new curriculums of the 1950s, showed that they were conceived and developed as self-contained packages, designed to be swallowed whole by schools and teachers. They were quite deliberately not adapted to the schools' curriculum or to teachers' concerns; this meant that rates of adoption were generally low and that the incidence of what sponsors viewed as misuse was relatively high.[12]

If these considerations account for the absence of much innovation in teaching, then one would expect teachers' work to be much more innovative when these conditions were absent. As a matter of fact, teachers in scores of colleges, universities, and private schools work under much different conditions than most schoolteachers. Their teaching loads are much lighter. They either make up their curriculum themselves, or they have a large role in devising them with colleagues. They have a great deal of time to prepare classes yet to come and plenty of time to reconsider those just presented. They use the books and other materials they choose. They are rarely supervised or evaluated by anyone else. They have little paperwork and are held in higher esteem than teachers in the lower grades in public schools. For all of these reasons and others, then, their teaching should be appreciably different than what is observed in public schools—if the conditions of teaching cause what is observed in public schools. But virtually all reports on teaching in colleges, universities, and private schools suggest that it is remarkably similar to what is observed in public schools. Lecture and recitation are the rule. Many students are bored. Rote learning is the rule. When instruction is better at such places, it seems to be due to more selected and capable students and to teachers who know more about their subjects than to innovative pedagogy.[13]

I do not argue that teaching conditions have no effect on public schoolteachers' work. But these examples strongly suggest that these conditions are insufficient to explain the qualities in that work that have been so deplored by reformers or to account for teachers' resistance to adventurous instruction.

Flaws in Reform

A third explanation focuses on frailties in the reforms. One common view is that there have been inadequate resources to do the job: too little money, too few people, or both.[14] Another explanation points to heavy-handed administration, which frustrates reform by pressing it without consideration of teachers' concerns. Another points to rapid changes in political signals that dissipate the momentum of reform. Still another focuses on deficiencies in curriculum, in teacher preparation, and in technical support for reform.[15]

These are all arguments with understandable appeal for education reformers. And each is plausible, for at nearly any given time, reform has been hampered by such frailties. But if we step back a few paces, we can see problems with these explanations. Although public education does suffer with significant resource constraints, these have greatly diminished since World War I. Unit expenditures on education (adjusted for inflation) have grown astonishingly.[16] Class sizes have shrunk by nearly half. Books and other materials are abundant by any past standard and are much more lively and varied. Yet there is no evidence that change in instruction has become easier, or more rapid, as a result of these greatly increased resources. To persist with this explanation is thus to agree that practice will not change any time soon because there is no reason to expect even greater resource increases. Nor is it plausible to explain the slow pace of instructional reform with technical deficiencies, such as the lack of good alternatives in curriculum, good ideas about instruction, or good people in teaching or in teacher education. Many more improvements could be made in each of these areas, and others as well. But inherited patterns of instruction have persisted through the provision of the new curricula and other instructional improvements that reformers desired. They have persisted as well through dramatic improvements in the education of American teachers and in teacher education. If such past resource improvements had little or no apparent effect on teaching, how much more would be required to do the trick?

Incentives for Change

A fourth sort of explanation focuses on incentives. Free market economists and reformers of other persuasions have argued that incentives for innovation are weak because public schools are nearly devoid of competition. They are maintained by government grants and insulated from politics by layers of bureaucracy. As a result, schools are said to be relatively immune to pressures for performance.[17] Decisions about the adoption or use of innovations are not much affected by the organizations' need to survive or prosper, for schools will go on and salaries will be paid even if promising innovations fail or go untried.[18]

Whether or not markets for schooling would have the desired effects, other commentators have argued that the present organization of public schools creates disincentives for innovation in teaching. The U.S. school system is broadly inclusive, bringing in many students who care little for academic study. Community values typically support sports, socializing, and vocational learning over academic studies. These do nothing to enhance students' interest in intellectual pursuits or teachers' interest in inventive instruction. Virtually universal enrollment and compulsory attendance mean that education itself is an entirely ordinary and unspecial enterprise, and this also weakens academic commitment. Weak internal standards for promotion and graduation reinforce the sense that education is unspecial. In addition, they permit most students to get through, and out, with little effort. These factors further weaken incentives for demanding teaching.[19]

There also are strong economic and social pressures to attend school and few legitimate alternatives for those who find school distasteful. Many school administrators respond to this situation by setting the highest priority on quiet, orderly classrooms rather than pressing for serious learning and inventive teaching. These priorities are generally endorsed by school boards. Even highly motivated teachers, faced with many students who have little commitment to academic learning, must work within social and institutional constraints that do little to mobilize and much to discourage such commitment. These conditions do not preclude inventive and demanding teaching, but they often make it quite difficult. It is especially difficult for teachers to press academic work on unwilling students, for the lack of alternatives to school, the many social and legal pressures for attendance, and community and official support for many nonacademic features of schooling have made it perfectly legitimate to attend school without attending to education. Teachers who urge hard work on such students are in danger of becoming troublemakers; if they elicit a disruptive response, it will be seen as their fault. Many teachers settle for minimal academic work as a way to secure peace and quiet from the uncommitted.[20]

These arguments offer a plausible account of the social and organizational circumstances within which most schoolteachers work. But they do not seem sufficient to explain the glacial pace of change in teaching. There are, for example, schools that present a very different picture with respect to incentives but in which teaching seems little different. Many private secondary schools are neither compulsory nor unspecial. Students choose to attend. They can be thrown out if they are disobedient. Their families pay fees. And there is evident student and faculty commitment to the school and each other. Yet the teaching in such places is often little different than in compulsory public schools.[21] Colleges and universities often present the same puzzle. Many of these institutions are relatively selective. None is compulsory. Attendance is far from universal. Teachers are not responsible for student discipline. Many compete for students and funds in markets. Yet many students do minimal work, and many teachers require little in return for passing grades. Most teaching appears to be traditional lecturing, with little student participation. A great deal of it seems to be quite dull and to engage students minimally at best.[22] College and university teaching seems to have changed little during the course of this century. There is scant evidence that innovations designed to improve instruction have been adopted or used. Indeed, the evidence suggests less innovation here than in the lower schools. The argument from incentives is thus no more compelling than explanations that focus on the conditions of teaching, defects in reform, or problems of organization.[23]

What do these various explanations tell us about efforts to explain the slow pace of change in teaching? A first point is that the explanations have not been very compelling. Although each is plausible, there are equally convincing examples of traditional teaching that persists when the explanatory factors are reduced or removed. These explanations may point to conditions that support traditional teaching, but they seem insufficient to explain the existence of such teaching.

In addition, the explanations themselves seem odd in certain fundamental respects. For instance, each assumes that improvement and change are to be expected. Inquiries seek to explain the absence of change, to discern "barriers," "obstacles," or "impediments" to improvement. But where is it written that change will occur if only the "obstacles" are removed? It is easy to understand why such an assumption would be common among educators, in view of many reformers' insistence that "adventurous teaching" is possible anywhere. The idea that change is normal is particularly easy to understand among a people that embraces the idea of progress as avidly as Americans do. But why should researchers adopt these assumptions? Why should we accept that improvement is to be expected or that change is the normal state of affairs? It may seem un-American, but perhaps stability is to be expected in teaching. Instead of looking for barriers to change in educational practice, perhaps we should be exploring possible reasons for their persistence.

A related oddity is that each account assumes few barriers to adventurous teaching within teaching itself. All focus on barriers outside of teaching, in its circumstances. Yet to believe that any teacher can produce such classes is not to decide how easy it would be. Would it be easy or difficult? One very curious feature of virtually all reformist writing about teaching, from Dewey to Bruner, is that no one has tried to answer this question. Indeed, no one has even considered it worth asking. Theorists who seek to reform the practice of teaching write nearly exclusively about the practice of learning, not about teaching. Dewey, Bruner, and others offered extended accounts of how children learn, or should learn, but they gave little attention to how teachers teach, how they should teach, or the nature of teaching practice. One reason for this curiosity is that these theorists seem to have thought that they were writing about teaching when they were writing about learning—an assumption that nearly all psychologists in education make. Once the rules or laws of learning were figured out, it was assumed or asserted that teachers would simply have to follow them, and children would learn. Or perhaps books written according to the rules would be put into students' hands, and they would learn despite teachers' ignorance of the rules. This helps explain why so few reformers ever inquired about the demands on practice that adventurous teaching would make: They simply assumed that teaching followed from learning, that their analyses of learning had cracked the problems of teaching. It also helps explain why there has been little inquiry into teaching as a practice: into the problems that must be solved, into the skills, knowledge, and other resources required to solve those problems, and related matters. Such omissions may have been plausible in the first blush of enthusiasm for reform, but they seem indefensible after many decades of evidence that adventurous teaching is rare.

A last peculiarity in the explanations considered here is that they all accept a relatively narrow scholastic focus. Researchers and reformers see the sources of immobility in teaching in the schools' social, political, and organizational circumstances. This is understandable in light of reformers' view that adventurous teaching can be had anywhere, that if such teaching does not exist, it is only because schools have not tried to produce it. And it is particularly plausible in a society saturated with professionalism, for faith in the power of professions to change and improve life often leads to a narrowed focus on professional operations and agencies, in both research and reform. But it is no more self-evident that the main influences on instruction are to be found in schools than it is that the chief influences on health are to be found in hospitals and doctors' offices.

These points suggest several large problems in the ways that educators and reformers have seen the improvement of teaching and in the ways that researchers have explained the slow pace of reform. The problems have led me to reconsider both matters. And that has led me into the study of teaching practice in an effort to better understand the nature of this practice.

The Nature of Teaching Practice

Instructional Traditions and Reform

Contemporary instructional practices embody an ancient instructional inheritance. In this inheritance, teachers are active; they are tellers of truth who inculcate knowledge in students. Learners are relatively passive; students are accumulators of material who listen, read, and perform prescribed exercises. And knowledge is objective and stable. It consists of facts, laws, and procedures that are true, independent of those who learn, and entirely authoritative. These ideas and practices have deep and old roots in academic habit. By contrast, reformers have a very different picture of instruction. They see learning as an active process of constructing and reconstructing knowledge. They see teachers as guides to inquiry who help students learn how to construct knowledge plausibly and sensibly. And they see knowledge as emergent, uncertain, and subject to revision—a human creation rather than a human reception. These conceptions of instruction are a radical departure from inherited ideas and practices. They also are a relatively recent, still controversial, and very weakly developed product of modern intellectual culture.

Consider first the view that knowledge is purely objective—that it is discovered, not constructed. This notion has roots deep in medieval Europe. Recall that educated men of that age worked from hand-copied manuscripts that had survived the collapse of a glorious empire or found their way into Europe from more sophisti-

cated Eastern civilizations. Educated Europeans attached great
esteem and authority to these rare, often sacred texts. They studied
and copied them with great care, memorized and analyzed their
contents with minute attention and considerable deference. In
medieval reverence for the text, we find one source of later ideas
about the objectivity and special authority of written knowledge.[24]

The Protestant Reformation strengthened this tradition, for
reformers sought to get back to the holy old sources that the
Church had monopolized and to reorient worship accordingly.
Luther was probably more convinced of the absolute truth of holy
texts than were the bishops of Rome and more committed to literal
Bible study. Early Protestantism strengthened respect for the objectivity and authority of written knowledge, adding to medieval
foundations on that point.[25]

Some heroic histories of science have held that such respect for
intellectual authority was destroyed in the age of Newton and
Voltaire. But the religious sources of respect for the authority of
written fact endured for centuries. Most of Europe remained
Catholic, after all, and the Counterreformation was not exactly a
liberal movement. In addition, the individualistic fruits of the
Reformation grew very slowly within most Protestant denominations: Most were state establishments in which orthodoxy was
carefully guarded. Even in the more individualistic American
colonies, literal reading, remembering, and reciting seem to have
been the rule well into the nineteenth century. Little in the early
modern history of religion eroded respect for the authority of
written knowledge.

Early modern scientists did sometimes attack religious belief,
but science did not destroy respect for intellectual authority. Scientists and philosophers in the seventeenth and eighteenth centuries
worshiped a rational nature. They believed in the objectivity and
authority of sciences that would open nature's lawful heart to
investigators. The age of Newton and Voltaire began to replace
reverence for the authority of revealed text or established church
with reverence for the authority of objective and rational natural
facts.[26] And as the facts of natural philosophy were discovered, they
were written down in books. In an age in which scientific experiments were restricted to a tiny minority that had the required
knowledge, time, and money, the best that literate men could do

was read. The written materials of science became a new doctrine. They were studied and recited as faithfully, and often as mindlessly, as the old doctrines. The revolutions of modern science of course radically changed the conception of knowledge, how it was derived, and where its authority lay. But these revolutions did little to disturb reverence either for the objectivity of fact or for the authority of the books in which facts resided.

During most of the modern age, then, there was little argument about the objectivity of knowledge, nor about the great authority of such knowledge, even though there was dispute about which sort of knowledge was true. In all of the European and American traditions, religious and scientific, knowledge was believed to be factual, objective, and independent of human distortion. Only very recently have these old and deeply rooted ideas been broadly questioned.

A second element in our old scholastic inheritance is the idea that teaching is telling. In medieval Judaism and Christianity, the teacher was a voice for authoritative knowledge, which originated elsewhere. He was a pipeline for truth. The teachers' assignment included codifying and clarifying established knowledge in written commentaries on texts, resolving in the commentaries disputes between authorities or among students, and passing knowledge on to students in tests and lectures. Teachers were the center of instruction.[27]

Teaching as telling appears to have survived early modern Europe more or less intact. Philippe Aries has shown that in a small circle of elevated families, more gentle practices of child rearing began to grow in the late middle ages or early modern era.[28] But the character of school instruction remained traditional, and formal instruction was limited to a modest fraction of the population.[29] Churches were the only institutions of popular teaching until the nineteenth century, and there seems to have been no more room for give-and-take with the laity in Calvinism and Lutheranism than in Catholicism.

Traditional instructional practices persisted through the Enlightenment. Although this may seem contradictory for an age of reason, nearly all schools began as religious establishments. Teaching was heavily influenced by the traditional pedagogy that teachers had seen as students in school, university, and church.[30] In addition, the Enlightenment view of mind as a blank tablet, ready to be inscribed by experience, did little to dislodge the inherited idea that teaching was the didactic telling of truths.

The dominant Western traditions of teaching had a strong didactic cast, then, well into the nineteenth century.[31] In both religious and secular practices, teachers were persons of authority. They had special knowledge. Their task was to pass this knowledge on, intact, to students.

The notion that learning is a passive process of accumulation, a third element in our scholastic inheritance, was quite consistent with these views. The idea that people learn by listening, reading, practicing, and remembering made perfect sense in medieval Europe, when knowing meant taking possession of material already extant. The idea that quiet attention, obedience to teachers, and recalling and repeating material were evidence of learning was probably reinforced by early Protestantism.[32] In addition to their textual literalism, the new denominations were obsessed with human sinfulness. In Calvinist and Lutheran doctrine, growing up meant learning to control devilish impulses. Protestant doctrine portrayed upbringing as a contest for young souls in which didactic instruction and strict discipline were needed to tame the wild spirits. Children who wanted their own way were viewed as willful, disobedient, or devilish. Obedience was a sign of religious virtue.[33]

The qualities in children that have been celebrated in more recent traditions of pedagogical reform—independence of mind, spirited inquiry, and a willingness to strike out on one's own—were thus identified with sinfulness in early modern Europe. The new philosophies of the European Enlightenment reversed this view radically in one sense: Children were pictured as innocent rather than sinful. But childish minds also were portrayed as passive receptors; a powerful new instruction was needed to replace the old ecclesiastical messages. The idea that children could learn the right lessons, if only left to themselves, appeared only later.

All the extant evidence about instruction in the seventeenth and eighteenth centuries supports this account. Methods varied, but most teaching proceeded as though learning was a passive process of assimilation. Students were expected to follow their teachers' directions rigorously. To study was to imitate: to copy a passage, to repeat a teacher's words, or to memorize some sentences, dates, or numbers. Students may have posed questions in formal discourse, and perhaps even embroidered the answers. But school learning seems to have been a matter of imitative assimilation.[34]

Compared with this venerable inheritance, traditions of reform were born yesterday. The notion that children have distinctive ways of thinking, and that they will learn better if these are taken into account, seems to have appeared in America only in the early nineteenth century. The idea spread in succeeding decades, but slowly. In the middle of the century, a few school reformers— Horace Mann and Bronson Alcott among them—argued for a gentler pedagogy and respect for children's uniqueness.[35] A few contemporary authors of teaching handbooks and school texts made similar arguments.[36] The new tradition was enriched by the importation of Froebel's ideas later in the century, by a growing volume of homegrown writing about a new pedagogy after the Civil War, by the establishment of a few normal schools dedicated to a gentler pedagogy, and by the growth of the child study movement.

By the time John Dewey began writing about education, about a century ago, new conceptions of childrens' thinking and learning were thus becoming more available. Instructional experiments also were reported more frequently. More than a few teachers must have had a brush with these notions, for the texts and handbooks went through several printings, and there were articles and reports in educational and popular magazines. In addition, some teachers attended the reformist normal schools or their summer institutes.

But these were early ripples, not a tidal wave. Turn-of-the-century reports from higher education and professional meetings suggest that the new ideas were far from common. And contemporary accounts of classrooms revealed that the gentler pedagogy had made at best small dents in traditional practice.[37] In addition, the new traditions had just begun to develop when educators were swamped by a real tidal wave: a deluge of elementary students, including huge numbers of immigrant children, washed into public schools late in the last century. One reason this slowed the new tradition of pedagogical experiment was that educators had to scramble simply to keep from sinking under the tide of bodies. Another was that most schools responded to the tide with batch-processing methods of instruction and school management.[38] On both counts, educational expansion created barriers to the progress of a new pedagogy that had not existed before.

Traditions of instructional reform developed further during the twentieth century, and the process continues today. The notion that learning is a process of active construction rather than passive assimilation, for example, is still quite novel. John Dewey advanced a version of this view in the early years of our century when he argued that school curriculums should encourage children to reconstruct the great heritage of extant knowledge by a process of guided reenactment. But he did so in an age when most scientists and fans of science pictured knowledge as solidly objective and enduring, when the reigning psychology pictured the mind as more a passive receptor than an active creator of knowledge, and when Dewey and other reformers agreed that most school learning was in fact passive—that students added nothing to it, even with what psychologists now term students' "misconceptions." The objectivity of scientific knowledge had not yet been called into serious question, and other limits on scientific understanding did not begin to appear until decades later. The more radical notion, that scientific knowledge itself is constructed, not simply discovered, that science is more a feat of disciplined imagination than of quarrying hard facts, has begun to gain some scientific acceptance only in recent years. And the idea that minds actively construct knowledge is only beginning to be explored in psychological research and to be broadcast in educated opinion (despite earlier philosophical intimations and announcements).

I have argued that recent efforts to make teaching more adventurous are a modest and contemporary chapter in a much larger and older story. Our struggles over Dewey's progressivism, discovery learning, and related reforms are only a few episodes in a great collision between inherited and revolutionary ideas about the nature of knowledge, learning, and teaching. The collision began only a few centuries ago, though with the wisdom of hindsight, we can now see some earlier intimations of recent ideas. In the perspective of this historic clash, recent reform ideas resemble early manifestos in a long revolution or fumbling first steps down an unfamiliar path. It seems possible or even likely that these episodes will turn out to be only the first chapters in a much longer saga. If so, we could expect to learn much more about both traditional and innovative instructional doctrines as the arguments sharpen and as some advocates on both sides try to practice what they preach. But we also can expect that such learning from argument and practice will be slow. After all, efforts to sort out the intellectual content and practical implications of both traditions have only just begun, under the pressure of conflict and challenge. This is true even in the United States, the nation most deeply committed to the new pedagogy, where efforts to try the new ideas out in practice are isolated and fragmentary. Other countries, like France, Germany, or Spain, remain largely untouched by new instructional ideas and practices. It seems reasonable to suppose that we are working on the frontiers of this great change and are far from a mature grasp of what the new tradition implies for our understanding of instruction, let along for the practice of learning.

Social Organization of Practices

By itself, of course, the great age of one tradition or the youth of another proves nothing. Revolutions occasionally seem to sweep everything before them. But there is no sign of such a revolution in instruction, even though reformers have repeatedly proclaimed it. What is more, traditions of practice do not exist in an academic vacuum. All instruction subsists within social organizations, and they can affect the progress of new ideas and practices. Families, neighborhood gangs, and factory work groups are all organizations in which instruction occurs, almost all of it informal teaching and learning. Schools are another sort of organization, one that is dominated by formal instruction and scholastic learning. Reformers work on schools, but the extent of congruence between scholastic and informal instruction could influence the progress of reform. In addition, most schools are part of larger educational organizations that we call school systems. One way these systems can influence practice is by affecting the transmission of knowledge about practice—including critiques of inherited views, ideas about reform, and examples of improved practice. This is particularly salient to any discussion of reform because many changes in practice require new knowledge. The instructional reforms discussed here certainly do, at least so the reformers have argued.

Popular and Scholastic Practices. Many practices are organized as very distinctive specialties. Plumbing is an example. Few nonplumbers do much repair or installation. Entry to practice is generally quite restricted. Legal requirements for municipal approval of repairs and installation often virtually mandate the use of master plumbers. And the tools of the trade are costly to acquire and not easily mastered. As a result, relatively few adults know much about plumbing, and few children learn much about it. Teaching also is organized as a specialized craft. There are restrictions on entry to practice. Becoming a teacher is fairly costly. The work is commonly conceded to be difficult. And there seems to be a good deal of specialized craft knowledge.

Despite these specialized features of teaching, there also is an extraordinary amount of unspecialized instruction. Most adult Americans are unlicensed teachers in a great range of matters. This work includes everything from such basics as teaching children language and the conduct of social interaction to such ubiquitous incidentals as teaching children and other adults how to ride a bike, drive a car, tune a television, or purchase groceries. The extraordinary amount of unspecialized instruction signals an equally broad range of unspecialized learning.[39]

It seems likely that we learn a great deal about teaching and learning from these popular practices. This matter has been little probed in academic research on teaching, but there is a good deal of indirect evidence.[40] Decades of study show that family and community influences on children's learning are more powerful than the schools' influences.[41] These results are consistent with evidence on the political attitudes that schools try to teach. Many studies show that family and community influences on the development of these attitudes in students outweigh those of schools.[42] In addition, children communicate among themselves about the content and methods of instruction, and there is plenty of evidence that they influence each others' academic learning. It seems likely that this pattern also holds for children's learning about teaching and learning. It is difficult to see how they could be so strongly influenced by community and family in the content of instruction and not also be influenced by the modes of instruction themselves. How could students learn from the message without learning from the medium?

What do children learn about teaching and learning from these popular practices? Systematic evidence is spotty, but it suggests that family and community instruction is mostly traditional. Studies of child rearing find that didactic instructional practices are very common. Parents are less likely, for instance, to explain than simply to tell children what to do. They are less likely to question than to command.[43] Studies of attitudes about education also find that traditional ideas and values, such as belief in strong discipline and acceptance of established authority, are very common.[44] These studies also show that traditional practices and attitudes are most common among less urbanized, more religious, or working-class or lower-middle-class Americans.[45] Children from these sectors of society are highly likely to arrive in school with well-formed and distinctly traditional attitudes about teaching and learning. Research on child rearing also shows that the parents who are most likely to employ elements of the new pedagogy at home, or to support it at school, are highly educated and cosmopolitan. But even these seem to be a minority of such parents: Most seem to have quite traditional ideas about what should be taught in schools and how. Finally, the relatively few schools that adopt the new pedagogy generally enroll children from unusually advantaged homes.

These points fit with my historical account of knowledge, teaching, and learning. Both suggest that the old scholastic inheritance has been transmitted at least as much by informal as by formal instruction. Philippe Aries, among other scholars, argues that this inheritance rests on popular practices of teaching and learning that are conservative in character and have been passed down unwittingly from medieval times.[46] These popular traditions have been slowly eroded by more cosmopolitan instructional ideas and practices in the last few centuries, but the old ways are still firmly established. One reason is that the new pedagogy seems to be rooted in a distinctively cosmopolitan and upper-middle-class style of family life, in which parental discipline is relaxed, in which children have plenty of money and free time and need not work, and in which personal independence is highly valued. The spread of the new pedagogy outside of school thus seems to depend at least partly on the expansion of both economic affluence and cosmopolitan moral and political values to new segments of the population. Although there has been some expansion of this sort, there is little evidence of great change. Most high school students still work, and a very large fraction do so for a significant amount of their time.

Most parents' attitudes about child rearing still seem to be quite traditional. Although prosperity has increased, income distribution has changed only slightly and inconsistently during this century.

Another reason for the slow spread of the new pedagogy is that it is a regular target of political attack. Pressure groups and public officials frequently press traditional ideas on school boards, administrators, and teachers. Parents often press them on schools when they find that they cannot understand their children's homework. Campaigns against frills, newfangled methods, and educational reform have been a recurrent feature of American school politics since the inception of public education. Many educators and local districts carefully avoid new ideas and practices, and teachers who might embrace them.

Most reformers have assumed that traditional instructional practices are rooted in teachers' bad habits, and that they are obsolete, boring, and stupid impositions on children. In a sense, this is not surprising—reformers have been broadcasting for roughly a century the idea that children are naturally adventurous learners who would be so in schools if traditional teachers would only get out of the way. But my account suggests that, more frequently than not, traditional teaching in schools echoes and reflects popular practices outside schools. If so, the conceptions and practices that reformers wish to replace are not simply the impositions of bad old boring teachers, as Dewey and most reformers since have asserted. The instructional practices that reformers wish to eliminate contain views of knowledge, teaching, and learning to which many parents, teachers, and students have deep loyalties. In many cases, it is the reform ideas and practices that are an imposition. What is more, these old views and practices can be reasonably defended (and have been, by I. L. Kandel and William Bagley, for instance), even if they are unpopular in many academic circles.

Reformers also have concentrated on schools in their efforts to improve instruction. They have tried to change teaching methods, texts, academic knowledge, and instructional organization. This too is unsurprising: Most reformers have been academics of one sort or another, committed by profession, if not experience, to the efficacy of academic work. They could hardly revise family life. Despite that, my account suggests that school instruction floats on a sea of popular practices and that these practices have historical life of their own. It also suggests that popular instructional practice is largely traditional. Efforts to reform school teaching subsist within a society in which unspecialized and largely traditional teaching and learning go on everywhere. The old scholastic inheritance is passed across the generations, outside the stream of formal schooling, by families and communities, as well as inside it, by teachers and students. These popular instructional practices slow the reform of academic practice. It seems painfully—and professionally—short sighted to believe that our old scholastic inheritance could be easily or quickly changed merely by changing scholastic learning and teaching.

School System Organization. I noted earlier that another way in which social organization can affect instructional reform concerns the transmission of knowledge about reform. School systems vary considerably in their capacity to gather and transmit knowlege about practice, or the improvement of practice. Some systems (the United Kingdom, Singapore, and some states in Australia, for instance) employ formal inspection as a way to collect and spread knowledge about good instructional practices among teachers and schools. Other school systems have no such avenues of internal communication. Some systems are large and decentralized, which makes communication difficult, other things being equal. Others are small and centralized, which can reduce barriers to the exchange of knowledge.

The organization of U.S. education generally seems to impede communication about practice. American schools sprawl over so large a country and are organized in such a decentralized and fragmented fashion that it may not be accurate to describe them as a system. Although there is plenty of communication within and around these schools, there appears to have been only sporadic and limited exchange of knowledge about practice and the reform of practice. Communication about progressive reforms has been especially limited.

Most of the intellectual inspiration for Progressive reforms of instruction has emanated from academic intellectuals in elite institutions of higher education. John Dewey, Jerrold Zacharias,

Jerome Bruner, W. H. Kilpatrick, and Theodore Sizer are among the leading figures in these traditions. They and many of their colleagues concerned with improving schools held posts at Columbia, Harvard, the University of Chicago, Massachusetts Institute of Technology, Brown, and other pinnacles of academic excellence. Institutions of this sort also are the sources of most academic research, whether in the sciences, the social sciences, or the humanities. They were the institutions from which much criticism of public education as mindless and boring was launched during the Progressive era, the 1950s, and the last decade or so. They were the intellectual source of the curriculum reforms of the late 1950s and the places in which most of the curriculum development was carried out. They also are the institutions in which the new cognitivist or constructivist psychology, presently regarded by many academics as a basic rationale for instructional reform, flourishes. These institutions are thus the center of the academic universe. Their faculties have great prestige.

But prestige does not easily translate into influence on practice. For one thing, precisely because these institutions are at the top, they are quite remote from the thousands of higher and lower schools in which nearly all teaching and learning occurs. One reason is that the social distance helps to preserve the great status of those at the top. Faculty hiring is an example. Graduate students trained in the best institutions tend to work in such places, but students trained elsewhere rarely find their way to faculty positions at the top. They much more often wind up in the sorts of less selective institutions from which they came. If graduate training is an influence on instructional practice, that influence rarely seems to cross the great divide of academic status that separates a few dozen research universities from thousands of lesser institutions.[47] And of course only a tiny fraction of public school teachers are graduates of the highly selective institutions at the top. Most schoolteachers are educated in unselective institutions in which mass education is the order of the day.[48] The education of faculty in lower and higher schools thus offers few ways for critics of traditional instruction in the great colleges and universities to influence teaching practice.

But even if we restrict ourselves to ideas about practice, the elite centers are less influential than their great prestige might suggest, for these great institutions have devised a unique mission: research and the production of new knowledge. Their distinction is due partly to their faculties' discoveries and academic production and partly to their education of new producers and discoverers. But the mass of colleges and universities, and nearly all elementary and secondary schools, exist to teach, to provide day care, to prepare students for further specialized education and work, and to grant degrees. Producing new knowledge is not a major and often not even a minor part of their work. As a result, staying in touch with new knowledge that has been produced in the academic centers is not a high priority for their faculties. It is, in fact, superfluous for most purposes of life and work in the academic hinterlands. Some use it as a way of "keeping up" and staying in touch.[49] But for those who do not write—which is the huge majority of U.S. teachers, whatever their institution—it is a matter of personal preference, not occupational necessity. Most teachers in the academic hinterlands have no good reason save curiosity to consume faculty production from the central academic institutions. This restricts the influence of critical writing about traditional instruction, or research on instruction or learning, that is done at the great research universities.[50]

Another reason that the great centers of learning have contributed little to the reform of instructional practice is that their faculties are not known for great interest or accomplishment in this practice. Teaching is not the highest faculty priority at these universities, nor are many of them noted for excellence in instruction. Even the study and improvement of teaching is something that evokes either ambivalence or hostility from most faculty. In addition, most teaching in these places, excellent or not, is traditional lecture and recitation, as it is nearly everywhere in American higher education. All reports on instructional practice suggest that it is only infrequently either student centered or exciting. It appears that college and university instruction has changed little for generations.[51] So even if the barriers to the transmission of ideas or practices I have described were much more modest, the examples of pedagogy that faculty at the great universities presented would be little different from what their less eminent colleagues do.

In fact, only a handful of educational institutions, higher or lower, assign a high priority to cultivating the reforms of instruction discussed here. Bennington, Sarah Lawrence, Bard, and a handful of sister colleges are centers of such practice, as are Shady Hill, the Cambridge School, the Prospect School, and a few dozen other elementary schools.[52] This is a small and quite selective group of institutions; most are private, charge sizable fees, and admit only academically able students. They have succeeded in keeping traditions of student-centered practice alive for several generations, which has been no mean feat. But the circle of institutions has not expanded much during that time and may have contracted. In addition, only a few efforts have been made to educate new recruits in this sort of teaching.

So the great academic centers, from which the most potent attacks on traditional pedagogy have been launched, are not well situated to influence instruction in most educational institutions. Nor are they places in which the new pedagogy is particularly cultivated. Efforts to nourish that pedagogy are made in other schools, but they are few in number, selective in character, and small in influence. The social organization of U.S. schooling seems to reinforce traditional teaching and to retard the spread of reform ideas and practices. John Dewey might have seen in this situation those gulfs between theory and practice that he so often deplored, but the gulfs seem wider and their existence more settled now than when Dewey began deploring them.

From this perspective, Dewey and the other left-wing progressives resemble nothing so much as early missionaries. Like many people of the word, these emissaries directed their hopeful messages toward a strange and unfamiliar land. As such people often do, they assumed that preaching, along with a few examples of good works, would carry the day. The curriculum reformers of the 1950s were also academic missionaries. And like most of Dewey's allies, they chose to preach from their high home ground rather than to work in the strange lands they wished to convert. The word can be powerful, especially among those who live by ideas, such as academics at the great research universities, among them most of the early left-wing progressives and most current critics of traditional instruction. But much history and many studies reveal the very modest effect that doctrine—whether scientific or revealed—has on practice. It is not surprising that many reformers have seemed to cry in an academic wilderness.

Although some may find this account discouraging, I have not argued that reforms of instruction have failed or that they will. I have instead tried to place these reforms in a perspective that might be useful to both reformers and those who study such work. I argued earlier that those who seek to encourage adventurous teaching and learning work at the frontier of historic collision between traditional and innovative conceptions of instruction. And I argued that reformers also work at the edges of deep social divisions: between a few agencies that offer scholastic instruction and many that instruct informally and often traditionally and between the few select centers of innovative instructional thought and practice and the great mass of unselective agencies of teaching and learning.

Estimates of historical position and social situation are always imprecise and often contested. But if one can never know certainly where one stands in history or society, one always makes estimates, thoughtful or not. And one often acts accordingly. Different estimates can yield very different conceptions of what is possible and what is to be done. These matters have rarely been discussed in the movements for instructional reform, at least partly because reformers unthinkingly assumed that victory would quickly be theirs. They have assumed that they worked close to the culmination of a great but swift change, that history was not only on the side of reform, but was pressing vigorously at its back. My argument, that the advocates of adventurous instruction work on new historical and social frontiers, leads to some rather different views about the nature of reformers' work and the problems that reformers face. My account implies that reformers are probably working near the beginning of a great, slow change in conceptions of knowledge, learning, and teaching and in a time of instability in ideas on all these matters. Those who begin a long revolution have different tasks than those who conclude it. The early work calls for exploration of alternatives, invention of many forms knowing that only a few may succeed, experimentation, and creation of examples that suggest the possibilities for change. One task is to develop a durable strategy of reform. Another is to create a tradition of change. Another is to nourish the knowledge and commitment that may sustain both. Still another is to probe what may seem an overwhelming opposition, to discern its weaknesses and strengths, and to use that knowledge in shaping strategies for further change. But at the end of a long revolution there is little time for exploration, experimentation, and invention. The top priorities are to take possession of disputed institutions, to consolidate power and ideology, and to dispose of old enemies.

Different estimates of historical position also yield various evaluations of the success of reform. It would be unwise to assess the beginnings of a revolutionary movement in terms appropriate for its conclusion, among other reasons because that could only create an illusory sense of failure. But there is reason to suspect that this has happened in American research on instructional reform and that it has had just such defeating effects. Researchers have for the most part simply accepted reformers' assumption that adventurous teaching would be easy because adventurous learning was natural. There has been little discussion of what standards of success and failure to apply. The Romantic view that the new teaching would be sweet, and its success swift, has contributed to the conclusion that instructional reform has been slow and has perhaps gone sour. Our understanding of instructional reform, and reformers' work, might profit from more exploration of these frontiers and the nature of work on them.

Teaching Practice and the Risks of Reform

I noted earlier that there has been little analysis of teaching as a practice. Although many researchers have studied teaching, few have considered the nature of this practice. Few have explored the distinctive features of teaching or compared this practice with others. Few have tried to figure out what the key problems of this practice are. Few have tried to understand what sorts of resources—skill, knowledge, and others—are useful in solving those problems. Many useful perspectives have been brought to bear on teaching, but few have tried to cultivate a perspective that is rooted in the distinctive features of this practice.

In addition, the Romantic assumption that adventurous learning is natural has kept most advocates and students of reform from trying to understand what the new instruction might require of practice. Though reformers have deplored the sad state of teaching in American public schools, they have seen no great obstacles to improvement. They have argued that teachers simply had the wrong books, used the wrong methods, worked under the wrong conditions, or had the wrong sort of education. Like most good school haters, reformers have assumed that the problem lay in bad institutions or in the nasty old past. Once the institutions were changed, or curriculum pointed in the new direction, children and teachers could adventure off together. Everyone believed that such teaching would be very different, but hardly anyone thought it would be very difficult.

The intellectual designs of research and reform have therefore embodied a sort of mutually reinforcing blindness. Few reformers have probed their own program in ways that would have allowed them to understand its intellectual content or its implications for practices of teaching and learning. And few students of teaching have considered this practice in a way that would give them a basis for understanding—or even a curiosity about—the demands that reform would make.

Teaching: An Impossible Profession. Teaching is a practice of human improvement.[53] It promises students intellectual growth, social learning, better jobs, and civilized sensibilities. Teaching is one member of a modest but growing family of similar practices; psychotherapy, organizational consulting, some parts of social work, and sex therapy are a few others. Practice in all of them is quite unique. Practitioners try to produce states of mind and feeling in other people or groups by direct work on and with those they seek to improve. Emotional peace is one example of the results sought, and knowledge of arithmetic is another. Others include organizational effectiveness, improved management, or refined enjoyment of sex.

These ambitions, and the practices that embody them, are distinctively modern. Practices of human improvement are children of the belief, invented only recently in human history, that humanity can make itself over, that individual and social problems can be solved by the application of human expertise. These practices are living testimony to our faith that ignorance, poverty, corruption, anxiety, and other problems that have plagued humanity for time out of mind will yield to organized knowledge and skill.

Practices of human improvement thus embody, in many small ways, the great problems of defining and delivering human progress and of deciding about the adequacy of what has been achieved. These are problems with which most modern governments have wrestled painfully, inconclusively, and often at great cost in time, money, hope, and even lives. They are among the chief problems with which the great modern social theorists and philosophers have grappled, with less effort and cost but no more settled results. Regardless of this mixed and difficult record, practitioners of human improvement must solve and re-solve their modest versions of these same problems many times a day in classrooms, clinics, consulting sessions, and other settings.

Practices of human improvement are therefore inherently problematic. Practitioners in them of course have much to do that is ordinary and even mundane. But their work brings them face to face with some of the most distinctively modern problems: the meaning of progress, the means of achieving it, and the difficulties of knowing what we have done, how well, and how we did it, among others. These practices all are what Janet Malcolm called impossible professions, though she wrote only of psychoanalysis.

Why? Wherein lies the impossibility? It arises from the great difficulties of deciphering and delivering human salvation. These difficulties appear in three problems that lie at the heart of all these practices. One is that although they promise personal betterment to clients, the nature of these improvements is uncertain. The means of producing them are unsteady and often mysterious. There usually is considerable conflict, inside practice settings and outside them, about both the nature of improvement and the ways to achieve it. The practitioners' assignment is thus to produce what they typically cannot define with any precision, and to do so in spite of their frequent inability to be sure how results are produced when they are or to know why things go awry, as they often do.

Not all improvements are equally uncertain. Behavior therapists attack obesity, smoking, drinking, and other troublesome habits with relatively clear and simple results: weight loss, an end to smoking, decreased alcohol consumption. Such definitions of results make it possible to frame treatments that also are relatively clear and simple: schedules of predictable positive reinforcements for reducing the unwanted behavior and negative reinforcements for indulgence. By contrast, traditional psychotherapists and analysts define the results of their practice in more complex and ambiguous terms: understanding the sources of fatness or the causes of smoking and drinking and coming to terms with the problem. This may mean losing weight, but it might also mean accepting oneself as stout. Such relatively complex and ambiguous results lend themselves to equally complex and ambiguous treatments: probing early experience in order to uncover the source of problems, reliving early feelings about problems by both recalling them and projecting them onto the therapist or analyst, making the old problems lively in the present, providing material to work through toward a more fruitful personal development.

Although uncertainty and dispute attend all conceptions of human improvement, then, the ends and means of each practice of human improvement can be defined in ways that reduce or increase uncertainty. One way to affect the difficulty of practitioners' work is to manipulate the degree of uncertainty in its results. Individual practitioners and clients often regulate their work together in this way, and sometimes entire streams of practice are similarly regulated.

A second general problem of human improvement is that practitioners depend on their clients to achieve any results. In most practices, practitioners rely on their own skill and will to produce results. They depend on clients or customers for approbation, applause, purchases, and the like. But in psychotherapy, teaching, and related practices, clients co-produce results. Students' and patients' will and skill are no less important than practitioners'. No matter how hard practitioners try, or how artfully they work, they can produce no results alone. They can succeed only if their clients succeed. This connection between practitioners and clients can produce astonishing accomplishments, when will and skill are combined in a common effort. But they also can produce terrific tensions. The possible achievements stimulate hopes for ambitious improvements in clients and practitioners, for the successes would be a great victory for both. But the possible failures encourage great caution, for if clients fail for having reached too high, practitioners will have little to show for their work save loss and even anguish.

There are many variations within and among practices in the acuteness of practitioners' dependence. In addition, even when dependence is acute, practitioners have devised some ingenious means of distancing themselves from clients' struggles. But there are limits to the distance practitioners can create. They cannot work without clients, so great distance is impossible. In addition, it is difficult to find indices of practitioners' success that are secure against clients' failure, precisely because of the promises these practices make for the improvement of others. Workers in these practices depend upon their clients and are vulnerable to them in ways unknown in any other human work.

Dependence and uncertainty interact. Practitioners who define improvement in complex and ambiguous terms increase not only the uncertainty with which they may have to deal, but also their vulnerability to clients, for the clearer and simpler a result is, the more likely clients are to achieve it with modest effort. Such results are appealing to many practitioners, for they promise at least modest success without the risk of great vulnerability to clients' abilities, interests, or momentary whims. More complex and ambiguous results require much more from clients, and often from practitioners. Practitioners who urge such results on clients—or who are urged toward them by clients—often hesitate to bank so much of their own success on a client's difficult performance. But whatever they decide, when practitioners weigh choices between more and less uncertain objectives, they also weigh how much they are willing to depend on their clients' will and skill.

Finally, human improvement is regularly difficult, quite apart from these two other problems. Even little children who want to learn multiplication often have great problems and learn little. One source of the difficulty is that such improvements can require much mental effort and emotional energy. They do not come naturally. Even if one learns multiplication in it simplest form—rote memorization of "times tables"—most students must work hard to learn the combinations and to hold them in memory. They must additionally remember all the rules and operations that govern the multiplication process so they can correctly manipulate the many large numbers they cannot memorize. Such work also requires emotional commitment simply because of the volume of work and the extended application required to learn. Students must willingly mobilize the mental forces needed to remember the material and to use it correctly. That commitment almost surely increases as students' capacity to remember declines; if so, the less able learners are, the more emotional commitment they must make to the work in order to learn. Furthermore, students must do these things more or less on trust, in the unconfirmed faith that the often unintelligible operations will be useful to them one day. The less able students are, the more important trust becomes. Mobilizing and maintaining such energy, commitment, and faith are rarely easy. Good teaching and intelligent materials help, and clumsiness in these departments can make things more difficult. But good instruction does not eliminate the mental and emotional difficulties of learning, any more than technically refined rockets eliminate gravity. They only overcome the contrary forces more efficiently than clumsier alternatives.

If one seeks to learn more complex versions of multiplication, by understanding number groups and gaining insight into their combination, some of these difficulties may recede. But others increase. Some students find it difficult to abstract from groups of things to groups of numbers. Others struggle with the notion of groups of groups. Others have trouble getting beyond an additive concept of multiplication. Some can puzzle their way through these matters, but find it difficult to match mathematical understanding to the algorithms commonly used to teach and do multiplication.

Educational improvement thus can become more difficult as it becomes more attractive and adventurous. One way to reduce difficulty is to avoid more difficult conceptions of results. Mechanical learning of multiplication offers students less intellectual power than understanding mathematical groups and their combination, but it takes less mental effort. The old Romantic assumption, that adventurous learning is easy because it expresses children's natural curiosity, finds little support here. This point holds for all practices in this family. Patients often enter behavior therapy, for instance, in order to cope with problems of overeating. That requires recognition of a problem and mobilization of the commitment and energy to do something about it. Neither is easy. In addition, behavior therapy is by definition uncomfortable: physically painful, emotionally stressful, or both. But it is probably less difficult to suppress overeating within a schedule of rewards and punishments than it is to probe personal history in order to locate the sources of gluttony and, by understanding and working through, overcome them. Physical punishments and rewards may be painful, but responding to them requires less emotional and intellectual investment than deep and sustained self-examination.

A second source of difficulty in human improvement is that it is often risky. Psychotherapy that probes gluttony not only requires great mental effort, but it also demands that clients explore painful childhood deprivations. Clients must recall and relive experiences that once terrified them and that are still vital enough to keep them gorging. That is risky in part because of the terrors that those old experiences held and in part because patients cannot know at the outset, or even much later in treatment, whether they will succeed. Often they are quite uncertain at the end of treatment. Facing the old terrors can be bad enough; after all, one has learned to live with them, even if painfully. Reliving them may only make things worse, disturbing and perhaps destroying a difficult equilibrium. Even worse, perhaps one will face them in vain, causing much anguish but no progress. Patients who wish to change face a dual risk: the loss of familiar if problematic versions of themselves along with the failure to become the people they wish to be. Students regularly face similar risks. Doing a little multiplication, even doing it badly, may not be entirely satisfying. Many students wish to do more or better. But their present accomplishment is something they achieved. Often the error-ridden algorithms work in spite of themselves; and even if they work irregularly, they represent some accomplishment, something that was learned at a personal cost. Such achievements are not cast aside lightly, at least by their creators. But to make the commitment to learn more, or a different version of multiplication, often looks like just such a decision. At least, it is to admit tacitly that what has been achieved is not enough, that the student one has become is in some sense inadequate. At the same time, as students weigh a possible commitment to learn more, many fear that they will fail. If they cannot master the skills and ideas that they wish to learn, or that they have been told they must learn, they risk not becoming the person they wish to be or have been told they should become. These small struggles, often enough to reduce students to tears and sometimes enough to provoke major anxiety attacks, have been little explored. At least part of the reason is that old American faith that learning is natural, that the best things in life are free.

Another way that practitioners can reduce the difficulties of human improvement is thus to reduce the risks. Teachers often do this by defining knowledge in clear and tidy ways, by teaching material in small increments that make modest departures from past knowledge, and by organizing lessons so that most students will perform decently, even if they learn little. Worries about the risks of improvement are of course not equally distributed across learners. Some students are so able, or so confident, that they seem almost oblivious to risk. But many others lack such confidence, ability, or both. Many strongly prefer mechanical learning precisely because it reduces risk by packaging knowledge in relatively discrete and manageable form. They find the unintelligible little packages greatly preferable to larger packages and more uncertain sense-making, precisely because those small packages are tidy and easily managed. We may know that these little packages of facts and algorithms offer less gain, but students know that they present less risk. Students' aversion to risk is doubtless part of the explanation for the difficulties encountered in various efforts to make learning and teaching more adventurous. Students resisted not because the curriculum was weak or the teaching inept, but because they were put off by the risks that the teaching opened up. Romantic advocates of intellectual adventure, and many students of such reforms, have ignored such problems, in part because they accepted that adventurous learning was natural, and mechanical learning was an unnatural imposition on the young. The aversion to considering risk may help explain why, in studies of the implementation of such instruction, only factors external to learning—teachers' techniques, school organization, curriculum, and the like—are held responsible for implementation problems.

Problems of difficulty and dependence interact. When teachers devise very taxing lessons, they create opportunities for students to make large intellectual leaps forward, and this holds out the promise of great success and satisfaction for all concerned. But such lessons also increase the probability that students will demur, avoid the challenge, ask for less demanding assignments, resist, or rebel. This would close off much chance of success for practitioners. The risks and difficulties of human improvement create contrary incentives, pulling practitioners and clients between stiff demands on the one hand and modest requirements on the other.

As practitioners struggle over appropriate ambitions for their clients' work, then, they also struggle with their own chances of professional success and satisfaction. Their practices present many opportunities to help others and many occasions for what seems selfless endeavor. But because their clients' successes and failures are in some respects their own, even practitioners' most selfless work is a vehicle for their professional success and satisfaction. The humans they improve include themselves.

Influences on Solving Problems of Human Improvement. My analysis implies that practitioners of human improvement face competing pressures. The promise of improving others, clients' wishes to improve, and their own desire to succeed as professionals all pull practitioners toward more demanding programs of betterment. They offer incentives to struggle with large uncertainties and to encourage clients to pursue difficult and risky improvements, for if practitioners and clients risk only a little, they can never gain much for themselves or each other. But ambitious and demanding improvements increase the uncertainty with which practitioners and clients must deal. They increase the difficulty and risk of the work, therefore increasing the chances that clients will be reluctant to try or be unable to make much progress. Taken together, these considerations pull practitioners toward less risky and demanding programs of betterment. Such conflicts, between ambitions for success and the risks they open up, and fear of failure and the safer approaches to which they lead are endemic to practices of human improvement.

But if these conflicts are found everywhere in these practices, they are not everywhere the same. Practitioners' personal resources—their knowledge, skills, commitments, and other resources—affect the sorts of improvements they seek and the success they achieve. In addition, the social arrangements of practice also affect the ease or difficulty of solving these common problems.

One set of social arrangements is organizational. Agency selectivity is one crucial feature of the organization of practice. It seems fair to say that practitioners who work in selective agencies are more likely to wind up with capable clients than those who work in open admissions schools, clinics, or social agencies. But if there are different degrees of selectivity, there also are different sorts. Elite colleges and universities are much more selective than community colleges and state universities, if we consider the ratio of applicants to vacancies, but they seem to employ similar approaches to selection of students. By contrast, psychoanalysts in private practice probably have a much lower ratio of applicants to vacancies than elite universities, but they may screen more effectively for purposes of practice. Elite institutions of higher education accept only a small fraction of those who apply, and are therefore designated as highly selective. Yet they accept many students who seem academically average at best, partly because the admissions process mediates a large list of competing demands for students arising from alumni, different academic departments, sports departments, extracurricular activities, and concerns for future alumni fund raising. These schools are very selective if one thinks of the ratio of applicants to vacancies. But they accept a great range of students because the selection criteria vary to reflect the wishes of many different internal constituencies. This also is the case, though not as markedly, at much less selective state universities. As a consequence, professors in elite schools are more likely, on average, to wind up with students who are capable and willing to take on hard academic work. But even though selectivity in the academic elite is extreme in one sense, most teachers in such schools have no part in the process, and many are at least partly dissatisfied with the results, for many students who wind up in their classes are undistinguished, at least in that subject, and are uncommitted to it as well.

By contrast, psychoanalysts in private select their patients themselves or with the help of matchmaking colleagues. There are no committees, and if there is conflict in selection criteria, it is internal to the practitioner. Analysts screen for commitment, capacity to pay, emotional fit, their own professional interests, and other things. But they do so to satisfy only themselves, including their conflicts. They are therefore much more likely than their colleagues in state mental hospitals to wind up with capable patients who will work hard, take risks, and have a good chance to succeed in treatment. Analysts employ a different sort of selectivity than college admissions, with rather different processes and purposes. Because it is more closely tailored to the purposes of practice, and is carried out by practitioners alone, it seems likely to produce a better fit between practitioners and clients than college admissions.[54]

Client choice is another salient feature of the organization of practice. Some practitioners work with clients who are compelled to accept their services; others work with clients who eagerly sought them out. The chances that clients will be willing to work hard and take risks would seem to be greater in the second sort of situation than in the first. Although this may be true in a superficial way, the effects of client choice are powerfully mediated by agency selectivity. Psychotherapists who practice in state mental hospitals and many teachers in public high schools work with clients who chose their services. Yet the benefits of client choice in these cases are often modest because both sorts of practitioners work in compulsory agencies with unselected clients, or clients who are selected for their acute problems. Student choices in such high schools often reflect a preference for little or no improvement rather than for hard work and big changes. And client choice in state hospitals may have little effect because most potential clients have few problems that are treatable by psychotherapy or analysis. By contrast, student choice of teachers in schools that are very selective is more likely to reflect a commitment to a particular subject or approach to teaching, for in such places, students are at least partly screened for academic ability and interest in schoolwork. As a result, students' choices are more likely to lead to mutual willingness of students and teachers to work hard and take risks, even though teachers often have little influence over who takes their classes. But even closer matching of client and practitioner can be observed in more selective situations, as in the work of some private tutors, teachers in music conservatories, or professors in graduate or professional departments of elite universities. In these cases, client choice combines with selectivity to produce more or less close approximations of mutual choice. And the combination of such choice with the effects of specialized selection increases the probability that clients and practitioners will work hard, take risks, and succeed.

If we regard these organizational arrangements from what I earlier called a perspective of practice, we can see that they are resources of practice, for differences in selectivity and client choice can ease or exacerbate problems that practitioners face. Consider teachers, therapists, or consultants whose work is so organized that they see only clients who have been carefully and mutually selected. It seems fair to say that organizational arrangements that produce such matching greatly ease the three problems of practice sketched earlier. Risk and difficulty are eased, for instance, in part because clients are selected for their capacities to take on difficult work and succeed in it. Practitioners' dependence on clients also is eased, in part because their clients are carefully selected for their willingness to work and for other qualities that make it likely they can succeed. Practitioners take relatively modest risks in work with such clients, even in pressing them for ambitious improvements. One reason is that their clients are so capable and committed. Another is that, in such selective situations, there frequently is a queue of at least equally talented applicants waiting for their chance. If some clients fail to perform, practitioners can take others on instead.

Another way to put this point is that resources of practice often exist in a trade-off relationship with practitioners' personal resources. In the sort of situation just described, practitioners need not rely heavily or entirely on their own personal resources to produce good results because the organizations in which they work provide many compensating resources. But consider, by contrast, teachers or therapists who must treat anyone who applies or who must practice with clients who have been compelled to see them. They work without the benefit of such organizational resources as selectivity and mutual choice, which makes it much more risky and difficult for practitioners to press clients for serious improvement. This might be attributed to the likelihood that few clients have much interest in improvement in such circumstances or little capacity. Or, more generously, one might attribute it to circumstances that make hopeful clients hesitate to attempt improvement. Or one might point to both difficulties. But whichever interpretation one chooses, the problems of practice are greater in this second case. If practitioners are to produce results that match those in more selective agencies, it will be because they do it much more on their own. They would have to work heroically, without much assistance from organizational resources and often in spite of many obstacles due to organization. In cases of this sort, practitioners must draw deeply on their personal resources to compensate for the lack of resources that organization can provide.

Social conventions about results are a second set of social arrangements that affect solutions to the problems of practice. Such conventions arise from theories about social problems and their treatment, professional doctrines about practitioners' work, codes established by licensing boards, and the requirements of other public agencies. These conventions are not like items on a shopping list—easily entered and just as easily altered. But they are made by men and women nonetheless, and changed by them as well.

One such convention concerns the allocation of responsibility for producing results. In most practices of human improvement, clients are assigned primary responsibility for producing the results of practice. Organizational consultants, for instance, offer their services to firms and agencies that wish to improve performance, to increase efficiency, or to improve communication. But the consultants' responsibilities are limited. They define and locate problems, explore and explain their nature, and suggest solutions. Some consultants offer assistance in producing the results in the sense that they provide training of various sorts. But they are consultants, technical assistants, helpers; the organization is in charge of execution. This arrangement is mutually beneficial for various reasons. But one consequence is that consultants' responsibility for results is greatly attenuated.

The same sort of thing can be said of psychotherapies. As varied as these therapies are, most assign primary responsibility for results to patients. Traditional psychotherapies have elaborate theories of disorder and treatment that center most attention on the patients' work. In order to struggle successfully with neurotic problems, patients must rediscover salient early experience. They must recall and relive it. Patients must transfer old feelings to the therapist. They must work through old feelings and new insights with the therapist or analyst so as to comprehend and defuse the old barriers to development. Patients also must overcome resistance to all of this and more. In all these endeavors, therapists are guides, helpers, invaluable companions, wise counselors, and even patient victims of transference. But however helpful they may be in these various roles, therapists are not chiefly responsible for results. The results of therapy and analysis are primarily the patients' work. In most therapies, practitioners are cautioned to avoid feeling that they can produce results and to avoid giving patients the slightest hint that they could, for most treatments rest partly on the theory that patients must accept responsibility for their problems, feelings, and improvement. Therapists, it is believed, could not do the patients' work without destroying much chance of growth in their clients and perhaps even making things worse.

Social conventions about results in school teaching are very different: Teachers are assigned heavy responsibility for students' learning. It is commonly assumed that all children can learn if only they are well taught. Inherited ideas about the efficacy of schools and the ease of learning have combined to create the sense that students will learn if only teachers will instruct. These ideas about schoolteachers' efficacy and responsibility are unique among practices of human improvement. They are unique even within teaching. Tutors and teachers in selective colleges, universities, and private schools are not assigned such heavy responsibilites. Their students are expected to share the responsibility for learning; often they are expected to learn well even when teachers instruct badly.

These beliefs about schoolteachers' responsibility for results affect their struggles with the common problems of practice. For instance, they enhance teachers' dependence on students because they tighten the link between students' and teachers' success. The belief that students are primarily responsible for learning and that teachers are only their guides and helpers loosens it. One might think it wise to keep this link tight, to enhance incentives for teachers to help students succeed. Although true in a general way, these matters are never worked out in general ways, but always in particular situations. Success can be defined in many ways, and these are sensitive to the organizations in which teachers work as well as to beliefs about results. For instance, in schools that assign both students and teachers heavy responsibility for results, teachers often push their charges more and take more risks. One reason for this is that such schools usually accept only students who agree to a sort of social contract, who accept a large responsibility for performance as a condition of admission or continuation. Some exclusive secondary schools fit this description, but so did the Harlem Street Academies and other schools that take only children who have failed elsewhere.

Why does a more equally shared responsibility for results give teachers leeway to press students harder? Part of the reason is that teachers everywhere depend on their students for success. If this dependence is managed under circumstances in which students are obliged to work hard and try to succeed, and in which they will be held accountable for not trying, teachers have a basis for expecting commitment to the purposes of their practice. They can manage their dependence on students for success by pressing students to try hard, to do their best. But if teachers must cope with this dependence under the assumption that students' learning depends heavily on them, and in circumstances in which it is difficult to hold students responsible for trying hard and doing their best, teachers can be quite vulnerable to students' disinclination to work. Just such circumstances exist in the compulsory, mass-enrolled U.S. public schools. In this situation, one rational way for teachers to cope with their dependence on students—to increase the chances of their own success by producing success for students—is to find criteria of success that most students can achieve with relative ease, for if they pressed students very hard, many might fail. Some might resist, or even rebel. Either or both would be problematic. The convention that teachers are primarily responsible for students' learning in a mass-enrolled, compulsory system creates incentives for teachers to accept students' values, ideas, and ambitions. It pushes them toward definitions of knowledge and learning that make it easy for many students to succeed.

Considered from a perspective of policy, my point is that the promise of success for all in a universal system creates pressures to avoid failure, for the greater the failure rate, the less the system has kept its promises. And because it is easier to avoid failure by reducing criteria of success than by stiffening them, other things being equal, such promises tend to push systems of this sort toward easier standards. Considered from a perspective of practice, my point is that, when assigned heavy responsibility for clients' success in such a universal service, practitioners' dependence encourages them to redefine success in terms acceptable to most clients. Some recent efforts at making schools more "effective" have focused, quite typically, on ways to stiffen teachers' responsibility for learning, without a parallel stiffening of students' responsibility.

A second social convention about results that affects practitioners' problem solving concerns the extent of consensus about the results of practice. Some schools or societies are torn by conflict over the aims of education; others display much agreement. In Japan, Singapore, France, and other nations, there has been relatively little dispute about the results of schooling. In addition, the consensus is expressed in a few systemwide examinations devised by teachers and others close to the system. The exams control school leaving and transitions within the first twelve grades. Consensus about results also can be observed in some schools or school systems in the United States, the result of deliberate action by teachers, parents, and school heads.

The degree of consensus about results affects practice. For example, it influences the extent of uncertainty with which teachers and students must cope. Systems marked by broad consensus on a few criteria of results give considerable focus to instruction. If students dissent from the established purposes, teachers and classmates will point to the exams, to their great importance for school and career, and to the great weight that the community, the school, or society attaches to them. If teachers wander off the curriculum, students will say similar things to the teacher, the head, each other, and parents. Consensus about results also eases teachers' dependence on students: they need not attend closely to students' arguments about issues of purpose or their lack of commitment to common purposes. Instead, consensus about results encourages students and teachers to work together toward a given common goal: doing well on the test. The existence of a common purpose that is taken seriously by society, that is clearly expressed in a criterion, and that is linked to curriculum helps to mobilize cooperation between students and teachers.

Social consensus about results is thus a resource of practice. As I noted earlier, these resources exist in trade-off relationships with practitioners' resources. Teachers who work in systems or schools that have settled on results need not spend great energy or time mobilizing students' agreement on this point. Society has, in effect, settled it for them. But teachers who work in schools or systems that are torn by conflict over the purposes of schooling are deprived of this resource. They must spend considerable energy on uncertainty and dispute about results, and they are more vulnerable to students as a consequence.

The United States is such a system, or collection of systems. It is riven by disputes about the results of schooling. Many Americans esteem education but others assign it low importance. Even among those who esteem it, there is deep disagreement over what sort of education counts, why, and how much. As a consequence, there is a small blizzard of tests and other results standards. Most systems use at least several different tests, and more are added regularly. Recently, many states and localities have added tests of "minimum competency" to others already extant.

A few tests create modest pockets of consensus; the advanced placement exams and curriculums are one example. But most complicate matters rather than simplifying them. They create confusion about what teachers and students are supposed to do and how well they are supposed to do it. Some of this shows up in local arguments about which tests students and teachers should be working toward. Some shows up in teachers' own conflicts about what they should be doing. This situation deprives teachers and students of resources of practice. Disagreement about results increases uncertainty and the need to struggle with it in classrooms. It also increases teachers' dependence on students, for teachers have no solid external criterion of results to which they can point and around which students can mobilize their own sense of purpose. Teachers and students must work out, by negotiation and persuasion, results that are agreeable to all or most. This naturally gives students a large voice. In these cases, teachers and students must settle for themselves problems that would elsewhere be settled for them by society or their school.

All practices of human improvement face impossible problems, arising from the many difficulties of defining and delivering on promises of personal and social betterment. But all practitioners do not face equally difficult versions of these problems. Those who work in highly selective settings, in which they choose clients and are chosen by them, are less vulnerable to clients than those who work in unselective situations. Those who work in institutions marked by strong consensus about results need not struggle with as much uncertainty about the ends and means of practice as those who work in a crossfire of argument. In these cases and others, social arrangements help solve the common problems of practice for some practitioners but exacerbate them for others.

Another way to put this is that, in theory, the problems of teaching are not at all unusual when compared with other practices of human improvement. But in fact, school teaching is distinguished by the extent to which social arrangements heighten the common problems of practice. Private tutors, graduate professors, and most psychotherapists practice in highly selective settings that ease the impossibilities of their work by presenting them with capable and committed clients. But most schoolteachers work in compulsory and unselective institutions in which there are few qualifications for entry and in which practitioners and clients have few opportunities for mutual choice. These circumstances heighten the impossibilities of practice by presenting schoolteachers with many clients who are relatively incapable and uncommitted. Practitioners in both sorts of setting struggle with uncertainty and dependence on clients, but therapists and others do so with considerable assistance from the organizational resources of practice. Schoolteachers have little assistance from that quarter.

In many nations, these problems of teaching are eased by a strong social consensus about the results of practice and by a plain focus on one or two examinations. But in the United States, the ends and means of schooling are a matter of terrific dispute. Schools and school systems with a clear and settled view of purposes reduce uncertainty and ease teachers' vulnerability to students. But in most American public schools, these problems are compounded by persistent dispute about what teachers should do and how they should do it. Thus, the dominant social arrangements of practice in teaching tend to increase both uncertainty and practitioners' dependence on clients.

These circumstances create powerful incentives for practitioners to reduce the uncertainty with which their work abounds and to limit the extent of their dependence. The most efficient way to achieve these ends is to adopt very conservative instructional strategies. One common strategy of this sort is to simplify work so that most can manage it and all can achieve some success. Another is to define knowledge in rigid ways so as to reduce or drive out most argument. Still another is to manage classrooms in ways that reduce the probability of uncertainty or dispute. These are all common properties of school teaching in this country.

In addition, schoolteachers are assigned heavy responsibility for producing results; practitioners' responsibilities in all other practices of human improvement, and elsewhere in teaching, are less marked. These responsibilities intensify teachers' vulnerability to students. They also make any uncertainty terribly problematic because it looms as a large obstacle to success. The unbalanced responsibility for results in U.S. school teaching strips away even more of the social and organizational defenses commonly available to practitioners in other practices of human improvement. This multiplies incentives for teachers to adopt conservative approaches to practice.

One bit of fallout from my argument, then, is that, without ever considering the content of curriculum or the organization of schools or classrooms, we can see powerful pressures that drive schoolteachers toward extremely conservative instructional strategies. Like every other practice of human improvement, school teaching is an impossible profession. But unlike all the others, the social circumstances of school teaching tend to strip practitioners of the protections that help make practice manageable for most therapists, university professors, organizational consultants, and others.

I find this account useful in an analytic sense because the extreme situation of this one practice illuminates the entire family to which it belongs. And the common properties of human improvement practices put many features of teaching in a helpful perspective. But as a practical matter, it is painful to observe so many people who are so committed to improving others producing so much frustration and so little effect. It is particularly painful to observe that these difficulties arise in part from Americans' distinctive optimism about the efficacy of teaching, the glories of learning, and the possibilities for human improvement through schools.

Demands of Adventurous Teaching. Adventurous instruction makes distinctive demands on teachers. It opens up uncertainty in classroom content and conduct. It increases the difficulty of academic work for students, partly because the work becomes riskier. And it invites instructional interactions that enhance teachers' dependence on students. In these ways and others, such instruction brings teachers into much more vivid contact with the common problems of practice. I do not mean that such teaching cannot be done, or done well. I mean only that ways to relinquish the old instruction must be found and new strategies devised at the same time. Neither is easy.

Consider the problems of uncertainty and difficulty for students. Learning to "discover" or "understand" a subject often seems to entail getting students to hold several different, sometimes seemingly divergent views of a topic in mind at once. In the case of multiplication, this might be reflected in the study of various ways to represent the combination of number groups. To solve the problem of multiplying ten times twelve, for instance, students might be asked to invent different ways of working the problem. Some might begin by adding twelve ten times. Others might add twelve five times, repeat it, and add the products. Still others might multiply twelve by two, repeat that five times, and add the products. Others might multiply ten by ten, and then ten by two, and add the products. Each is a plausible though somewhat unconventional way to do and represent multiplication. Seeing the array, and discussing it, might advance understanding of what multiplication is about. But it also would multiply uncertainty about the topic. That would be a nearly inevitable result, at least in the short run, of confronting different versions of multiplications. It also would be a likely result of inviting students to explore the meaning and merits of various representations, for such explorations would dramatize the many different ways in which this simple arithmetical matter can be viewed. Increased uncertainty would be especially likely if, as most advocates of such teaching argue, students probed these points in discussions, considered each others' versions of the procedure, and challenged each others' reasons for representing multiplication in one way and not another.

Such work can be fascinating, and students could learn a great deal about multiplication and mathematical reasoning from it. But in order to do so, they would have to tolerate considerable uncertainty: about the nature of arithmetical problems, about the procedures for solving these problems, about what the answers are and what an answer is, and about how implausible answers can be detected and plausible answers defended. If done well, this would lead to questions about the nature of arithmetic and what it means to know it. That would be all to the good; if done carefully, such work can be immensely illuminating. But it requires students to find ways to embrace uncertainty, to adopt trying out (i.e., hypothesis framing and testing) as a way of life in learning. To do so, teachers and students must devise instructional strategies that enable them to manage and capitalize on the higher levels of uncertainty. Such strategies are available, but they make unusual demands on teachers and students. Though they have been little investigated, there is no evidence that they are easy.

Adventurous instruction also is more difficult than conventional teaching. One reason for this, just sketched, is that simplified conceptions of knowledge and learning require less mental effort than what we call understanding or problem solving. Although some students find rote learning frustrating, their frustration does not arise from its difficulty, but from what they see as its superficial and boring qualities. Another source of greater difficulty is risk. Adventurous pedagogy invites students to share their ideas, arguments, intuitions, and mistakes with classmates and teachers. Although one can learn much from collective debate and scrutiny, it entails an extensive exposure of self. Students may find this especially problematic in classrooms in which a large and possibly competitive audience watches and listens. Instruction of this sort requires that teachers find ways to engage students more fully in learning, but it also requires that they find ways to reduce or otherwise manage the possible personal risks of such greater engagement. It is no mean trick to intensify engagement at the same time as easing its risks. Teachers and students do have strategies that permit them to cope with this curious requirement. Although they have been little explored or even described, there is no evidence that they are easy.

This brief discussion suggests that efforts to make instruction more adventurous strike close to the problematic heart of teaching. Teachers who try to work in this style must become adovates for uncertainty, trying to open up varied conceptions of knowledge. This ordinarily increases the difficulty of their work, in part because so many students seem allergic to it, at least initially. In order to succeed with such students, teachers must take on a large agenda: help students abandon the safety of rote learning, instruct them in framing and testing hypotheses, and build a climate of tolerance for others' ideas and a curiosity about unusual answers, among other things. Teachers who take this path must work harder, concentrate more, and embrace larger pedagogical responsibilites than if they only assigned text chapters and seat work. They also must have unusual knowledge and skills. They require, for instance, a deep understanding of the material and modes of discourse about it. They must be able to comprehend students' thinking, their interpretations of problems, their mistakes, and their puzzles. And, when they cannot comprehend, they must have the capacity to probe thoughtfully and tactfully. These and other capacities would not be needed if teachers relied on texts and worksheets.

In addition, teachers who seek to make instruction more adventurous must take unusual risks, even if none of their students resists, for if they offer academic subjects as fields of inquiry, they must support their actions and decisions as intellectuals, not merely as functionaries or voices for a text. They must appeal to rules of inquiry, methods of proof, and canons of evidence for resolving disputes and settling uncertainty about the solutions to problems rather than appealing to the textbook or the authority of their office. In order to do so, teachers also must be prepared to share authority, for how could students become active inquirers if their ideas and solutions were not taken seriously, accepted if plausible and well defended, and rejected only if demonstrably implausible? If academic subjects are to be taught as fields of inquiry, students must become inquirers, learning how to frame problems and decide disputes rather than learning how to get the right answer. They must therefore be encouraged to assume the authority that comes with intellectual competence rather than to fly blind on the authority of text or teacher.

When teachers embark on an adventurous approach to pedagogy, then, they open up an entirely new regime, one in which students have more autonomy in thought and expression and much more authority as intellects. But such autonomy and authority are difficult for many students and their teachers. They find it unfamiliar at least, unsettling, and even threatening. None of this is required if teachers proceed in the standard instructional format: They can rely on the authority of text, or on their official position, to cope with uncertainty or dispute about knowledge or procedure.

Another result of adventurous instruction, therefore, is that teachers must depend on their students much more visibly and acutely, for if students are to become inquirers, if their knowledge is constructed rather than merely received, they must take a large responsibility in producing instruction. It is, after all, their ideas, explanations, and other encounters with the material that come to compose much of the subject matter of the class. If students do not pick up these broader intellectual and social responsibilities, most adventurous approaches to instruction simply will not work. But if students do pick them up, teachers will depend on these students more to produce the class. Teachers must rely less on their own protected performances in lectures or recitation or on materials that they control, such as texts and worksheets. They must accept their charges much more fully as co-instructors. There are strategies that teachers use to work in this way, though they have been little explored. Teachers must find ways to help students expand their intellectual authority while seeming to reduce or change their own authority. Teachers must find ways to extend their own dependence on students while seeming to relinquish many central instruments of influence in the classroom. Teachers must make themselves more vulnerable, yielding to students the opportunities to inflict painful wounds, in order to help them become more powerful thinkers. Such work can be exhilarating and rewarding, but it is not easy.

Conclusion

Teaching is a practice of human improvement. It promises intellectual growth, humane awareness, economic opportunities, civic consciousness, and many other virtues. Like other practices in this new family of human endeavors, teaching is an impossible profession. I do not mean that teaching cannot be done. I mean that each of these practices is a medium in which we now struggle with essential but insoluble problems of human nature and destiny. Nor do I mean that teachers are really theologians or philosophers *manque*; there is much in their work that is ordinary. I mean only that teaching has become an occasion for coping with these insoluble problems. In earlier ages, the problems were solved elsewhere, and if teachers dealt with such issues, they appear mostly to have rehearsed and passed on the answers. But in a secularized world, in which human progress is the highest good, the practices that deliver such progress inevitably become a battleground for struggles about the meaning of progress, about the means to achieve it, and about how much we have achieved.

One issue that bedevils work in all these trades, then, is how the purposes of improvement will be defined and what means will be employed to realize them. I noted that the ends and means of teaching can be construed in very ambitious and adventurous terms or in rather simplified and routine terms. This impossible practice can therefore be constructed in a rather easy and routine manner or in a very difficult and unpredictable manner. I frame this point in a larger analysis of efforts to explain why teachers in the United States have mostly chosen to construe the ends and means of their work in a rather traditional and often quite limited fashion. In addition to my historical and sociological comments on this matter, I tried to answer the question with reference to the nature of teaching practice itself. I argued that human improvement makes distinctively difficult demands on practices and practitioners. Because the central issues of practice are both insoluble and unavoidable, ways must be found to cope. Ways must be found to offer practitioners and clients opportunities for improvement, but to do so in a fashion that does not commit them to endless struggle with insoluble issues, for they are not philosophers or theologians, debaters, or analysts. They are practitioners who seek specific improvement for specific persons.

In search of these ways of coping, I compared teaching with other practices of human improvement. I sketched some of the means of coping found in other practices. Most psychotherapies, for instance, delegate extensive responsibility for results—including decisions about when therapy has succeeded, and can end—to patients. Most practices of human improvement are quite selective: Clients and practitioners choose each other, and clients are usually selected with an eye to their commitment and other capacities for success. These and other ways of coping with the impossibilities of such work arise from various social arrangements of practice: conventions about results, and the organization of practice chief among them. I termed such arrangements "resources of practice," in part because, like practitioners' personal resources, they help solve the common problems of practices of human improvement. But unlike practitioners' resources, these arrangements advance the purposes of human improvement without requiring much or any attention from practitioners. In consequence, they permit practitioners and clients to dig deeply into their work together if they wish, more deeply than if these resources were reduced or removed.

School teaching is distinctive, however, because it lacks most of these resources of practice. Most schoolteachers confront the insoluble problems of human improvement relatively naked, enjoying much less assistance from the social resources of practice than most of their colleagues elsewhere. This situation raises the costs, for teachers, of ambitious efforts to help their students improve.

Part of my argument, then, is that if we consider teaching from a perspective of practice, we can see many reasons why teachers consistently make conservative choices about instructional strategy, for lacking many resources of practice to support and protect their efforts at human improvement, teachers are thrown back on their own resources. Because the particular improvement in which teachers specialize is intellectual growth, academic and social learning, these personal resources consist of how they represent knowledge, define learning, and organize knowledge and learning in their classes and the personal conviction, determination, and generosity they bring to such matters.

My analysis does not entirely explain conservatism in teaching. Teachers' work is influenced by its social circumstances, and if all Americans had been educated as John Dewey wished, teachers' pursuit of adventurous instruction probably would be easier. But my account may add something to our understanding of teachers' strategic choices and to the difficulties they have had in efforts to make instruction adventurous, for such instruction invites teachers to open themselves to the great problems that lie at the heart of their work, to frame a pedagogy that embraces uncertainty, to increase the risks of learning and teaching and to enhance their vulnerability to students. Such work has been done and can be done more, but it runs against the grain. In all practices of human improvement, practitioners and clients find some protection from the impossible problems they confront. In most of these practices, they are built into the social arrangements that surround practitioners' work. In school teaching, though, those protections are wanting. As a result, practitioners establish other protections in the ways that they deploy their resources.

Because this chapter is part of a celebration of a new academic center for the study of instruction, it seems appropriate to close with some questions. In reconsidering efforts to promote exciting instruction in these pages, I have posed questions that usually have gone unasked: What does it take to carry off adventurous teaching? How do teachers who do it well manage to do it? What strategies do they use and why? I like the questions partly because we have nearly everything to learn about the answers, which seems odd for a people as enthusiastic about such teaching as Americans. And I like them partly because they call attention to explaining the successes of adventurous teaching. This seems more appropriate to our historical situation, and it may help to advance this distinctive tradition of thought and practice.

Notes

1. Carl Kaestle, *Pillars of the Republic* (New York: Hill and Wang, 1983), chaps. 4, 5, 6; David K. Cohen, "Loss as a Theme in Social Policy," *Harvard Educational Review* 46 (November 1976): 553–571.

2. Mark Twain, *Life on the Mississippi* (New York: Bantam, 1945), p. 44.

3. Twain was one of the greatest school haters, but he was hardly alone. James Fenimore Cooper's *The Last of the Mohicans* celebrates many of the same ideas. And despite Thoreau's arguments for education, he was no fan of schools.

4. Edward Eggleston, *The Hoosier Schoolmaster* (New York: Arno Press, 1962).

5. Both *The School and Society* and *The Child and the Curriculum*, two of Dewey's most popular books, depict what he called the "old education" as the result of misguided ideas about learning and teaching. In these and other writing, Dewey seems to assume that once teachers understand what he sometimes called the "laws of psychology," they would be in a position to set things right. This impression is reinforced by the account offered in Katherine C. Mayhew and Anna C. Edwards, *The Dewey School* (New York: Atheneum, 1966), chaps. 2, 3, 4. The book reveals that Dewey and the teachers had no idea how difficult it would be to teach as he wished. Dewey confirms this in memoranda to the authors.

6. Larry Cuban, *How Teachers Taught* (New York: Longman, 1984), pp. 1–11. Though I raise some questions, I am much indebted to Larry Cuban's work in this book and in his several thoughtful essays.

7. Dewey had many important colleagues, and he drew on a modest tradition of child-centered theory and practice. In some ways, he seems more a great

codifier and rationalizer of this tradition than an inventor. But he was the first great philosopher and psychologist of adventurous learning and the first in this tradition who spoke to a national audience.

8. Larry Cuban draws on many of these in *How Teachers Taught* and in his more recent *Teachers and Machines* (New York: Teachers College Press, 1986).

9. There has been an outpouring of research along these lines in the past fifteen or twenty years. One of the seminal studies was Paul Berman and Milbrey McLaughlin, *Federal Programs Supporting Educational Change*, vol. 7 (Santa Monica, CA: Rand Corporation, 1977). Another was Karl Weick, "Educational Organizations as Loosely Coupled Systems," *Administrative Science Quarterly* 21 (March 1976): 1–19. Because most research on American education is not comparative—either across types of institutions within the United States or across nations within the same type of institution—the awkward issue presented here has not been much explored.

10. These points are regularly rediscovered in the wake of success i ve efforts to change teaching. Many of them are nicely summarized, for the current reforms, in Michael Sedlak, Christopher Wheeler, Diana Pullin, and Philip Cusick, *Selling Students Short* (New York: Teachers College Press, 1986), pp. 99–130.

11. Cuban, *Teachers and Machines*, pp. 51–71.

12. Many critics of these reforms correctly note that the reformers did not take teachers' views into account in planning their work. But this was no oversight. Many of the academics who pressed the reforms and devised the new materials regarded teachers as the problem and sought to write books that would work in spite of teachers. See Arthur Powell, Eleanor Farrar, and David K. Cohen, *The Shopping Mall High School: Winners and Losers in the Educational Marketplace* (Boston: Houghton Mifflin, 1985), pp. 282–292.

13. Ibid., p. 213.

14. This theme is an old one in United States education. It is being picked up again in the wake of critical assessments of the most recent wave of educational reform. See, for example, William Snider, "Broader Focus Said Key to Next Wave of Reform Drive," *Education Week*, 22 April 1987.

15. On curriculum change, see, for example, Neal Gross, Joseph Giacquinta, and Marilyn Bernstein, *Implementing Organizational Innovations* (New York: Basic Books, 1971). On the 1950s curriculum reforms, see Powell, Farrar, and Cohen, *The Shopping Mall High School*, pp. 282–292. On administration, see Berman and McLaughlin, *Federal Programs Supporting Educational Change*.

16. Explaining the failure of reform has been an important theme in American educational research since the turn of this century, when reformers and commentators first noticed that instructional innovations were not having much effect. Such work picked up again in the early 1930s, partly as a result of worries about the schools' response to the strains of rapid growth and depression era constraints. And research on the impact of innovation developed into a sizable social science industry in the late 1960s, when a large and quite unprecedented program of national educational reform seemed to flag or flop.

17. See, for instance, Milton Friedman, *Capitalism and Freedom* (Chicago: University of Chicago Press, 1962); Center for the Study of Public Policy, *Education*

Vouchers: A Report on Financing Education by Grants to Parents (Cambridge, MA: Center for the Study of Public Policy, 1970).

18. Some reply that even if education were organized as a market activity, incentives would be relatively ineffective, for education does not have results that can be easily summarized in things produced, services performed, net sales, or profit and loss—unlike most private firms and some public organizations. Nor are production processes well understood or easily controlled by teachers or managers. As a result, strong market incentives might well produce confused signals, encourage teachers and students to do the simplest sort of work, or both.

19. Philip Cusick, *The Egalitarian Ideal and the American High School* (New York: Longman, 1983); Powell, Farrar, and Cohen, *The Shopping Mall High School*, chap. 5.

20. Ibid.

21. Powell, Farrar, and Cohen, *The Shopping Mall High School*, p. 213.

22. Frank Newman et al., *The Second Newman Report: National Policy and Higher Education* (Cambridge, MA: MIT Press, 1973), pp. 10–11, 40–41. See also the references in footnote 51.

23. In addition to these counterexamples, direct evidence on the effect of incentives is thin. The preceding sketch draws on the work of historians, organization theorists, economists, and other commentators. But these studies contain little direct evidence on the effects of incentives on teaching or learning. Instead, there are inferences (often large) from data collected for other purposes, data-free organizational theorizing, sociologically recycled economics, and interview studies in which direct testimony about motivation, commitment, and rewards is taken on its face. The skimpy evidence does not mean that incentives have no effects, but it certainly opens up doubt about the claims sketched previously. Note as well that incentives are the resource of the 1970s and 1980s: reform in these decades has focused on tighter requirements, improved social climates for achievement, and other noneconomic resources. Yet enthusiasm for the efficacy of these resources is no more solidly based than enthusiasm for those resources that were popular in earlier decades: more experienced teachers, better books, newer schools, more equipment, and the like. In fact, the current assumptions about the efficacy of incentives bear an eerie resemblance to assumptions about the power of "objective" resources in the 1950s and 1960s, just before the deluge of contrary evidence.

24. Ernest C. Moore, *The Story of Instruction* (New York: Macmillan, 1938), chaps. 3 and 4.

25. Frederick Eby and Charles F. Arrowood, *The Development of Modern Education* (New York: Prentice-Hall, 1934), pp. 71–72, 82–100, 128–137.

26. Ernst Cassirer, *The Philosophy of the Enlightenment* (Boston: Beacon Press, 1955), pp. 3–15.

27. See, for instance, Harry Broudy and John R. Palmer, *Exemplars of Teaching Method* (Chicago: Rand McNally, 1965), chaps. 4, 5, 6; Philippe Aries, *Centuries of Childhood* (New York: Knopf, 1962), p. 262.

28. Aries, *Centuries of Childhood*, p. 61.

29. Ibid, part II, chaps. 5, 6, 7.

30. Ibid.

31. These points are consistent with the testimony of those early reformers who sought to change traditional teaching. In the late eighteenth and early nineteenth centuries, Rousseau and Pestalozzi represented their child-centered ideas as unprecedented deviations from ancient practices of didactic lecture and mechanical recitation. British advocates of more gentle and child-centered instruction reported that rigid rote teaching was the rule there, four to six decades later. And contemporary American reformers of similar persuasion bemoaned the rigidity of teaching-as-telling, at about the same time. Although vanity may have inclined these innovators to play down the sources of their own inspiration, the evidence in their accounts is quite consistent with everything else we know about teaching at the time.

32. There was, in fact, a drastic tightening up of discipline in school as a consequence of the Reformation. See Aries, *Centuries of Childhood*, pp. 252–262.

33. See Eby and Arrowood, *The Development of Modern Education*, and Broudy and Palmer, *Exemplars of Teaching Method*, pp. 69–70. Medieval approaches to teaching seem to have begun as formal occasions in which instructors told knowledge to students. But the rise of scholastic philosophy, which focused much attention on the problems of harmonizing church teachings with increasingly diverse and secular knowledge, gave rise to new approaches, especially to formal disputation. This changed teaching, at least in some respects. Abelard, though celebrated in many modern accounts for his liaison with Heloise, was much more noted by contemporaries for his recognition of fundamentally contrary views of important religious issues, his efforts to harmonize these issues through a sort of dialectical method, and his brilliance in disputes with other scholars concerning these issues. The method of dialectic that he helped pioneer became central in scholastic philosophy. Disputation played a noteworthy and perhaps central role in university teaching in the twelfth and thirteenth centuries. Teachers seem to have employed it among themselves and perhaps in work with students, and students who wished to be certified as university teachers themselves (to become doctors) had to demonstrate their competence in disputation of a thesis that they prepared. It appears, however, that these forms became stylized and perhaps arid by the later Middle Ages. Disputation seems to have played no part in instruction in Protestant churches or schools.

34. Broudy and Palmer, *Exemplars of Teaching Method*, chap. 6; Aries, *Centuries of Childhood*, pp. 262, 266–268.

35. Robert L. Church and Michael W. Sedlak, *Education in the United States: An Interpretative History* (New York: Free Press, 1976), chap. 4.

36. See, for instance, David P. Page, *Theory and Practice of Teaching* (Syracuse, NY: Hall and Dickson, 1847).

37. Barbara Finkelstein, "Governing the Young: Teacher Behavior in American Primary Schools" (doctoral dissertation, Columbia University, 1970), pp. 13–101. See also the observations reported by Joseph Mayer Rice, *The Public School System of the United States* (New York: Century, 1893).

38. David Tyack, *The One Best System: A History of American Urban Education* (Cambridge, MA: Harvard University Press, 1974), pp. 177–216.

39. Although the social organization of instruction described here is not unusual, it is not inevitable either. Some societies have very weakly developed school systems, and in such cases, nearly all instruction is unspecialized. Other societies have very highly developed systems of schooling and child care, which sharply restrict unspecialized instruction. Some kibbutzim in Israel, for instance, deliberately have removed children from their homes and made child rearing a communal responsibility, carried out in separate facilities by somewhat specialized caretakers. Although the purpose was to reduce social inequalities and build community, one effect was to replace unspecialized parental instruction with more specialized and formal instruction by child care workers. There are similar developments in the United States, though for quite different reasons. Formal, institutional child care has greatly expanded in recent decades, in part as a result of more women working. An increasing fraction of children therefore receive appreciably less instruction from parents and appreciably more from teachers and from young peers. In some cases (home care, most obviously), informal instruction from child care workers simply substitutes for parents' informal instruction. But in other cases, children receive less informal and more formal instruction because they attend formal child care agencies that give a prominent place to schoollike teaching and learning.

40. Most academic research on instruction focuses on school instruction, as though researchers assumed teaching and learning were limited to academic establishments. Academic investigations of instructional innovation also have been restricted to schools. Researchers have considered change only in school instruction and have tried to explain nonchange only in terms of various features of schools' organization, management, or political economy. And they have done so despite all the evidence that popular influences on learning are very important, perhaps more important than academic influence.

41. See, for instance, Harvey Averch, Stephen J. Carroll, Theodore S. Donaldson, Herbert J. Kiesling, and John Pincus, *How Effective Is Schooling? A Critical Review and Synthesis of Research Findings* (Santa Monica, CA: Rand Corporation, 1972).

42. For example, Richard M. Merelman, *Political Socialization and Educational Climates* (New York: Holt, 1971), pp. 90–108.

43. See, for instance, Melvin L. Kohn, *Class and Conformity* (Homewood, IL: Dorsey, 1969), chaps. 6 and 7.

44. Opinion surveys regularly turn up large majorities of the population who express traditional views on matters of discipline, morality in schools, and teaching. The Gallup surveys, published periodically in *Phi Delta Kappan* for more than a decade, are the most accessible current source.

45. Kohn, *Class and Conformity*.

46. Aries writes, for instance, that traditional conceptions of childhood persisted, virtually unchanged, in the French and British working classes from the sixteenth and seventeenth centuries into the nineteenth century. The workers' social isolation from the aristocracy and upper middle class meant that innovative child-rearing ideas and practices, which originated among advantaged families, had little effect on workers. Medieval attitudes and practices thus persisted

virtually unaltered into the nineteenth century among most French and British families. See Aries, *Centuries of Childhood*, pp. 334–336.

47. Christopher S. Jencks and David Riesman, *The Academic Revolution* (Garden City, NY: Doubleday, 1969), pp. 12–27.

48. It seems likely that this pattern will not be eased by the current reform movement. In fact, as "better" institutions get better still by tightening up teacher education requirements, their share of the teacher education supply will probably shrink, and an even larger fraction of the coming teacher force will be educated in the less selective institutions. It is thus quite possible that the net result of reform will be a teaching force that is less well educated, on average.

49. Heavy teaching assignments in the many institutions of mass higher and lower education offer many incentives to read little and write less. This difference in organizational mission and individual work greatly impeded the influence of ideas, produced at the center, on thought and practice at the periphery.

50. Jencks and Riesman, *The Academic Revolution*, chaps. 8–12.

51. Though there is a large literature on college teaching, in which it is agreed that most teachers lecture and that most do an uninspired job, there seem to be no surveys of teaching method. Two recent overviews of the field are William McKeachie, ed. *New Directions for Teaching and Learning* (San Francisco: Jossey-Bass, 1980), and Michael J. Dunkin, "Research on Teaching in Higher Education," in *Handbook of Research on Teaching*, 3d ed., ed. Merlin C. Wittrock (New York: Macmillan, 1986), pp. 754–777. For some historical observations, see Frederick Rudolph, *Curriculum: A History of the American Undergraduate Course of Study Since 1636* (San Francisco: Jossey-Bass, 1977), pp. 88–89, 94, 232–233.

52. Rudolph, *Curriculum*, pp. 275–276.

53. This section draws on a book in progress, tentatively titled *Teaching: Policy and Practice*.

54. The fit would doubtless depend at least partly on the strength of demand for therapists' services, but there seems to be no evidence on this point.

3

Constancy and Change in Schools (1880s to the Present)

Larry Cuban

The British historian Isaiah Berlin divided people who dealt with ideas into two kinds: hedgehogs and foxes. Hedgehogs are those people who pursue unrelentingly one idea. They grab and shake an idea, chewing and grinding it thoroughly before ever letting go. Foxes are people who leap from idea to idea, juggling many simultaneously, seldom staying long with one before scurrying to another. I am much closer to a hedgehog than a fox. The paradox of change amid stability (or is it stability amid change?) has nagged at me for well over a decade as a practitioner and academic, as a teacher and superintendent.[1]

One sign of my enduring embrace of this puzzle is a photograph I discovered in the National Archives while researching a book called *How Teachers Taught*. That photo intrigued me so much that I used it on the first page of that book and in a subsequent one called *Teachers and Machines*, which pursued the issue of durability in teaching practices. This photo captures for me the contradiction of change amid stability that we observe daily in our lives with a smile, an annoyed shrug, or a wink.

The photo was taken in 1927. It shows a teacher with a pointer in her hand motioning to a globe of the world while speaking to seven elementary students seated in two rows of bolted-down desks. Textbooks are spread before three of the students. Behind the teacher is printed on a blackboard "Today's Aerial Geography Lesson." Above the blackboard is a clock. The lesson is being taught in an airplane.

The mix of the most advanced technology of the day blended with a traditional form of instruction is the persistent puzzle that intrigues me. This photo captures for me the contradiction that I have wrestled with during the last few years.

Let me break apart the contradiction of constancy amid change in schools by making four statements, each of which is supported by ample evidence that researchers, informed policymakers, and practitioners would probably endorse.

● At certain times, under particular conditions, bands of reformers have been strikingly successful in transforming the shape, reach, and practice of schooling.

● Teachers and principals have adopted classroom and school changes frequently over the last century.

Yet in the face of these changes:

● Innovation after innovation has been introduced into school after school, but the overwhelming number of them disappear without a fingerprint.

● Widespread resistance to change by teachers and administrators has marked the history of public schooling.

These apparently contradictory statements call for examples. First, there have been successful school reforms. Let me add quickly that by "success," I mean changes designed, initiated, implemented, and incorporated into routine school operations. The face of American schooling, to offer one example, was transformed, "restructured" in current lingo, by the introduction of the graded school, an import from Prussia. Horace Mann, Henry Barnard, Calvin Stowe, and other mid-nineteenth-century reformers railed at school inefficiencies, the ineffectiveness of untrained teachers, a fragmented, uncoordinated curriculum, and scattered schoolhouses with children of all ages jumbled together in one room in American cities and villages. They urged upon school boards, legislators, and teachers the merits of classifying pupils by age, providing trained teachers with separate rooms, and ending the inefficiencies of mixing all ages of children in a classroom where a teacher had little time to work with each child.

Not until 1848, however, did the first graded school appear. The newly built Quincy School in Boston had twelve classrooms, each holding fifty-six students, and an auditorium accommodating seven hundred pupils for eight grades in the school. Every teacher had a separate classroom, every student a separate desk, and all could pay attention to the same subject matter at the same time. From classifying students by age and providing self-contained classrooms for each teacher to address specific parts of the curriculum, it was not long before reformers and administrators developed a uniform course of study and examinations to enable students to move easily from one grade to another.[2]

Between 1856 and 1864, for example, Chicago Superintendent William Wells divided over fourteen thousand children into ten grades and assigned 123 teachers to those grades. Wells expected teachers to follow the same schedule for reading, spelling, and arithmetic. In 1862, he issued *A Graded Course of Instruction to Teachers with Instructions to Teachers* outlining what had to be covered in each subject and how teachers should teach the content.[3]

By 1890, in cities across the nation, what was considered to be modern was a graded elementary school with a uniform curriculum, textbooks geared to each subject in the curriculum, tests, promotions, and a teacher sitting at her desk in her room. The graded elementary school became the conventional wisdom. School boards and superintendents embraced that wisdom, budgeted funds, and built such schools; and teachers and principals staffed them. The innovation of the graded school in pre–Civil War America became standard practice by the turn of the century.

Since then, reforms to alter the elementary school and self-contained classrooms, such as nongraded programs or open-space architecture, have made occasional dents in these forms, but they persist nonetheless as the basic structural arrangement for American schooling. Thus, an innovation initiated almost a century and a half ago to organize space, time, teachers, and subject matter to deal productively with large numbers of children endures as the basic structural arrangement for schooling. That is the mark of a successful reform.

Although I use the graded elementary school as an example, other successful changes engineered by coalitions of reformers have also transformed schools. The comprehensive high school, introduced by efficiency-minded Progressives in the early decades of the twentieth century, applied the principles of specialization and standardization embedded in the graded elementary school to those turn-of-the-century small high schools preparing students for college. The comprehensive high school with varied curriculums has been attacked often since 1945 but endures as the fundamental way of providing schooling for teenagers. Other reforms, such as consolidating small rural schools into larger units, governing schools through a trained superintendent and small school boards, vocational curriculums, and programs for the disadvantaged such as Head Start, Chapter 1, and Upward Bound, have also succeeded.

If my first example suggested how innovations launched by reformers could be embraced by school boards and superintendents and still endure over time, I do not wish to suggest that teachers and principals have seldom initiated changes in their schools and classrooms. In my research on how teachers taught over the last century, I have read many teacher-written accounts of their classroom work. In working as an administrator, I have sat in hundreds of classrooms. I was repeatedly struck by the willingness of these teachers to alter routines and try other approaches if it met *their* criteria for classroom change. Teachers implicitly asked practical questions of proposals for change made by others or of their own innovations. Seldom aloud or in writing, they nonetheless asked: Is it simple? Can it be used in more than one situation? Is it reliable? Is it durable? Will doing this cost me more in time and energy than it will return to my students? Will it help me solve problems that I have defined as problems? If an innovation passed muster on these practical questions, one could bet that the teacher would try something new, and, if it worked (i.e., met these criteria), it would transform some classroom routines.[4]

Consider some of the commonplace practices that teachers have adopted: chalkboard, worksheets, overhead projector, grouping in the lower grades. Also consider the many less obvious, less dramatic alterations that teachers make in their classrooms: a teacher who decides to change her strategy for questioning students to include queries that require fuller responses and to wait a few seconds longer for answers, the teacher who brings plants and animals from the neighborhood into a biology class, the teacher who writes short stories for her students to read and critique, or the teacher who has students in one class make up the test for students in another. These are nothing dramatic that would shake professional journals or arouse a standing ovation; yet modest teacher-initiated changes occur quietly and go unrecorded.

Principals also frequently initiate unnoticed changes. A principal finds her sixth-grade and first-grade teachers willing to establish a tutoring program for older students helping younger ones. Or a principal gets the staff to agree to end those clanging bells to change classes. Or numerous principals, having been appointed to schools in need of salvaging and knowing little about what the research says should be done, proceed to convert disasters into high performers. The literature on effective schools is studded with instances of self-directed change.[5]

The point is clear: Frequently, teachers and principals initiate, adopt, and incorporate changes into their daily routines, although they often go unobserved beyond the schoolhouse door.

Now, consider the following two opposite statements about change. First, innovation after innovation has been introduced into school after school, with the overwhelming number of them disappearing without a fingerprint.[6] How many examples do you want? These are my candidates for an article in a professional journal entitled "Whatever Happened to . . . ?"

Programmed instruction
Flexible scheduling
Individually Prescribed Instruction (IPI)
Differentiated staffing
Program Planning and Budgeting Systems (PPBS)
Open classrooms
New math

For those with imperfect memories or who suffer from amnesia of pre-1950 reforms, try these:

Core curriculum
The Dalton Plan or contract teaching
The Winnetka Plan or individualized learning
Life adjustment curriculum
The platoon system
Classroom radio

The history of school reform is littered with the debris of discarded changes. I am reluctant to spend too much time on this statement because its truth is recorded in the experiences of those who have simply worked in schools over the last three decades.

Let me turn instead to the last statement about change in schools: Widespread resistance to change by teachers and administrators marks the history of public schooling. Let me mention just a few instances of resistance to support the statement.

To cheerleaders for machine technology in classrooms, such as instructional television, the use of film, or computer-assisted instruction, teacher response has been less than enthusiastic. Surveys reveal minimum penetration of classrooms. Because teachers determine usage of machines, they have often become the target for charges of foot dragging.[7] Note further another example of the reluctance of many teachers assigned to teach in open space schools built in the 1970s to accept higher levels of noise and full disclosure of their teaching to colleagues, administrators, and parents. Frequently in such settings, bookshelves, movable chalkboards, and partitions replaced the missing walls and converted open space into self-contained classrooms.[8]

Similarly, principals react slowly to demands for changes in practices. Sandwiched between district office mandates and teachers upon whom they are utterly dependent to achieve school goals, many principals argue that they are so severely constrained by district regulations, parental expectations, and teacher needs that simply keeping the school operating stretches their limits. The energy necessary to mount schoolwide changes is limited and channeled to managing the existing arrangements in such a manner as to cause little notice from the district office or school board. Compliance, not change, is the first commandment of survival.[9]

I argue that all four of these statements—two of which counter the others—are accurate. How, then, can I explain the persistence of reform in the face of durability in practice? Many of you have probably figured out that such constrasting statements may be due simply to different views of change.

Conceptions of Change

So much has been written about the nature of change that I hesitate to enter that river of words that stretches back over two millenia. But I said "hesitate," not "refuse."

Equating Change and Improvement

Explicit analysis of change and its meaning can be traced back to the Greeks, although I suspect that biblical scholars can point to similar wrestling among Old Testament figures. It was Heraclitus (540–480 B.C.), for example, who said that "nothing endures but change." The Greeks and their intellectual heirs in the Renaissance, the Enlightenment, and the twentieth century thought about change as growth. The metaphor of organic development seen among plants, animals, and human beings became harnessed to notions of change. Connected to the metaphor of change as growth are the concepts of life cycles (birth through death) and progress. Change as growth implies that there is a purpose and direction and that change is inevitable. From these concepts unfolds the notion of evolutionary change as improvement.[10]

Yet change may or may not be progress. Take the middle-aged, obese fellow who is anxious to reduce from three hundred to one hundred eighty pounds. Over two years, he loses one hundred fifty pounds but gains back one hundred forty. He lost weight; he changed. But he has not improved. He is still fat.

Determining progress also depends upon the goals and mental map of the person making the judgment. Another example might help. I have already referred to the massive expansion of public schooling between the mid and late nineteenth century. Tax-supported common schools took in boys and girls from cities and farms, migrants and immigrants. Buildings went up. Teachers were hired. The school year lengthened. With more children attending classes, more children graduating, and more children from different cultures sitting in classrooms than before, these presumed improvements were linked to a growing, maturing system of public schooling. These changes can be viewed as incremental, positive developments in achieving a schooling appropriate for citizens in a democracy.

In the eyes of other observers, however, what appears as improvements may be viewed as calculated efforts by those with social and economic power to design and impose a schooling that will shape children's beliefs, values, and behavior in directions appropriate to social needs as defined by those in power. These changes, then, are seldom seen as improvements, but impositions of the powerful upon the weak.

To still others, such changes in the schools—the graded school, different curriculums, longer school day, and particular teaching practices—could be viewed as inventive responses by pragmatic citizens, administrators, and teachers to the demographic changes sweeping across the nation in the middle and late decades of the nineteenth century. These changes, to such observers, are neither progress nor imposition of elite values upon working-class and disadvantaged populations, but imaginative adaptations in coping with swelling numbers of children.

A more specific example to underscore the same point is to read Cremin's *Transformation of the School*, a history of progressivism, and Callahan's *Education and the Cult of Efficiency* and consider how both dealt with the innovation called the Platoon School in Gary, Indiana, before World War I.[11] Cremin sees it as a progressive innovation in the spirit of democratizing and improving schools; Callahan condemns it as an import from the business sector that contained an efficiency mentality that worsened schooling for Gary children.[12]

First-Order and Second-Order Changes

Let me define what I mean by first-order and second-order changes by using an example sadly familiar to each of us.[13] In the mid 1980s, the National Aeronautics and Space Administration (NASA) experienced grave setbacks with the tragic destruction of the *Challenger* shuttle and two unmanned rockets within three months. By all accounts, an agency that had soared with the successes of lunar landings, shuttle flights, and space walks staggered to a halt with the deaths of seven astronauts and two rocket failures.

With public awareness of a complete performance collapse, NASA's new leaders had to define the problems clearly: In engineering terms, was the *Challenger* accident a design problem, a lapse in quality control, or some mix of the two? Defining the problem accurately becomes crucial because a definition will chart the direction for changes in NASA's goals, formal structure, and relationships with government contractors and Congress.

Similarly, for issues facing schools, there is a need to determine clearly whether problems are framed as design or quality control issues (or some combination of the two). For schools, what engineers would call "solutions aimed at ending quality control problems" I call "first-order changes." These are intentional efforts to enhance existing arrangements while correcting deficiencies in policies and practices. Those who propose first-order changes assume that the existing goals and structures of schooling are both adequate and desirable.

First-order changes in schools include recruiting better teachers and administrators, raising salaries, allocating resources equitably, selecting smarter textbooks, adding (or deleting) courses to (or from) the curriculum, scheduling people and activities more efficiently, and introducing more effective forms of evaluation and training.

First-order changes, then, try to make what exists more efficient and effective without disturbing the basic organizational features, without substantially altering how adults and children in schools perform their roles. The compensatory programs of the 1960s and since, including Title I of ESEA and Chapter 1, are instances of first-order reforms. The current school effectiveness movement and its swift spread into state-driven reforms of the 1980s, with their emphasis on high expectations, time on task, strong instructional leadership, academic performance in basic skills, and aligning goals with curriculum, texts, and tests, is a more recent instance of first-order reforms.

"Second-order changes," or what engineers would call "solutions to design problems," seek to alter the fundamental ways that organizations are put together because of major dissatisfaction with present arrangements. Second-order changes introduce new goals, structures, and roles that transform familiar ways of doing things into novel solutions to persistent problems. The point is to reframe the original problems and restructure organizational conditions consistent with the reframed problems.[14]

Some specific examples of second-order changes are moving from the one-room schoolhouse with one unsupervised teacher and children ranging in age from six to sixteen to a graded elementary school with a principal, self-contained classrooms, and a formal curriculum. An example of second-order changes in curriculum and instruction is when teachers and principals choose to embrace a pedagogy rooted in a vision of children as individuals who need to learn to make their own decisions, as learners who need to connect what occurs outside the school with classroom activities, and as pupils who need to discover and create knowledge rather than absorb it. Teachers and administrators with such visions organize schools, classrooms, lessons, and curriculums consistent with those beliefs. Roles and relationships in such classrooms and schools and how time and space are allocated and used all shift in response to these beliefs.

Presently, a few proposed reforms have the capacity to alter fundamentally the design of schools. Consider, for example, vouchers for parents, open enrollment plans for districts (that is, the elimination of neighborhood schools), or school-based management designs that permit school staffs to make budgetary, personnel, and curricular decisions. In each instance, the intention is to alter a basic part of the design of schooling through enlarging choice and autonomy or rearranging how schools are funded, thus altering school governance and operation.

Generally, since the turn of the century, school reform has been a series of first-order changes. On occasion, particular second-order reforms have been attempted in uncoordinated fashion, such as student-centered instruction, nongraded schools, team teaching, or open space architecture, with little enduring effects other than occasional adaptations of these efforts by individual teachers and principals.

The last two decades provide ample illustrations of first-order changes backed by the full force of state and federal law and dollars. From the National Defense Education Act (1958), the Elementary and Secondary Education Act (1965), and the Edu-

FIRST-ORDER REFORMS

- More Dollars
- New Curriculums
- Raising Standards for Teachers
- Longer School Day
- More and Better Evaluation Tools
- Efficient Schedules
- After-School Programs
- Career Ladder
- Merit Pay
- Better Texts
- Smaller Classes

IMPROVING QUALITY CONTROL

STRUCTURES

- Compulsory Attendance
- Graded School
  —Self-Contained Class-room
  —Segmented Curriculum
- Formal Authority Vested in District School Board by State
  —Delegated to Superintendent, Principals, Teachers
- Hierarchical Authority Produces Goals, Policies, Routines that Frame Roles, Relationships, and Work Behavior of Teachers, Principals, and Superintendent

SECOND-ORDER REFORMS

- Nongraded School
- Open Classroom
- Vouchers
- Community-Run Schools
- Teacher-Run School
- School-Based Management
- No Attendance Boundaries
- Open-Space Schools

ALTERING DESIGN OF SCHOOL

Figure 3–1
Reforming Schools

cation of Handicapped Children Act (1974), policies and billions of dollars spent since the late 1950s produced first-order changes in schools. Consider the following:

- new specialists who pull children out of classes to receive additional help (such as reading experts, Chapter 1 teachers, bilingual, and vocational education staff)
- procedural changes that guarantee due process for handicapped students covered by P.L. 94–142
- new classification systems for categorizing children (limited English-speaking, gifted, and handicapped) and for certifying teachers (English as a second language, teachers of the gifted, teachers for the learning disabled or severely retarded)
- expanded testing to determine student performance[15]

All these changes altered existing rules, modified practices, or further specialized staff. The reforms created new constituencies that could be easily monitored but hardly dented existing organizational structures. Nor did any sustained modification of the curriculum or classroom instruction occur from these federal efforts. Neither was intended or sought.

Federal efforts to reform schooling suggest first-order changes that led to further strengthening of the existing design of schools. Schools were seen as failing to provide necessary resources, much less quality services, for certain children and, worse, excluding groups entirely. Federal policymakers tried to improve equal access to schooling rather than to transform the structures, roles, and relationships within states, districts, and schools. These first-order changes were far from trivial. Expanding access and opportunity for unserved children is a massive and essential task consistent with the overall goals of a democracy.[16]

The changes that have occurred from these federal interventions have been overtaken in the 1980s by activist state governments filling the vacuum created by the Reagan administration's ideology of reducing the federal role. State after state has introduced omnibus reforms aimed at improving public schools. Governors, legislators, and superintendents mandated a longer school day (and more days in school), higher graduation standards, more tests, and tighter linkages between these tests and what is taught in classrooms. Further, many states legislated higher entry-level teacher salaries, merit pay schemes, competency tests for new and veteran teachers, and stiff evaluation procedures.

Are these first-order or second-order changes? The bulk of these state reforms aim for quality control, to make the present system more productive, and not to disturb basic roles and arrangements in schools and classrooms. The historic design of public schooling instituted in the mid-nineteenth-century urban schools, with all of its additions, remains intact. Thus, two decades of federal and state interventions seem heavily loaded toward first-order changes, toward strengthening existing structures of schooling.

Categorizing Changes

Changes in schooling can be categorized as touching the core or the periphery of schooling.[17] By "core" or schooling, I refer to the structural elements that form the program scaffolding of an institution in which most children and youth complete their career as a student. These core programs school the ordinary child—that child who adults assume is basically uninterested in learning yet who is expected to finish a dozen years of schooling. Some call this "schooling for the masses"; in derogatory terms, it is "batch processing." David Cohen and his colleagues call the high school "a supermarket."[18]

These core programs, aimed at moving students who were viewed as incapable or uninterested in sustained academic performance, are deeply embedded in such daily routines and commonplace events as report cards, homework, telling children when they can go to the bathroom, worksheets, rows of desks, and reading groups. Few of us think twice about such familiar markers to the classroom and school terrain. For the vast majority of students and teachers, this is the educational mainstream, the way schools have been and should remain.

But students who have difficulty adjusting to school routines, who enjoy the practical and the concrete, the handicapped, the disadvantaged, and the gifted—in short, those who do not easily fit into the mainstream—are pushed to the margins of the school.

Specialized programs emerge. These are usually small, special settings on the fringes of what other students experience: the school-within-a-school for the academically talented, the continuation school for those who cut classes and taunt teachers, the Chapter 1 rooms where students work in reading and math labs, the program for pregnant teenagers in the tiny house next to the junior high school, the suite of rooms in the basement where forty handicapped children work with three teachers and aides but no administrator, the two floors of the high school that have auto body, carpentry, and electronics classes.

In these peripheral settings, innovations in pedagogy, instructional materials, grouping, allocation of space and time, and relationships among teachers and between teachers and students often (but not always) find a home. This occurs because they are at the margins. These teachers and program administrators can take chances. Little inspection by school or district administrators occurs. Test results and other coin-of-the-realm performance measures are seldom applied. So in many of these fringe settings, an observant visitor might find a very different climate, a closeness in personal relationships between students and teachers seldom achieved in mainstream classrooms. In brief, one could find second-order changes precisely because these programs are at the edge, inhabiting the margins where fewer people (who are quite different from the mainstream) and dollars are involved. The insulated edges often become nesting places for second-order reforms.

Although second-order changes have seldom penetrated the core of schooling aimed at the average student, for more than half a century some structural changes have found a home in these peripheral programs. It is possible, then, in the same high school, for example, to see a mix of strikingly stable, durable forms of instruction, curriculum, and organizational arrangements sharing space with fundamentally different classrooms and experiences for youth.

Making Sense of the Contradictions

How can it be that successful reformers have fundamentally altered the shape, reach, and practice of schooling, yet innovation after innovation has disappeared from schools, barely leaving a trace? How can it be that teachers and principals have frequently modified their classrooms and schools yet are viewed as primary resisters to reform?

I have suggested that part of the puzzle is in one's frame of reference about change. One viewer's improvement is another's backward step. That is, although change occurs continuously, notions of improvement reside in the heads of participants and observers. Progress to some may appear as superficial or even detrimental to others, given their different ideas about the purposes of schooling.

For example, some of those in the midst of state-driven reforms aimed at improving test scores and other productivity measures of schooling consider gains in student performance on standardized achievement tests, numbers of students taking academic courses, and increased attendance as benchmarks of excellence and pragmatic political responses from a system of schooling where standards had slid downward for years.

Yet these very same outcomes can be interpreted differently by others who are less interested in student productivity and more interested in equity or improved reasoning skills. To achieve gains in academic productivity, important goals for schooling, such as reducing the number of dropouts, particularly among the ethnic poor and those very bright students who find recitation, fact-filled textbooks, and constant test taking uncongenial, may get sacrificed. Moreover, the quest for higher test scores often shoves aside another equally important goal of improving the reasoning and problem-solving skills, both of which demand different teacher approaches and materials.[19] So, for a current reform movement, judgments about whether such changes are indeed improvements will vary.

Although this distinction between change and improvement helps, it still does not account for the actual existence of counter-forces to change. After all, if change is constant, few seem to seek it out; probably, the only person who welcomes change is a baby with wet diapers.[20] My second distinction about first- and second-order changes may help.

A number of second-order reforms established the dominant structures of schooling between the mid-nineteenth and early twentieth centuries. Coalitions of reformers successfully initiated, implemented, and institutionalized such fundamental changes as the graded elementary school and the comprehensive high school. In establishing these institutions, for example, reformers created formal structures that shaped roles, relationships, and the daily practices of schooling that each generation of parents since 1945 has come to view as traditional, even legitimate. The self-contained classroom, the graded curriculum, the fifty-minute period, frequent testing, the reliance upon textbooks and worksheets, and the governance of schools have become institutional benchmarks of what proper schooling is.[21]

Since the turn of the century, periodic efforts to introduce changes have succeeded if they enhanced these structural elements (e.g., better textbooks, tests, and different curriculums; more time in school; higher teacher salaries; and compensatory education). Such successful reforms were essentially first-order because they aimed to improve the quality of what already existed, what had come to be called "traditional schooling," and not to alter the existing organizational structures. In effect, each wave of first-order reforms strengthened traditional structures, giving further legitimacy to existing school practices. It comes as no surprise, then, that many educators and citizens who received their schooling in these settings and attributed their success to such structures found them congenial and worth defending when faced with second-order change.

Unsurprisingly, many reforms aimed at altering these very same structures (second-order in their intent) failed. Consider open space architecture, informal education, team teaching, widespread use of films, programmed learning, and other electronic media, differentiated staffing, flexible scheduling, and other erratically introduced reforms. Many foundered on the shoals of flawed implementation; many also tripped over the resistance of teachers and administrators, who, unconvinced by the unvarnished cheers of reformers, saw little gain and much loss in embracing second-order changes, except in special programs at the margins.

Although I note the very real resistance to certain reforms and the strengthening of stability in structures and practices by first-order changes, the distinction between the core and the margins of schooling suggests that a mix of both first- and second-order changes has indeed penetrated these stable institutions continually. Small alternative schools, magnets, and programs for the special child and those keen to acquire practical skills leading to jobs without ever seriously disturbing the legitimacy of the entire enterprise inhabit the edges of schooling, leaving mainstream students to move through routines remarkably akin to what their grandparents experienced in places called schools. Hence, constancy and change abide in schools. Reforms of both orders persist, given the varying goals of reformers and tastes for improvement.

The Significance of Understanding Constancy and Change in Schools

As an academic hedgehog and a veteran practitioner wrestling with the puzzle of stability and change, I have come to appreciate the infinite complexity of trying intentionally to change either part of or a whole organization. Organizations, I have discovered, have plans for reformers.

Where I am now in my thinking about the paradox of organizational change amid stability is that if policymakers and practitioners were to make the distinctions I have made about change, a more complex view of what the problems are in public schooling might emerge. I have found that defining problems is far more important than generating solutions.

I am unpersuaded that my distinctions are the only ones or the most significant; I do know, however, that they permit me to map more faithfully problems associated with preserving in schools what is viewed as worthwhile and changing what appears to be unworthy. By acknowledging that change is continual and that the enduring structures of schooling help account for the persistence of many traditional practices, we obtain a richer, fuller, and more subtle picture of the complex institution of schooling.

Consider the most common goal of school reform over the last century: changing teaching behavior. Already mentioned is the staggering inventory of efforts aimed at altering what teachers do in their classrooms. Reformers, however, seldom asked the basic questions: How do teachers teach? What is constant and what has changed in their teaching? Why do they teach the way they do?

Instead, reformers desperately seeking improvement—as they define it—jump to the question: How *should* teachers teach? In doing so, these policymakers and practitioners often tasted disappointment. Annoyance with teachers grew. The policymakers lamented, if *only* teachers were more responsive, if *only* teachers understood the importance of this or that reform, if *only* teachers worked harder.

Thus, asking the wrong question first produced a succession of failures in implementing classroom changes and the inaccurate conclusion that intransigent teachers were to blame. Asking prior, more fundamental questions about why teachers teach the way they do and what innovations they had embraced and rejected results in a very different analysis.

What I am describing is reframing a problem. By defining the problem initially in terms of how to get teachers, for example, to install new technologies in their classrooms, we frame solutions in terms of getting *teachers*, individually or in groups, to alter routine behaviors. Such a definition of the problem assumes that all that is necessary to get teachers to use instructional television, computers, and other machines is to convince them to do so. Alas, it ignores the power of organizational settings, cultural norms, and the individual teacher's beliefs in shaping classroom behavior. Reframing the problem of how to get teachers to use more technologies is to reexamine how classrooms and schools are organized to reduce incentives for teachers to use machines.

Similarly, policymakers deeply interested in improving student performance in critical thinking, moral behavior, and academic achievement, yet unaware of these distinctions and the paradox of change amid constancy, might eagerly offer solutions to the problems of schools in politically feasible terms such as raising teacher salaries, extending the school day, getting more computers into classrooms, adding more tests for children, publishing test scores, or cutting class size. Such solutions speak to an amnesia about earlier school reforms and a misunderstanding of the potency of organizational settings upon how people behave.

I argue that if both policymakers and practitioners understood the inherent contradiction of constancy amid change and could appreciate varied conceptions of change, a very different dialogue about what problems beset schools and how they might be solved would occur. But a sense that some issues in schools are intractable within the current organizational arrangements might also arise. The persistent reappearance of certain issues would suggest deeper, culture-bound factors.

Furthermore, for those advocating structural (or second-order) changes in schools, a stronger, even pessimistic, feeling that nothing could be done about these problems might grow. Although these feelings might suggest despair about what can be achieved in reforming schools, I believe that viewing constancy and change as I have actually encourages optimism about what can and cannot be done within current organizational structures. Surely, understanding more fully the origins of constancy and change and the distinctions that I made about conceptions of change might lead to scaled-down notions of the possible. Yet down-sized but vivid aspirations are critical *if* they can be achieved. Small victories are victories nonetheless. This argument for modesty in appeals for restructuring schools should be weighed against the unalloyed cheerleading that accompanies so many attempted reforms, the overpromising, and the inexorable wave of disappointment that frequently hardens into an acid rain of cynicism—the most corrosive of fallouts from failed reforms.

In short, what becomes significant is the reframing of fundamental questions about change in schools: What are the goals of desired changes? What blocks these goals? What should remain as it is? What have previous efforts at change achieved? Why did they fail? How do existing structures help or hinder desired changes? Wrestling with the puzzle of constancy and change is my way of trying to figure out exactly what problems in schools need to be solved and why. This is no trivial task.

Notes

1. Isaiah Berlin, *The Hedgehog and the Fox* (New York: New American Library, 1957).

2. David Tyack, *The One Best System: A History of American Urban Education* (Cambridge, MA: Harvard University Press, 1974), pp. 44–45.

3. Ibid., pp. 45–46.

4. Larry Cuban, *Teachers and Machines* (New York: Teachers College Press, 1986).

5. Charles Teddlie. Carolyn Falkowski, Sam Stringfield, Stephanie Desselle. and Robert Garvue, *Louisiana School Effectiveness Study* (Baton Rouge: Louisiana State Department of Education, 1984).

6. Michael Kirst and Gail Meister, "Turbulence in American Secondary Schools: What Reforms Last?" *Curriculum Inquiry* 15 (1985): 169–186; David Tyack, Michael Kirst, and Elisabeth Hansot, "Educational Reform: Retrospect and Prospect," *Teachers College Record* 81 (Spring 1980): 253–269.

7. Cuban, *Teachers and Machines*.

8. Larry Cuban, *How Teachers Taught* (New York: Longman, 1984).

9. Seymour Sarason, *The Culture of the School and the Problem of Change* (Boston: Allyn and Bacon, 1971); R. Bruce McPherson and Robert L. Crowson, "Sources of Constraints and Opportunities for Discretion in the Principalship," in *Effective School Leadership: Policy and Process*, ed. John J. Lane and Herbert J. Walberg (Berkeley, CA: McCutchan, 1987).

10. Robert Nisbet, *Social Change and History* (New York: Oxford University Press, 1969).

11. Lawrence Cremin, *The Transformation of the School* (New York: Vintage Books, 1961); Raymond Callahan, *Education and the Cult of Efficiency* (Chicago: University of Chicago Press, 1962).

12. Where do I stand on change and improvement? I divorce the two concepts. Improvement is in the eye of the beholder. One's beliefs and values shape views of whether change helps or hinders people. I assess changes separate from such notions while remaining aware of my values and beliefs. So I do evaluate certain changes as beneficial or detrimental while explicitly indicating what I prize and believe. To me, then, change is not necessarily improvement. To reform may or may not yield progress. It depends upon who does the judging.

13. Paul Watzlawick, John Weakland, and Richard Fisch, *Change: Principles of Problem Formation and Problem Resolution* (New York: W. W. Norton, 1974).

14. For schools, "the structure" refers to the formal and informal goals used to guide funding and organizing activities; who has authority and responsibility and how the schools are governed; how time and space are allotted; how subject matter in the curriculum is determined; who determines which students attend what classes and how those classes are organized; how the different roles of teachers, principals, and superintendents are defined; how such formal processes as budgeting, hiring, and evaluating are determined and organized. These structural elements are linked, in some cases tightly, in other instances less so, but alterations in one or more usually produce vibrations in the others.

15. Tyack, Kirst, and Hansot, "Educational Reform: Retrospect and Prospect."

16. In making this point, I want to make sure that no mistake is made in interpreting this distinction between first-order and second-order changes. I attach no particular value to one being better than the other. Recall my earlier point that change is not improvement and that improvement is in the eye of the beholder. Of course, I have my preferences for why change should occur, under what conditions I prize stability, and under what circumstances certain kinds of changes are most appropriate; such preferences simply mirror the goals that I see most appropriate for public schooling in the last decades of this century. I do not question the intentions of those who boost first- or second-order reforms, only their understanding of what they are attempting to change.

17. Arthur Powell, Eleanor Farrar, and David Cohen, *The Shopping Mall High School: Winners and Losers in the Educational Marketplace* (Boston: Houghton Mifflin, 1985).

18. Ibid.

19. Cuban, *How Teachers Taught.*

20. Von Roger Oech, *A Kick in the Seat of the Pants* (New York: Harper & Row, 1986), p. 125.

21. Brian Rowan and John Meyer, "Institutionalized Organization: Formal Structures as Myth and Ceremony," *American Journal of Sociology* 83 (1977): 340–363.

4

Assessment in the Schools: Purposes and Consequences

Samuel Messick

One often hears that many teachers and school administrators—and, needless to say, many students—complain that there is too much testing in American schools, especially because test results are frequently not well used, are overused, or are misused. In point of fact, however, the attitudes and beliefs of teachers and students about testing are more complicated than such blanket indictments would imply and must be interpreted in light of the perceived impact of the test information on students and teachers themselves.

As an instance, in surveys of elementary and secondary school teachers, the majority reported that standardized tests are as accurate as (or more accurate than) other indicators as measures of student potential and that test scores are educationally important, especially for student placement and the planning of teaching at the beginning of the school year.[1] In contrast, the majority of teachers also maintained that the use of standardized achievement scores is a relatively poor way either to evaluate students for promotion or to evaluate the effectiveness of teachers.[2]

In regard to student perceptions of testing, survey data indicate that, in general, students report positive consequences—such as being placed in an advanced group, deciding to go to college, and deciding on a future job—as a result of testing rather than negative consequences. Yet at the same time, the majority of secondary school students consider it unfair to use standardized tests in promotion, admissions, and hiring decisions—that is, in decisions that affect their own current or future well-being.[3] It is interesting to note that, because of low correlations among the total set of fairness judgments, one cannot point to a particular type of person who is generally negative toward the use of tests but can only say that some students dislike tests in certain situations and some in other situations. "There seems to be no single source of grievance about test usage, nor is there any identifiable group of people who are antagonistic to test use in all situations."[4]

Thus, the utility and fairness of testing in the schools is perceived by different parties in different ways, in part as a function of how the use of the test information might influence their own position and prospects. But these different viewpoints should not be simply discounted as mere defensive concomitants of the apprehension over evaluation that attacks students, teachers, and administrators alike. Rather, these different viewpoints are more constructively treated as multiple perspectives on the purposes and consequences of testing, as examples of a broader array of differential perspectives on the values of testing in education.[5]

Purposes of Testing

As ordinarily conceptualized, the two main purposes of testing in the schools are to assess developed abilities or aptitudes of students and to assess student subject-matter achievement. Such information is presumably needed so that instruction may be geared to the entry-level knowledge and abilities of the students. This may be accomplished by a variety of procedures ranging from the individualizing of instruction to simply tuning classroom activities to the average student ability level.[6] As a midrange example, in the aptitude-treatment interaction tradition, students might be assigned to differential instructional treatments that capitalize on their strengths, compensate for their weaknesses, or remediate deficiencies in skills important for subsequent learning.[7] But there are many other educational purposes of testing in the schools as well as concern, not just with developing abilities and knowledge but with fostering interest, motivation, and social sensitivity or interpersonal skills.

Assessing Affective as Well as Cognitive Outcomes

Assessment of student cognitive abilities and information-processing skills might include measures of perception and attention, language comprehension and production, memory, visualization, reasoning, knowledge representation, restructuring and problem solving, fluency of ideas, and evaluation or judgment skills. Assessment of educational achievement might include measures of reading, writing, mathematics, subject-matter knowledge and skills, domain-specific problem solving, skilled motor performance, and discourse skills in various contexts. These cognitive abilities and educational achievements are highlighted in school testing because they represent important learning outcomes at particular instructional levels and because they facilitate (and forecast) subsequent learning. Tests designed to tap developed abilities and aptitudes primarily serve purposes of prediction, classification, and readiness diagnosis. Tests designed to tap achievement primarily serve purposes of certification of student learning, program evaluation, and remedial diagnosis.[8]

However, not only student cognitive abilities and achievements are important to assess, but student affective characteristics as well. This is so because affective characteristics—especially dimensions of attitude, interest, and motivation—not only are desired outcomes of schooling, but they too are facilitative (or debilitative) of current and subsequent learning.[9] Nonetheless, affective characteristics are rarely assessed in school testing—not because they are deemed unimportant, but because their valid measurement is a promise of the future. It is crucial, however, not to lose sight of affective and personal/social outcomes of education, because otherwise the abilities and achievements that can be validly assessed currently might warp the whole enterprise in a hypercognitive direction.[10] This is crucial because the purposes of education that are hard to test for also tend to be hard to teach for and, in the absence of valid outcome measurement, hard to judge whether and how well they are taught for. Thus, the purposes of testing in education are, or should be, intimately tied to the purposes of education itself.

As an illustration of the short shrift explicitly afforded affective objectives and outcomes in education, consider the powerful facilitator of both school and nonschool learning that psychologists call "intrinsic motivation"—that is, motivation for learning and performance for its own sake. Intrinsic motivation is internally driven as in such forces as curiosity and interest, which operate not only in the absence of external reinforcement but often in the face of negative reinforcement. In the research literature on this topic, two primary determinants of intrinsic motivation are prominent, namely, the opportunity to develop and exercise competence and the expression of self-determination.[11]

Given the purported power of intrinsic motivation in fostering learning and performance, the two objectives of competence and self-determination should be accorded the same status in education as the concepts of health in medicine and justice in law. Yet self-determination ordinarily has about the same status in education as the concept of comfort in architecture, and for much the same reasons. Self-determination is typically treated as a desirable but latent by-product of education, not as a manifestly driving objective. In this case, I would argue, it is not so much that the lack of valid assessment of self-determination has hampered educational practice as that the lack of explicit educational purpose has obscured the need for test development in this area. The message here is that full consideration of the purposes of testing in the schools should embrace not only the many purposes that testing has traditionally or primarily served, but also important or emergent purposes that testing might or should serve.

Multiple Testing Purposes and the Resultant Need for Trade-Offs

Standardized testing has long served a multitude of purposes in American schools.[13] For example, tests are used to assess student learning, both in terms of the achievement level attained and in terms of gains in achievement over the school year. Tests are used to assess potential learning ability or readiness, to monitor progress, to diagnose reasons for failure, to judge degree of mastery, to place students in advanced or special programs, to provide a basis for school marks, to provide a basis for individualizing instruction, to identify under- and overachievers, to guide students in their choice of specific school subjects and in their choice of curriculums, to guide students in their decisions about postsecondary education and in their choice of specific colleges, to guide students in occupational and vocational choice, to inform institutions of higher learning about their applicants for admission, to inform prospective employers about job applicants, to inform students about their own abilities and achievements, to inform teachers about the abilities and achievements of their students, and to certify minimum student performance for graduation. Other reasons include testing to assign students to sections in a course by achievement level or in a grade by ability level, to meet state testing requirements, to select students into a school or program, to make school-to-school comparisons, to help in informing and counseling parents about student progress and prospects, to evaluate programs and curriculums, and to evaluate teacher effectiveness.

Compressing this litany of testing purposes, we find that the major functions of testing in the schools include assessing student abilities and achievements; diagnosing learning difficulties; grouping students for instruction; placing students in special or advanced programs; informing students, teachers, and parents about student strengths and weaknesses; counselling students and parents; selecting students for schools or programs; and evaluating program and teacher effectiveness. In brief, tests are used for instructional improvement, certification of student achievement, placement, guidance, selection, and evaluation. These are traditional and familiar testing purposes, but they are not exhaustive. For example, tests are used not only for student, teacher, and program evaluation but for system evaluation, monitoring, and reform as well—as in statewide assessments and the National Assessment of Educational Progress.[13] Tests are also used to clarify and operationalize educational objectives and to set realistic standards of excellence.[14] Tests may also serve to assure equity of access to desirable programs and to needed student services.[15]

Given this mind-boggling multiplicity of testing purposes, it is not surprising that each test or each test administration is pressed into multiple uses. Although a given type of test information may in some sense be relevant to multiple purposes, it is not often *optimal* for multiple purposes or, indeed, for more than one or a limited set of related purposes. As a result, some educational purposes are typically well served by tests while others are less so or not at all. Furthermore, the tests are then criticized for not performing effectively in jobs they were not constructed to do. This suggests that more testing may be needed in the schools, not less—but a greater diversity of testing, not necessarily a greater amount. Trade-offs must be recognized in the future allocation of testing resources so that comprehensive and integrated testing systems can serve multiple educational purposes optimally. For the present, however, testing in the schools is not only less than optimal; it is also disjointed. It is not only that some educational purposes are well served by standardized testing while others are less so, but the pursuit of some purposes via testing may be contrary to attainment of other purposes. This makes it clear that not only the intended purposes of testing must be addressed, but also the consequences of testing.

Consequences of Testing

Because standardized tests vary in quality, test scores are often misused, and apprehension over being evaluated leads affected parties to stress drawbacks and limitations of the appraisal, often defensively but nonetheless possibly legitimately, potentially harmful consequences of testing have long had to be contended with on the educational scene. Let us first confront some criticisms of testing that are so generalized in nature as to be virtually systemic in their import, and then let us consider the charge that standardized test scores are often misleading because they fail to take account of local circumstances.

General and Context-Specific Consequences of Testing

The general criticisms hold that testing leads to permanent status determination, to narrow conceptions of ability, to domination of education by tests and testers, and to mechanistic evaluation and decision making.[16] More pointedly, it is argued that standardized tests place an indelible stamp of intellectual status on a student, predetermining subsequent learning outcomes and irreparably impairing self-esteem and educational motivation; that the narrow conception of ability and achievement tested for encourages pursuit of only these limited goals and reduces the diversity of talent and skill; that tests determine what is taught, control the curriculum, and limit student and teacher options; and that quantitative test scores encourage impersonal, inflexible, and mechanistic processes of evaluation and decision making, thereby diminishing individual freedom and choice.

Such criticisms of the ways in which tests can be inappropriately interpreted and used focus attention on the fundamental problem of test misuse. But it is important to recognize that the test itself should not automatically be blamed for such misuse—although some tests, by virtue of incomplete or inadequate supporting materials and training, may indeed facilitate misuse. It is also important to recognize that the test could and should be interpreted and used in other more appropriate and valid ways.[17] Educational tests should be used to facilitate improvement of cognitive abilities and achievement levels, not to limit or fix them, because nothing impairs self-esteem and motivation like low school performance. Tests should serve to broaden conceptions of human potential, because assessment of differentiated cognitive abilities and school achievements beyond traditional verbal and quantitative measures highlights the multiplicity of consistent individual differences and the diversity of talent. Tests that reflect the objectives sought by the school should be selected so that any influences of testing on teaching and the curriculum will be in the desired direction.[16] Finally, tests should be used not to impose decisions but to inform decisions, thereby enhancing self-determination and personal choice.

Another fundamental criticism of testing in the schools is less systemic and more local in its consequences. This is the criticism that individual test scores are often invalidly interpreted because they are viewed in isolation rather than in context. Indeed, to the extent possible, test scores should be interpreted in light of the students' motivation, cooperation, and adaptive behavior in the assessment setting—as well as of nontest adaptive behavior in other settings—and in light of the student's family and cultural background, learning opportunities, primary language, handicapping conditions, and whatever other variables are salient in particular instances. But taking context into account implies the need for an even broader array of valid information about students and their circumstances than standardized testing programs typically afford. It suggests the need for comprehensive assessment in context.

Consequence of Comprehensive Contextual Assessment

To see what a concern for context might entail, let us examine the kind of comprehensive assessment in context that has been recommended as a basis for special education referral because its key features apply more generally to the basic issue of local score interpretation.[19] To set the stage, the contention that specific score inferences are relative to context has three main implications: first, the need to consider the student *as* context when particular student functional characteristics are appraised against the background of his or her other characteristics; second, the need for direct assessment *of* context, especially of the measurement context and the environmental contexts of social and educational experience; and third, the need for focused assessment *in* context to appraise functional student characteristics under realistic conditions of functioning, especially as they operate in response to instruction.[20] Accordingly, the system of comprehensive assessment in context recommended for special education has three main aspects—namely, assessing achievement in relation to student characteristics, in relation to sociocultural environments, and in relation to the quality of instruction.

Let us begin with the last feature first because it poses some prior questions in regard to the interpretation of achievement test scores. The point is that individual student achievement should be appraised in relation to the quality of instruction received, for only then can we discern what the scores specifically mean and what import for action follows therefrom. There is a certain circularity in this view, to be sure, because student achievement is to be appraised in relation to the quality of instruction, yet the effectiveness of instruction is typically evaluated by means of standardized achievement tests. The way out of this bind is to obtain independent indicators of instructional quality in addition to average achievement test scores.

The following four types of evidence of instructional quality have been suggested in the case of special education referral, but they are to be applied to regular instruction as well as special programs.[21] First, there should be some evidence that the school is using programs and curriculums shown to be effective not just for students in general but for the various ethnic, linguistic, and socioeconomic groups actually served by the school in question. Such evidence, indeed, might be derived from standardized achievement score distributions, not just means and standard deviations, separately compiled by subgroups. Second, there should be evidence that the teacher has implemented the curriculum effectively for the student in question—for example, that the student receives appropriate direction, feedback, and reinforcement; that the student has been adequately exposed to the curriculum by virtue of not having missed many lessons due to absence or disciplinary exclusions from class; and so forth. Such evidence might include teacher and school records as well as observational data provided by a school psychologist, educational consultant, or resource teacher. Third, there should be objective evidence that the student has not learned what was taught while other students in the class are performing acceptably. This might be obtained using criterion-referenced tests tailored to the specific curriculum. Fourth, and most critical in special education referral, there should be documentation that systematic efforts were made to identify learning difficulties and strengths and to take corrective action or employ alternative instructional methods and materials. Relatively speaking, assessing achievement in the context of instruction contributes less to the interpretive meaning of the test score, which reflects what the student currently knows and can do, however it is attained, and more to the soundness of inferences for action based on the scores.

In contrast, again relatively speaking, assessing achievement in the context of student characteristics contributes more to the validity of score interpretation per se. The point here is that inferences about a particular student competency or attribute should be relative to the intrapersonal context of that student's cognitive and behavioral repertoire as well as to his or her intellectual and personality makeup, or at least to salient features of that makeup. Because the student constitutes a very complicated system of interdependencies, one must anticipate that certain student characteristics will influence or interfere with the assessment of other student characteristics—as when poor comprehension of test instructions, inadequately developed or deployed reasoning skills, uncorrected visual defects, or impulsive behavior degrade or otherwise distort the assessment of subject-matter knowledge and skills.[22] Although one ordinarily assumes in the assessment of educational achievement that the respondent is an attentive, well-motivated, intact organism in control of disruptive impulses and maladaptive behaviors, such assumptions should be evaluated in individual cases because the exceptions offer alternative explanations to incompetence as the meaning of low achievement test scores.

Comprehensive assessment in context facilitates such evaluation by including not only measures of developed cognitive abilities to supplement achievement test scores, but also screening measures for biomedical factors and for adaptive and maladaptive behaviors. Biomedical indicators are included to ascertain the extent to which a student's achievement might be affected by sensory, motor, or other physical impairment, as well as to signal appropriate avenues of remediation. Adaptive behavior scales are included for two reasons: (1) to identify emotional and behavioral deviance possibly disruptive of both test and classroom performance and (2) to appraise a variety of nonintellective adaptive strengths that might temper test-based diagnoses of academic difficulty. A number of other student characteristics that might function in this way could also be included, such as measures of affects, attitudes, beliefs, interests, personal and social needs and motives, temperament traits, coping and defense mechanisms, cognitive and learning styles, and social values.[23] The intent is to discern or discount plausible rival sources of low test performance to buttress the construct validity of local score interpretation and use.

In regard to the third aspect of the comprehensive system, assessing achievement in the context of sociocultural environments contributes with roughly equal force to the validity of both score interpretation and action inferences. The main point to be made here is that proposed educational interventions based on inferences about student functional characteristics, especially about competencies, should be relative to the experiential context of learning opportunities in the school, home, community, and culture to which the student has been exposed, as well as relative to the assessment context in which the scores were obtained. This distinction between the assessment context and the broader social and cultural contexts of learning and experience is stressed here because it is often overlooked in considerations of context and because the respective contributions to the validity of score interpretations and action inferences are different.

In order to clarify any consistent differences or irregularities in measurement that might obtain, characteristics of the examiner (whether the teacher, school psychologist, or outside test administrator) as well as of the test setting (whether the classroom, psychologist's office, or auditorium) should be systematically noted, especially as these may differentially elicit apprehension or defensive motivation or otherwise influence the student's spontaneous style of reponsiveness. Inferences about assessed student performance should be relative not only to examiner and setting effects but to the broader context of the measurement process and purpose as a whole. This means not just taking into account critical objective features, such as whether the test was speeded or unspeeded, but also rectifying interpretations of test performance in light of the student's general style of reaction to the test, the examiner, and the assessment situation. A number of personal characteristics that the student brings into the situation are especially germane, such as familiarity or prior practice with the particular type of test, achievement motivation, self-esteem, and proneness to evaluative anxiety. Because these factors in the social psychology of the measurement setting offer plausible rival interpretations for low test scores, they contribute directly to the local validity of score interpretation. That is, low test scores may not mean low competence but, rather, that something plausible interfered with the demonstration of competence.

With respect to the broader environmental contexts of social and educational experience, the major variables may be clustered for convenience in terms of influences related to the student's family, peers, classroom, teachers, school, and the larger community and culture surrounding them.[24] Such sociocultural factors may not contribute directly to the validity of score interpretations but, rather, to the soundness of action inferences based on the scores. That is, sociocultural experiences may not contradict that low test scores reflect low competence but, instead, offer plausible hypotheses as to why the competence is low. When implications for educational action are drawn from test performance, the reasons why scores are low should make a considerable difference. For example, in deciding how to intervene, it should matter whether the student—or the student's teachers, parents, or peers—thought the knowledge and skill required by the test were important or relevant.

Because no comprehensive assessment in context, however comprehensive in intent, can feasibly address all of these potentially important variables, choices should be made and trade-offs negotiated in terms of the major purposes of the assessment and the salient issues on the local scene. Nonetheless, such comprehensive assessment still may not be feasible, except for specialized purposes where the adverse consequences of invalid local score interpretations justify the effort, as in special education referral. Even in such intense-scrutiny situations, however, not all of the relevant contextual variables will prove to be well measured, nor will all measurable variables be unequivocally interpreted. Indeed, the feasibility of comprehensive assessment in context may depend on the eventual extensive deployment of computer-based assessment to render the collection and integrated use of multiple measures an effective reality.

Consequences of Testing for Teaching

Potential consequences of testing are often passionately pointed to, but plausible ramifications are rarely dispassionately examined. Consider the distillation of possible adverse testing consequences salient in the minds of teachers that emerged in an investigation by Darling-Hammond and Wise of teachers' views of educational standard setting as implemented through standardized testing:

> Teachers worry about standardized tests as an appraisal mechanism. They are concerned that the multiple-choice format is too limiting, that it cannot assess all the things they teach. . . . Teachers see standardized tests as altering the curriculum. Some of the effects are obvious: testing takes time; preparation for testing takes even more time; there is less time to teach; and there is pressure (perceived as both good and bad) on students and teachers to perform. Less obvious are the distortions introduced in the curriculum. Some teachers begin to emphasize the content they know will appear on the test. They begin to teach

in a format that will prepare students to deal with the content as it will be tested. . . . Teaching as if there is always a right answer is thought by some teachers to stifle creativity. More generally, that which is not tested is not taught.[25]

What an incredible indictment by teachers of *teaching* this last statement represents! If the impact of testing on teaching is of great concern, why is Ralph Tyler's admonition not heeded, namely, "to establish a testing program that faithfully reflects the objectives sought by the school. In this way, the influence of testing is to reinforce the other efforts of teaching."[26] Teachers evidently feel under pressure to match the content and form of their curriculum to the content and form of the tests, presumably so that their students will not be disadvantaged in test performance (or the teachers themselves disadvantaged if the tests are used in evaluating their effectiveness). But how does this pressure actually affect their teaching behavior, and what difference does it make whether they try to respond to the pressure or not?

In this regard, a recent study by Mehrens and Phillips, which assessed the differences in standardized test scores resulting from curricular differences in two school systems, is quite illuminating. It was concluded that the degree of match to the test of neither the curriculum nor the textbook series used had a significant impact on test scores, either statistically or practically speaking. In these authors' words:

Critics' concerns about teachers being unduly influenced by the objectives tested, and their concerns about large differences in test results due to differential mismatch between test and curriculum, seem to be unnecessary. . . . [Apparently,] teachers realize that students need to become generally competent. They realize that students cannot be taught only specifics. Students need to be able to generalize. Teachers realize that the specific objectives tested on a standardized achievement test are a small, but one hopes representative, sample of what students should be able to do. Evidently they teach toward the domain, not the sample. Evidently, if they teach from materials that weigh the subdomains differently from the test, lower scores do not result. This must mean that students generalize from the specific objectives taught, and that the tests measure these generalized learnings. That is what we wish to measure, because that is what we wish to infer.[27]

In this concern about the influence of the content and form of the test on the content and form of the curriculum, the impact of form may be more far-reaching and profound than the impact of content. That is, the ubiquitous multiple-choice format used in standardized testing may lead teachers to stress the development of memory and analytical skills as well as convergent thinking about right answers and to downplay the development of synthesizing skills and divergent thinking about alternative possibilities. The latter are more appropriately assessed by writing samples and by responses that are constructed rather than selected by students. This concern that test form may influence the form of teaching and learning is what Frederiksen calls the "real test bias." Such concern could be countered, of course, if standardized tests would rely more heavily on writing exercises and constructed responses, as in the National Assessment of Educational Progress.

One hopes that simply testing for writing, synthesizing, and divergent thinking will have an invigorating effect on the teaching of these skills because otherwise the students might be disadvantaged in test performance in a new and different way. The better the teaching and learning of synthesizing and divergent thinking skills, the more confident students will be in the exercise of these skills and the less anxious in their appraisal. This is important because evidence is accruing that students perform better on constructed-response items than multiple-choice items if they are low in anxiety but worse if they are high in anxiety.[29] Anxious students are evidently self-conscious about their performance as well as task conscious, allowing self-doubts and other disruptive thoughts to distract them from task processing. The conventional multiple-choice format seems more effective than a constructed-response format in maintaining attention on the task. But this problem might be alleviated in more educationally relevant ways by attacking a major source of evaluative anxiety, namely, by adequate preparation and skill development of students in the areas evaluated.

Another consequence of testing highlighted in the Darling-Hammond and Wise distillation is that testing takes time, leaving less time for teaching.[30] There is no question that standardized testing takes time. And, if testing is to include writing exercises and constructed responses, is to cover a broader range of objectives sought by the school, and is to incorporate background and contextual information to improve local score interpretations and test-based action inferences, then testing may need to take even more time. However, one of the promises of technology is that computer-based assessment will also be computer adaptive in the sense that the items and tasks presented to a student will be individually tailored to his or her performance level, thereby eliminating redundancy in answering items that are too easy and frustration in attempting items that are too hard. Such efficient assessment will take less student and teacher time than conventional methods, will permit the testing of more student attributes in a fixed time, and will facilitate the analysis and integrated use of multiple measures and context variables. More important still, computer-based assessment systems can be integrated with instruction so that testing serves a curriculum-embedded formative function in teaching as well as a summative evaluative function.

Consequences of *Not* Testing

Standardized testing in its typical current form has its limitations, and some adverse consequences may accrue to testing in the schools; therefore, one response is to improve testing (and teaching) to minimize unwanted effects. Another response is to eliminate standardized testing altogether from the educational scene. This latter stance is unlikely to be adopted, to be sure, but it is not quite out of the question, at least in the minds of some testing critics. It is important to recognize that *not* testing has consequences, too, and that this route to eradicating the limitations of testing also forgoes the benefits of testing.

According to Ralph Tyler,

> Tests are here to stay and their uses will increase. . . . Because testing can increase motivation and provide an additional source of reinforcement to learning, and because it can help clarify the objectives of the school and focus effort on them, testing should be used as a positive factor in the educational program. . . . Pupils and teachers . . . should have continuing experience with appropriate tests to gain confidence in their ability to learn and to perform and to utilize the reinforcement potential of tests as an important dynamic factor in learning.[31]

And as another sometime critic of testing points out, educational tests should not be strictly curriculum bound: "We should be interested in not just how much students know of what they have been taught, but also how much they know that they have not been taught. If students cannot learn without being taught, both they and we have a sorry future in this fast-changing world."[32] These are the kinds of beneficial functions of testing that would be lost if it were expunged from the schools, but there are many others. An important point is not that testing serves these functions perfectly or even optimally but, rather, better than proposed alternatives.

If tests were eliminated, the multiple purposes that testing currently serves would still exist and need to be addressed by other means. If objective standardized test procedures were not available, schools would likely revert to the uses of the past—namely, to subjective appraisals, which are notoriously affected by selective perception and memory as well as by personal and ideological biases. As a consequence,

> excellence in programs of education would become less tangible as a goal and less demonstrable as an attainment. Educational opportunities would be extended less on the basis of aptitude and merit and more on the basis of ancestry and influence; social class barriers would become less permeable. Decisions on important issues of curriculum and method would be made less on the basis of solid evidence and more on the basis of prejudice or caprice.[33]

In addition, without tests in educational and job-training programs, teachers and counselors would be forced to rely on observations of skills and deficiencies during the course of the activities. Although in many instances this might provide relevant information on which to base subsequent instruction, being unsystematic, it would also occur over an extended period of time. Ironically, teachers and students would thus be faced with what is tantamount to slow assessment, whereby valuable instructional time must be diverted to preliminary observation before specialized treatments can be sensibly applied.[34]

Furthermore, standardized tests and associated normative information provide an important way for teachers to acquire a useful appreciation of the multiple competencies and attributes that characterize student behavior and to develop needed sensitivities to the nuances of cognitive growth. Without standardized tests, an increased parochialism might spread throughout education because of the absence of normative perspectives as well as restriction in access to concrete exemplars of what other educators deem important to assess (hence to teach). Worst of all, there would be a dearth of comparable yardsticks for gauging the effectiveness of educational programs and for evaluating the equity of the educational system.[35] The upshot of all this is that the social consequences of *not* testing are extreme: Tests may be eliminated only at a cost, and a large part of that cost is a likely increase in discrimination and ignorance.

It must be remembered that objective standardized tests became popular in the first place because subjective appraisals by teachers and administrators were unreliable and lacked comparability across students and other affected parties. Objective standardized tests could be held to tough standards of reliability and comparability as well as validity and fairness. The very use of quantitative scores and the existence of elaborate psychometric and statistical machinery for analyzing them virtually invites such scrutiny because there are consensual procedures for evaluating validity, reliability, comparability, and fairness in such instances. Indeed, it is because tough standards based on hard evidence can be applied to tests that the limitations of testing are revealed and can be dealt with.

However, it is not the test scores per se but the inferences and actions based on them that are judged to be valid, reliable, comparable, and fair.[36] If inferences and actions in education are not based on test scores, they nonetheless will need to be held to these same standards but in the absence of directives on how to proceed. Thus, ultimately, the most insidious consequence of *not* testing in the schools is that validity, reliability, comparability, and fairness of educational inferences and actions will not be as efficiently or as forthrightly addressed, if addressed at all.

Notes

1. D. W. Dorr-Breme and J. L. Herman, *Assessing Student Achievement: A Profile of Classroom Practices*, CSE Monograph Series in Evaluation, No. 11 (Los Angeles, CA: UCLA Center for the Study of Evaluation, 1986); David A. Goslin, *Teachers and Testing* (New York: Russell Sage, 1967).

2. Linda Darling-Hammond and Arthur E. Wise, "Beyond Standardization: State Standards and School Improvement," *Elementary School Journal* 85 (January 1985): 315–336; Goslin, *Teachers and Testing*.

3. Orville G. Brim, Jr., David C. Glass, John Neulinger, and Ira J. Firestone, *American Beliefs and Attitudes About Intelligence* (New York: Russell Sage, 1969).

4. Ibid., p. 193.

5. Samuel Messick, "The Values of Ability Testing: Implications of Multiple Perspectives About Criteria and Standards," *Educational Measurement: Issues and Practice* 1, no. 3 (1982): 9–12, 20, 26.

6. Benjamin S. Bloom, *Human Characteristics and School Learning* (New York: McGraw-Hill. 1976).

7. Lee J. Cronbach and Richard E. Snow, *Aptitudes and Instructional Methods* (New York: Wiley, 1977); B. N. Lewis, "Avoidance of Aptitude-Treatment Trivialities," in *Individuality in Learning: Implications of Cognitive Styles and Creativity for Human Development*, ed. Samuel Messick (San Francisco: Jossey-Bass, 1976); Gavriel Salomon, "Heuristic Models for the Generation of Aptitude-Treatment Interaction Hypotheses," *Review of Educational Research* 42 (Summer 1972): 327–343.

8. Richard E. Snow and David F. Lohman, "Implications of Cognitive Psychology for Educational Measurement," in *Educational Measurement*, 3rd ed., ed. Robert L. Linn (New York: Macmillan, 1988).

9. Samuel Messick, "Potential Uses of Noncognitive Measurement in Education," *Journal of Educational Psychology* 71 (June 1979): 281–292.

10. Samuel Messick, "Structural Relationships Across Cognition, Personality, and Style," in *Aptitude, Learning, and Instruction*, vol. 3: *Cognitive and Affective Process Analysis*, ed. Richard E. Snow and M. J. Farr (Hillsdale, NJ: Erlbaum, 1987), pp. 35–75.

11. Edward L. Deci, *Intrinsic Motivation* (New York: Plenum, 1975); Edward L. Deci and Richard M. Ryan, *Intrinsic Motivation and Self-Determination in Human Behavior* (New York: Plenum, 1985).

12. Goslin, *Teachers and Testing*.

13. Edward Haertel, "Measuring School Performance to Improve School Practice," *Education and Urban Society* 18 (May 1986): 312–325; Samuel Messick, "Response to Changing Needs: Redesign of the National Assessment of Educational Progress," *American Journal of Education* 94 (November 1985): 90–105.

14. Samuel Messick, "Progress Toward Standards as Standards for Progress: A Potential Role for the National Assessment of Educational Progress," *Educational Measurement: Issues and Practice* 4, no. 4 (1985): 16–19.

15. Kirby A. Heller, Wayne H. Holtzman, and Samuel Messick, eds., *Placing Children in Special Education: A Strategy for Equity* (Washington, DC: National Academy Press, 1982).

16. Robert L. Ebel, "The Social Consequences of Educational Testing," in *Proceedings of the 1963 Invitational Conference on Testing Problems* (Princeton, NJ: Educational Testing Service, 1964). Reprinted in *Testing Problems in Perspective*, ed. Anne Anastasi (Washington, DC: American Council on Education, 1966).

17. Ibid.

18. Ralph W. Tyler, "What Testing Does to Teachers and Students," in *Proceedings of the 1959 Invitational Conference on Testing Problems* (Princeton, NJ:

Educational Testing Service, 1960). Reprinted in *Testing Problems in Perspective*, ed. Anastasi.

19. Heller, Holtzman, and Messick, *Placing Children in Special Education*; Samuel Messick, "Assessment in Context: Appraising Student Performance in Relation to Instructional Quality," *Educational Researcher* 13, no. 3 (1984): 3–8.

20. Samuel Messick, "Assessment of Children," in *Handbook of Child Psychology*, 4th ed., vol. 1, *History, Theory, and Methods*, ed. William Kessen (New York: Wiley, 1983), pp. 477–526.

21. Heller, Holtzman, and Messick, *Placing Children in Special Education*.

22. Messick, "Assessment of Children."

23. Messick, "Potential Uses of Noncognitive Measurement in Education."

24. Messick, "Assessment of Children."

25. Darling-Hammond and Wise, "Beyond Standardization," p. 331.

26. Tyler, "What Testing Does to Teachers and Students," p. 13.

27. William A. Mehrens and S. E. Phillips, "Detecting Impacts of Curricular Differences in Achievement Test Data," *Journal of Educational Measurement* 23 (Fall 1986): 195.

28. Norman Frederiksen, "The Real Test Bias: Influences of Testing on Teaching and Learning," *American Psychologist* 39 (March 1984): 193–202.

29. Alicia P. Schmitt and Linda Crocker, "Improving Examinee Performance on Multiple-choice Tests" (paper presented at the annual meeting of the American Educational Research Association, Los Angeles, 1981); Snow and Lohman, "Implications of Cognitive Psychology for Educational Measurement."

30. Darling-Hammond and Wise, "Beyond Standardization."

31. Tyler, "What Testing Does to Teachers and Students," p. 16.

32. W. M. Haney, "College Admissions Testing and High School Curriculum: Uncertain Connections and Future Directions," in *Measures in the College Admissions Process: A College Board Colloquium* (New York: College Board, 1986), p. 48.

33. Ebel, "The Social Consequences of Educational Testing," pp. 142–143.

34. Samuel Messick and Scarvia Anderson, "Educational Testing, Individual Development, and Social Responsibility," *Counseling Psychologist* 2, no. 2 (1970): 80–88. Reprinted in *Crucial Issues in Testing*, ed. Ralph W. Tyler and Richard M. Wolf (Berkeley, CA: McCutchan, 1974).

35. Ibid.

36. Lee J. Cronbach, "Test Validation," in *Educational Measurement*, 2nd ed., ed. Robert L. Thorndike (Washington, DC: American Council on Education, 1971); Samuel Messick, "Validity," in *Educational Measurement*, 3rd ed., ed. Linn.

5

Studies of Textbooks: Are We Asking the Right Questions?

James R. Squire

The sheer absence of trustworthy fact regarding the text-in-use is amazing. There is dissatisfaction with texts as with other aspects of education, but among the possible points of improvement there is inadequate evidence to tell where the greatest proportionate need lies. Thus, the literature seems to reflect empty controversy, with every participant certain that his responsibilities concerning the text are far better executed than are those of his opposite number.

So wrote Lee Cronbach and his associates over thirty years ago (Cronbach, Bierstedt, McMurray, Schramm, and Spaulding 1955). And so for the most part could write most critics of textbooks today. Despite more than three decades of diverse criticism and defense of textbooks, intensive study of the concept of readability, much criticism of basal reading programs, and the rise of concern with instructional design, research on textbooks and instructional materials remains largely fragmented and open to varied interpretation. Certain dimensions of textbooks have been carefully studied, often for predetermined purposes. The rise of systematic approaches to instructional design promised an era in which textbooks would support predictable learning, but the continuing diverse demands of the marketplace too often deflect attention away from excellence in instruction.

This chapter reviews ten major areas of research: historical studies of textbooks, readability studies, instructional design, visual design, evaluation of textbooks, the quality of instruction in texts, the uses of textbooks to study curriculum, the uses of textbooks in the classroom, textual analysis, and the process of selection. In every area, we see missed opportunity, but in many we also find unusual insights and, on occasion, promising direction for future study. Studies from the Education Products Information Exchange (EPIE) repeatedly indicate that a review of changing content and pedagogy in particular textbooks over the years offers a close approximation to changes actually occurring in our classrooms (EPIE 1976a, b). Given this fact, it seems surprising that researchers concerned with curriculum change have not submitted textbooks in all major disciplines to sustained historical review. Those curricular areas like mathematics and science, which have undergone repeated convolutions in emphasis, would seem particularly appropriate disciplines for study. A review of textbooks in literature could reveal the extent to which censorship, say, or sensitivity to human relations have influenced changes in curriculum. But such investigations are still awaiting researchers.

Historical Studies

During the past century, issues concerning textbook quality have periodically, if not continually, been raised by educational leaders. Townsend (1891) put "the textbook question" in 1891; the National Society for the Study of Education issued a yearbook, *The Textbook in American Education*, in 1931 (Edmonson 1931); the European Affairs Division of the Library of Congress (1948) reviewed international use; and the American Textbook Publishers Institute (1949) provided a status review. Cronbach and colleagues' (1955) critical review appeared at a special conference. Dessauer (1974) reviewed all aspects of investment, development, and distribution in publishing. Cole and Sticht (1981) edited a symposium on the status of textbooks for the Center for the Book of the Library of Congress, and UNESCO (1984) provided a subsequent review of the international uses of textbooks. For two years beginning in

1984, an annual report on the state of publishing was made available. Such status reviews concern themselves primarily with issues of the moment—economics, distribution, "thin markets," selection practices, censorship, and any passing issue of interest to many educators.

In addition, a small number of individual writers prepared summary reviews of the current textbook scene, most notably Black (1967), McCullough (1974), Benthal (1978), and Goldstein (1978). For the most part, such studies are limited to providing information about textbooks and instructional materials and, thus, have been limited in impact.

More interesting, at least for the perspective they provide, have been the historical studies, such as Elson's (1972) historical analysis of textbooks as "guardians of tradition." Woodward (1985b) and Graham (1978) studied the evolution of basal readers. But more influential by far are the detailed analyses of readers used during different historical periods embedded within Nila B. Smith's (1986) history of American reading instruction. Woodward (1987a) also traced the image of the teacher of reading (from professional to manager) as reflected in changes in manuals of two programs from 1930 to 1986. The history of textbooks in composition has been analyzed (Stewart 1978, Crowley 1985, Conners 1986), and Reid (1969) provided autobiographical reflections on his long-term career in developing textbooks in writing and in literature. Important insights into textbook development during the early part of the century emerge from the work of William S. Gray, a major leader in reading instruction who spearheaded the development of a basal series that by the end of the 1940s may have been used by more than 65 percent of all teachers (Mavrogenes 1985). Soltis (1987) found that the grammar in textbooks has not changed in one hundred years, but the implicit curriculum taught by grammatical exercises periodically changes to reflect current social concerns. Hirsch (1987) traced the decline in cultural content in readers through a cursory consideration of reading texts over the past two hundred years. Histories of individual publishing houses have also been published for most imprints and contain some valuable insights into changing conditions in publishing.

But many of the historical accounts, like the status studies, fail to illuminate because they lack a sustained point of view. More valuable in many ways, particularly in suggesting an alternative approach to analyzing changes in texts, is Chall, Conard, and Harris's (1977) incisive analysis of changes in textbooks over the last thirty years (in reading, literature, language arts, and science) in relation to falling SAT scores. By selecting widely used texts published every five years, and then tracing a decline in the level of challenge and an increased reliance on illustration to convey ideas, the study showed how textbooks became progressively easier and thus may have contributed to falling standards of expectation. More challenging books did not begin to appear until the early 1970s. Although the correlation of level of challenge in elementary school textbooks and its relation to falling SAT scores of high school students seems tenuous at best, Chall did demonstrate that ten years after the books in elementary school were simplified, national test scores declined. Finding the level of challenge increasing in the early 1970s, she predicted (rightly) that test scores would begin to rise in the 1980s. In this study, Chall and her colleagues suggested a method for analyzing changes in curriculum, instruction, and levels of expectation that might well be emulated in other curriculum areas.

FitzGerald's (1979) comparative analysis of American history texts, another approach, seems brilliant not only because of her analytical comments on the then available histories, but because she was able to trace the increasing neuterization and destruction of point of view in history textbooks over a period of decades by successfully analyzing changes in each edition of texts by Muzzey, Magruder, and others that had been used for several generations. FitzGerald seemed unusually stimulating in relating the political views expressed in history books to what she saw as a consensus (or lack of it) in American society. But this is not the only value of such study. If instructional materials inform 90 to 95 percent of all K–12 instruction, as Komoski (1978) has indicated, then neuterization of textbooks seemingly must reflect a similar neutralization in the basic instruction in history offered in our schools. The changes that do occur, however, occur slowly and are not likely to be of great significance from one copyright change to another (Woodward 1987b). Any student of change in instructional material is advised to deal with the sweep over decades, as did FitzGerald.

Readability and Style

Over fifty years ago, the publication of the influential *What Makes a Book Readable?* (Gray and Leary 1935) awakened researchers and educators to a constellation of factors that influence the reader's reaction to any text and ushered in an era in which the readability of instructional materials was seriously studied. The vocabulary load of schoolbooks, of course, had long been recognized as critical in instruction, and word studies had been appearing since early in the century (Miller 1916, Selke 1930, Hockett and Neeley 1936, Stone 1941, Olson 1965, Harris and Jacobson 1972, Rogers 1975, Heitz 1979, and Gionfriddo 1985). In many ways, these vocabulary studies and subsequent readability studies represent the first serious analyses of textbooks. Some publishers have even undertaken word frequency studies on their own, similar to the work of Thorndike and others long ago (see Johnson with Baumann, 1983).

Beginning in the 1940s, researchers sought objective ways to assess the level of challenge in instructional materials (Halbert 1943, Dale and Chall 1948, Taylor 1953, Chall 1958, Bormuth 1966, Beard 1967, Fry 1969, Klare 1975, 1984, Dawkins 1975, Sticht and Zapf 1976, Harrison 1980).

In addition to readability studies in basal reading, research in readability has been undertaken in such diverse fields as mathematics (Williams 1979), data processing (Render, Stair, Stearns, and Villere 1975), social studies (Johnson 1977), spelling (Hagerty 1981), language arts (Rowls and Hess 1984), and on a variety of college-level texts, particularly those used in two-year colleges, where the level of challenge poses unusual problems (Kurzman 1974, Keetz 1978, Jones 1981, Bent 1981, Johnson and Otto 1982).

From this work, a number of formulas for estimating readability of passages emerged and became widely used by the publishers of textbooks and trade materials for children and by those selecting the materials for use in schools. The Dale-Chall and the Fry formulas have been the most widely used, and the ratings frequently are considered by selection committees as one criterion in selecting graded material for the classroom.

The formulas have provided teachers, researchers, and editors with useful tools for estimating the difficulty of material and for determining, as both Bloom (1976) and Chall (1983) have reported, the importance of using challenging materials if children are to learn effectively (Morris and Johns 1987). Certainly, reliance on these formulas is widespread, although attitudes toward them vary with educator and publisher (Conard 1981). Indeed, Chall, Conard, and Harris-Sharples (1983) were even able to identify variation in the level of difficulty from subject to subject in a given grade or in classes intended for less able readers. Another reason the formulas are so widely respected when used correctly is that they have stood the test of time, and some of the pioneer researchers in the field, most notably Chall and Fry, continue to examine their uses and misuses. Indeed, as this is written, Chall has in press a newly revised readability formula.

Because the formulas tended to be based on quantifiable data— sentence length, vocabulary familiarity, or phonemic structure— writers and publishers inevitably found it relatively easy to select and/or adapt selections in textbooks to satisfy the criteria established for a given grade. Because school adoption committees increasingly required instructional materials to be at identified levels, publishers had no choice but to comply. With the school reform movement initiated in the 1970s, concern mounted with respect to textbook quality and particularly to the quality of writing and the adaptation of literary selections to fit the predetermined Procrustean yardstick of the readability formula (Anderson, Armbruster, and Kantor 1980, Rubin 1981, Davison and Green 1987, Duffy 1985, Duffy and Waller 1985). To many critics, it seemed that the readability formula tail was wagging the literary selection dog. To others, concept level or concept density seemed a greater problem than vocabulary or sentence length (Osborn and Bobruk 1981). Chall has publicly promised a formula for estimating concept level in her forthcoming book. Some researchers have also tried to relate the quality of the prose, as well as its readability, to effective or ineffective learning (Lantaff 1978, Mayer 1981).

Alternatives began to be advanced. Utilizing cloze technique and focusing on content area textbooks, the New York State Department of Education in cooperation with the College Entrance Examination Board (CEEB 1982) developed a new Degrees of Reading Power test intended to supplant conventional reliance on readability formulas. Content area textbooks in use in the state were "graded" to form grade level standards. Cloze procedure was used with students to estimate reading level. Grade level estimates were published for all textbooks in use in the state.

Armbruster and Anderson (1981), working at the Center for the Study of Reading, expressed concern with awkward prose structures in text materials, which they felt too often resulted from exclusive reliance on the set formulas, and called for "considerate" texts clearly written to promote comprehension (Armbruster and Gudbrandsen 1986). Their work has been particularly influential in the social studies curriculum as they have sought to identify the large variety of factors that influence children's reaction to text, not merely sentence length and familiarity of vocabulary. More "considerate," "user-friendly" texts were the ultimate aim.

If such a corrective was helpful to authors and publishers, so was the reminder that adaptations undertaken to improve readability scores frequently create problems in understanding (Beck, McCaslin, and McKeown 1981). Beck subsequently demonstrated that intelligent revisions in selections designed to improve coherence can pave the way to greater reader understanding even when readability formula ratings are increased (Beck, McKeown, and Omanson 1984). Baumann (1986) also has demonstrated how rewritten passages in content readers can increase comprehensibility.

The recent efforts to modify too rigorous a reliance on readability formulas are important, for surely quality of writing and style must contribute importantly to reader reaction. Binkley (1987) has recently pointed out how rewriting of history texts has often made passages less comprehensible for slow learners by eliminating connectives and elements that promote cohesive discourse. The study of Graves and Slater (1986) is encouraging. They demonstrated significant improvement in student understanding of standard text passages (on the Vietnam War) when passages from textbooks were rewritten by linguists, composition specialists, and particularly professional writers from *Time-Life*. Style of writing does make a difference! More studies stressing style of writing could result in strengthening the efforts of author and editors who seek to publish quality textbooks. The work on readability has been and will continue to be valuable when intelligently applied; but it offers no way of assessing clarity of expression and felicity in presentation of ideas. More emphasis on such factors in relation to the comprehensibility of textbook materials is urgently needed.

Visual Design: Typology and Illustration

Educational publishers are wont to talk about textbooks having to pass "the thumb test," the initial, cursory examination used by teachers and members of selection committees to screen the majority of texts submitted for consideration so that only a manageable number remains for serious study. Given the fact that this "thumbing through" rarely takes more than a few minutes, the art, illustration, typeface, and overall visual design have maximum impact, which is one reason why the first and the final signatures (i.e., thirty-two pages) in poorly designed texts are frequently more colorfully and abundantly illustrated than other sections.

Given the importance of the visual design in customer acceptance—and the impact it can have in supporting instruction—it is surprising that so few educational researchers have seriously addressed the problem. Tinker (1963) was one of the first to concern himself with visual design and learning, and individuals in England have addressed such considerations for the past two decades (Spencer 1968). For the most part, however, studies have been spotty. Frase and Schwartz (1979) manipulated two typographic designs to determine which facilitated comprehension, and Wendt (1979, 1982) demonstrated that changing column width, type size, and wording can affect reader response to physics textbooks.

Data reported thus far in several studies indicate that page layout and type size can make a difference. A number of exploratory studies, although far from definitive, suggest that graphic cues can facilitate learning (Pelletti 1974, Waller 1980, Hartley and Trueman 1981, Shebilski and Rotondo 1981). More definitive studies of visual layout undertaken jointly by textbook designers and educational researchers could substantially improve tomorrow's books, the more so if ways could be found to report teachers' and students' reactions to visual designs tested in schools. Such testing, now widespread in the publishing industry, yields proprietary information not likely to be shared within the industry. But the data collected might be published subsequent to the introduction of the instructional product, say two or three years after copyright.

The role of art and illustration in learning has concerned students of textbooks more than typeface, perhaps because it seems to require less specialized knowledge. One looks in vain for studies of the relationship between art style (e.g., realistic, fanciful, photographic, surreal) and learning, but any brief review of selected basal readers or social studies textbooks will indicate that attitudes toward illustration change from decade to decade. Indeed, only a few studies of readers' attitudes toward illustration have been reported (Gray and Leary 1935, Poulos 1969), even though publishers regularly test this dimension of their product.

How do illustrations affect comprehension? First asked fifty years ago, the question has long troubled researchers in reading (Goodykoontz 1936, Miller 1937, Weintraub 1960, Thomas 1976, Gutmann, Levin, and Pressley 1977, Willows 1978a, b, 1980, Duchastel 1980a, b, Flagg, Weaver, Fenton, Gelatt, and Pray 1980, Schallert and Tierney 1980, Brody 1981, Green and Olsen 1985, B.D. Smith 1986, Koenke 1987). In substance, most researchers report that illustration can either facilitate or hinder comprehension, depending on the nature of the visual, its location, and the extent to which it is designed to direct readers to the instructional focus rather than detract from it. Legenza and Knafle (1978) tried to summarize the components of illustrations with greatest appeal and reported that there are three key elements—the number of actions in an illustration, the number of children, and the number of people. The evidence is mixed, but it appears that a key factor may also be the way in which the illustration is used in teaching. Such studies would be more helpful to designers and selection committees were someone willing to provide an integrated summary of findings as guidelines for visual design.

One of the more widely discussed studies of the role of illustration was Samuels's report that color illustration can negatively impact children's learning to read at the primer level by directing attention away from words (Samuels 1970, Montare, Elman, and Cohen 1977). Samuels recommended the use of black and white illustrations. However, whether teachers will select primers without four-color art is a moot question. At least one publisher of a laboratory-developed reading program found strong customer reaction against the use of one-color art (Southwest Regional Laboratory 1976). This may well be an example of teacher attitudes, rather than those of children, controlling practice.

The presence or absence of illustration has been reported as desirable or undesirable in several subject areas. Chall, Conard, and Harris (1977) found a growing overemphasis on illustration rather than on printed text to be characteristic of textbooks in several areas where textbooks had become gradually less challenging between 1940 and 1970. In their content analysis of high school English textbooks, Lynch and Evans (1963) reported that copious illustration of literary works seriously impacted a reader's ability to visualize works as written. They recommended secondary school texts in literature without illustration. Who can, after all, see Marc Anthony as Shakespeare depicted him if first confronted by a photograph of the young Marlon Brando in a toga!

More recently, Bryant and others (1980) found that humorous illustration in textbooks has little effect on comprehension but has a negative impact on plausibility, even though such humor adds to a text's appeal. Woodward (1986) criticized the photographs in social studies textbooks as being more cosmetic than instructional. The failure or success of textbooks in integrating illustration, content, and instruction offers an avenue of analysis that could well be replicated in other curriculum fields.

A more recent study of maps, charts, and graphs in readers and social studies books, sponsored by the Center for the Study of Reading, suggests ways in which researchers of visual design can relate their studies to instructional purposes (Hunter, Crismore, and Pearson 1986). Focusing on how such visual displays are used in conceptual development, the researchers reported that seldom were incisive questions directed to readers or were readers provided data and encouraged to construct their own charts, graphs, and maps—a pedagogical strategy almost mandatory for solid conceptual understanding. Early work had demonstrated the usefulness of maps for learning geography, but later analysis seems to break new ground in considering how the visuals are used in teaching several important study skills. More attention to the instructional uses of illustration may result from this recent effort.

Instructional Design

Widespread concern with instruction (as distinct from curriculum) emerged in the 1950s and 1960s, with the creation of research and development centers by the U.S. Office of Education—and subsequently the National Institute of Education and the Department of Education—giving rise to a codification of procedures for instructional product development. Many of these emerged from federally sponsored attempts to produce better textbooks in areas of compelling national need (Baker and Schutz 1971, Anderson and Jones 1981, Dick and Carey 1985, Hartley 1985, Kemp 1985, Jonassen 1985). Basically, these reports summarize the practical experience of research-based developers—either in university or governmental laboratories—who attempt to make product development more systematic and learning more predictable.

The work is an important dimension of research in instructional materials because, in specifying how instruction should be designed (e.g., congruence of objective, learning activity, and test; varying massed and spaced practice), these specialists were also specifying how instructional products should be used. Their work has been especially powerful in its impact on such recent school emphases as programmed learning and mastery learning and on the "teaching effectiveness" studies where systematic emphasis is important. But the sum total of these reports has also influenced how commercial instructional materials are developed and evaluated. For a time, researchers published learner verification studies. (See, for example, Ball 1979.) Much of the work of practitioners like Madeline Hunter and Ethna Reid finds its roots in this work, as do the evaluative studies by EPIE and some of the research at the Center for the Study of Reading and the Institute for Research on Teaching (Schmidt, Caul, Byers, and Buchmann 1984).

Some of these studies have attempted to create guidelines for constructing effective texts (Zahn 1972, Hartley 1985, Brezin 1980). Others have explored the instructional effectiveness of including such instructional strategies as questioning (McGaw and Grotelueschen 1971, Armbruster 1987), embedding headings and processing aids (Holley et al. 1981), metadiscourse and use of refutation (Hynd and Alvermann 1986, Crismore 1983), teaching the main idea (Baumann 1986), teaching phonics (Beck and McCaslin, 1978) or coherence (Beck, McKeown, and Omanson 1984).

The importance of critical features in the design of instruction varies with purpose and with subject. A critical analysis of the long series of recommendations on instruction in each of our major curricular areas would today be a practical contribution, as would involvement of specialists on learning and teaching in subject areas in specifying and modifying recommended designs.

Evaluation and Review of Textbooks

If commercially prepared instructional materials are used as the basis for 90 to 95 percent of classroom time, as studies have consistently demonstrated (Komoski 1985), it is not surprising that the texts have been repeatedly evaluated from one point of view or another.

Many studies have involved content analyses, too unsystematically conducted by reviewers who were anxious to point to the inclusion or omission of particular aspects of content. This has been especially characteristic of studies motivated by social issues. Jenkinson (1979), who has studied more carefully than most the efforts to restrict the reading of children, identified more than two hundred outside groups attempting to influence schoolbooks in one state alone. Although articulate defenders like Jenkinson and the People for the American Way have emerged publicly only during the past decade, objections to selected textbooks have been voiced throughout our history and on some occasions have been answered. A celebrated early case involved the burning of an overly liberal social studies program during the late 1930s. The senior author of the series spent a year interviewing the book burners throughout America (Rugg 1941).

Concern about eliminating prejudice from books and improving intergroup relations emerged a decade later (Wilson 1948, Steward 1950). Attention to international understanding was also characteristic of textbook studies at that time (Quillen 1948).

During the 1960s, concern for multiethnicity and the fair depiction of black Americans and native Americans was followed by analyses of the depictions of Hispanic Americans and Asian Americans and of the role of females (Kane 1971, Jay 1973, Britton and Lumpkin 1976, Garcia et al. 1976, Arnold-Gerrity 1978, Sadker, Sadker, and Garies 1980). These concerns, often expressed by human relations committees, which in some districts monitored the selection of materials, changed the face of American instructional materials (Jenkinson 1986, Cole and Sticht 1981). Even a cursory comparison of textbooks published in 1987 with those published thirty years previously will reveal the impact of these studies.

Analysis of textbook content has covered many topics. At various times, concerned groups have analyzed the treatment of Jewish cultural history and the Holocaust; the role of Italians; the presentation of alternative life-styles; the inclusion of situational ethics and secular humanism; the expression of American free enterprise; the presentation of morality and ethical considerations; the appropriateness of language in textbooks; the nutritional soundness of the food mentioned; the teaching of religion, creationism, and evolution; the teaching of poetry; and a host of other minor issues (Hefley 1976, Chall, Karger, and Gregory, 1979, Doyle 1984, Woodward and Elliot 1984, Shapiro 1985). Still, when the Committee on Freedom to Read studied parent objections to schoolbooks in 1981, only 15 percent of the challenges were to textbooks or to materials used for instruction. The group concluded that educational publishers had learned to tailor textbooks to fit customer requirements (AAP, ALA, ASCD 1981). Some call this "precensorship." Tailoring texts to respond to perceived customer needs is an inevitable part of educational publishing, and virtually all major publishers conduct market studies to ascertain these needs even though this research is largely unreported in public documents.

Yet, major controversy concerning efforts to censor schoolbooks continues (Last 1982). Possibly the most intensive studies of schoolbook censorship were those that emerged during the mid 1970s from the community uprising against the language arts textbooks in Kanawha County, West Virginia, where the lack of parental involvement in text selection and the listing of liberal language arts textbooks for use in a conservative area inflamed local passions (NEA 1975, Hillocks 1978).

The growth in understanding of instruction and instructional design and the role of materials in furthering instructional intent has led during the past twenty-five years to demands for textbooks of greater quality.

Ruth Strickland (1964) was one of the first serious students of language teaching to call for children's literature of better quality in basal readers when she noted that the simplicity of the prose sentence patterns in primer stories impacted adversely children's growth in language, views similar to those documented later by Zimet (1972), Bettelheim and Zelan (1982), and Bruce (1984). Such criticism of textbooks, particularly in reading and language arts, mounted during the academic reform effort of the 1950s (Flesch 1957) and has again emerged during a similar critical period today.

Extensive studies of instructional problems in textbooks have only recently emerged on a wide scale. Collins, Brown, Morgan, and Brewer (1977) analyzed textbooks in relation to reading tasks. Braddock (1974), Donlan (1980), and Baumann (1986) studied the frequency, placement, and use of main ideas in social studies. Braddock's discovery that only about 40 percent of the paragraphs in social studies textbooks use topic sentences has been recently sustained by Baumann (1986). Seminoff (1981) and Hanus and Moore (1985) reported that the quality and placement of questions in textbooks enhanced learning. And Armbruster (1987) is now revealing the preponderance of factual or low-level questions in social studies and science. Beck and Block (1979) compared two basal reading programs, then analyzed the decoding activities in eight beginning reading programs. (See also Beck and McCaslin 1978.) Hiebert and McWhorter (1987) report a similar analysis of four beginning reading programs today. And Durkin (1987), in a new study of the teaching and testing of phonics in the kindergarden, finds serious neglect of language activities as teachers concentrate on phonics. Venezky, Kaestle, and Sum (1987) speculate that the preponderance of literature in basal readers and the lack of attention to higher-level processing of informational texts contribute to the inability of many students to reason.

Rose (1981) reported on ineffective composition texts; Schallert and Gleiman (1979) found teachers easier to understand than textbooks; and Copperman (1978) launched a broadsided attack on readers based less on documented research than on polemics.

Analyses of special instructional features in existing texts have also appeared. Attitudes and values reflected in primers were the focus of one study (Zimet, Wiberg, and Blom 1972), but the range of topics for such research has been broad: racial equality (Krug 1970), the work mode bias in readers (Luker and Jenkins 1973), styles of family living (Conway and Mechler 1983), depictions of Latin America (Andereck and Dixon 1983), portrayal of the handicapped (Baskin 1981), portrayal of the family (Kealey 1980), populism (Peiser 1973), phonics generalization (Sorenson 1982), writing in content books (Donlan 1980), writing process orientation (Graves 1977), images of social work (Leviton and Cook 1983), language experiences (Carstensen 1972), cultural diplomacy (Flack 1971), student interest (Pieroneki 1980), Central America (Anderson and Beck 1983), and discussion practices in reading methods books (Alvermann, O'Keefe, and Moore 1987).

Science, mathematics, and social studies textbooks, as well as basal readers, have their critics (Willis 1974, Crismore 1983, Hawkins 1973, Herron 1983, Pauling 1983, Armbruster 1985, Davis, Ponder, Burlbaw, Garza-Lubeck, and Moss 1985, Elliot, Nagel, and Woodward 1985, Woodward, Elliott, and Nagel 1986, Stigler, Fuson, Ham, and Kim 1986, Shymansky 1987).

Evaluative analyses have also appeared on textbooks in spelling (Gentry 1979, Stetson and Boutin 1982), writing (Koops 1975), Eberhard 1982, Dorrell and Johnson 1982), industrial arts (Negin 1982), and ecology (P. J. Thompson 1982). Still, with much of the recent cognitive research in reading and language development, it seems inevitable that many of the assessments would be of basal readers, as they have been for many years (Wrightstone and Lazar 1957, EPIE Institute 1974). Making these analyses more widely available to the profession could favorably influence selection decisions. Many appear in obscure publications not readily available to teacher-selectors.

Another problem is that authors have seldom been held as accountable for the quality of textbooks that bear their names as they are, say, for scholarly studies or research reports. Indeed, the authoring of a distinguished textbook is seldom taken into account when a candidate is being considered for promotion. Dora V. Smith once observed that not until literature written for children was seriously reviewed and the authors held accountable for the quality of their writing did literature for children begin to improve.

Much of the same is true of textbooks today. Not until authors find their professional reputation affected by the textbooks that bear their names will many of them attend to quality concerns.

A few recent studies have been so influential that they require separate mention. Durkin (1984) reviewed the teacher manuals in select basal reading series and reported that they spend little time teaching comprehension as defined by recent cognitive research. Osborn (1984a, b) found that the workbooks provided with basal reading series frequently violated basic instructional principles and did not systematically provide practice in applying concepts and skills taught in the lessons, findings subsequently supported by Anderson (1984). These studies have been enormously influential in directing improvements in basal reading texts, the more so because they have been so widely publicized to editors, selectors, and administrators (Osborn, Jones, and Stein 1985, Apple 1985, Woodward 1985a, Tyson-Bernstein and Woodward 1986).

One result of the widespread concern with improving the instructional quality of textbooks was the rise of Educational Products Information Exchange (EPIE), an agency established to evaluate texts and regularly publish a newsletter on textbook quality, which prepared comparative evaluations of textbooks in various fields, argued for field-tested learner verification of textbook effectiveness (a practice adopted in one state but now in the process of being questioned as valuable), and provided consultant service on the selection process when requested by school districts (EPIE Institute 1976a, b). Recently, the EPIE Institute has developed a computerized capacity to analyze desired instructional outcomes in relation to outcomes assessed and those included in text materials (EPIE Institute 1987).

Any reasonable study of the impact of these many kinds of evaluations on the content and design of textbooks will indicate rather clearly that highly focused, well-documented, well-publicized studies like Durkin's, Beck's, and Osborn's have had a decided effect on what is subsequently published and subsequently selected. Thus, researchers in subject fields other than reading would be well advised to focus their attention in textbooks on one or two highly desirable features and then to disseminate the findings as widely as possible.

Further, given the enormous variety—and vitality—of schoolbook censorship activities, well-documented in their many dimensions, a valuable contribution could be made by studying the historic impact of major social controversies on subsequent publishing efforts. Such impact has been relatively unexplored.

The Classroom Uses of Textbooks

Growing concern about the quality of instruction fanned by the teaching effectiveness studies (Berliner and Rosenshine 1987, Edmonds 1979) led in the 1970s to concern with what was happening in the classroom. When Komoski (1978) revealed data showing that more than 90 percent of class time is spent on textbook learning, researchers began to analyze seriously teachers' reliance on commercially prepared materials (Shannon 1983, Chapman 1983, Schmidt, Caul, Byers, and Buchmann 1984). Much of this initial work was in reading because of new concern about cognitive-based comprehension instruction. But researchers also studied the match between text and teaching in English (Applebee 1987, social studies (Fetsko, 1979), mathematics (Freeman, Kuhs, Porter, Knappen, Floden, Schmidt, and Schwille 1983b), and science (Shymanski 1987).

Some of the more significant studies are the prepublication and postpublication studies by individual publishers designed to improve the effectiveness of the texts. Most major publishers regularly do field tests on selected dimensions of their major programs or conduct follow-up studies after publication to guide revisions. Proprietary information, the data from such "learner verification" studies, is rarely reported, even though many insights concerning the uses of texts in schools could emerge if ways were found to report findings two or three years after publication, when the data become less commercially sensitive. Major publishers, after all, have not only authors, consultants, and staff to provide the technical expertise needed for such research, but maintain field staffs of up to two hundred representatives trained to visit schools and classrooms regularly and collect information on what is happening.

Among the more provocative published studies that could serve as models for research in other subjects are those undertaken by Durkin (1978), who visited selected classes and reported teachers spending little time teaching comprehension even when help for such teaching is provided in teacher's manuals. Subsequently, Durkin (1981, 1983) studied and criticized basal reading manuals as providing too little help for teachers, then published data on the lack of match between what teachers do and what manuals suggest. Because of the concreteness of her data, Durkin's findings have had a strong impact on teaching and on textbooks.

Continuing the analyses of classroom practices in reading, Mason and Osborn (1983) found 90 percent of all classroom reading time in grades 3–6 devoted to word-level or word-part processing; only 10 percent was devoted to sentence-level or discourse-level processing, where most comprehension occurs. This report, coupled with the finding that 75 percent of all primary reading time is spent on workbooks and skill drills (Anderson, Hiebert, Scott, and Wilkinson 1985), led to a renewed emphasis on strengthening material for skill practice (Osborn 1984b). Clearly, the recent analyses of reading, writing, and literacy from the National Assessment of Educational Progress, which show wide-spread incompetence of American students in reasoning, may be traceable to such lack of attention to thinking (Applebee, Langer, and Mullis 1987).

Growing concern with the importance of oral language in learning—discussion, reciprocal teaching, collaborative learning, and the like—has stimulated new interest in encouraging learning from textbooks through improved oral activities (Armbruster 1987, Davidson, Padak, and Wilkerson 1987, Padak 1987). Palincsar (1987) has demonstrated that reciprocal teaching through which groups of students discuss a text results in significantly increased comprehension. And a new comparative study finds the superiority of Japanese and other Asian students in conceptual learning ascribable to the time devoted to mathematics, to congruence of the learning activities, and to extensive verbalization of mathematical concepts (Stigler and Perry 1987).

Recognition of the importance of textbook teaching has stimulated efforts to improve use of such commercial material (Osborn 1984b). A pioneer effort in 1918 seemed to go largely unnoticed (Hall-Quest 1918), but recent efforts to promote metacognitive awareness of what is learned have had a decided impact on schooling (Brown, Campione, and Day 1981). Differences in how individuals learn from texts have also been studied (Wilson 1973).

Recently, Armbruster (1987) focused on the nature of questioning in social studies and science textbooks and reported that low-level, factual questions predominate, but that some variation occurs with the subject field.

These studies, particularly the cluster in reading, have helped to inform the profession of the qualities of good textbooks, as well as the need for sound staff development programs to promote better use of textbooks. At present, the research seems to have been particularly influential in teaching reading, perhaps because of the number of studies and of present-day dissemination efforts in this curriculum area (e.g., centers, assessment results, conferences). Valuable recommendations clearly could emerge if similar studies were conducted in other subject fields.

Textbooks as a Reflection of Curriculum

With the revelation that between 75 percent and 90 percent of classroom time is devoted to textbook teaching, a growing body of research has concentrated on analyzing textbook content and pedagogy as a substitute for other ways of studying curriculum and instruction at a particular time. The Educational Product Information Exchange reported on student knowledge of textbook content at the start and end of a school year (EPIE Institute 1976b). Chall found changes in textbooks over thirty years related to declining SAT scores (Chall, Conard, and Harris 1977).

A number of studies have reported the current status of subject teaching as indicated by textbook emphases. Walker (1976) used such an analysis to re-create the pre-twentieth-century curriculum. Applebee (1983) found the writing activities in content area textbooks particularly limiting. In England, Medway (1986) examined selected writing textbooks and methods textbooks to compare changes in teaching between 1958 and 1968. DeVecchi (1981) used the study of calculus texts as the basis for constructing a theoretic framework for the discipline. In social studies, Hahn, Marker, Switzer, and Turner (1977) used textbook analyses to determine which concepts derived from the "new social studies" were being used in the classroom and which were not. Elliott (1987) reviewed efforts to teach concepts about the Constitution in grades 3, 8, and 11 by analyzing textbooks. And in England, Arnot and Whitty

(1982) reported that text analysis is the best way to develop a perspective on the American curriculum; Schwartz and Allington (1977) compared American and West German basal texts as reflections of national schools.

A series of studies on elementary school mathematics, conducted at the Institute for Research on Teaching at Michigan State University, has identified the lack of match between textbooks and tests and the content elements that teachers actually select from textbooks (Kuhs and Freeman 1979, Schwille, Porter, and Gant 1980, Freeman et al. 1983b, Schwille, Porter, Belli, Floden, Freeman, Knappen, Kuhs, and Schmidt 1983. In every case, the textbook was seen as the curriculum. Similar analyses of the content and teaching apparatus in textbooks have also characterized the separate subject studies of the International Assessment on Education, although the data from these analyses (in literature, science, mathematics, and writing) usually have been circulated only privately and not in published reports.

Recent criticism of the impact of standardized tests and state assessment on instruction (Squire 1987) has spawned a series of studies on the relationships of texts and tests (J. Thompson 1982, Freeman et al. 1983a, b). These studies indicated a less than 50 percent overlap between the topics covered in elementary mathematics books and those on related tests, a lack of fit also reported by Bracey (1987). In a comparative study, Komoski has also revealed that only four of eighty-four possible subject attributes are taught or tested in the sixth grade of three states (EPIE Institute 1987).

A similar lack of fit between reading tests and texts has also been reported by Flood and Lapp (1986), who are particularly concerned that only certain types of reading are being assessed (narrative and exposition) and that tests demonstrate a lack of interest in exposition. Armbruster (1987) found a mismatch of text questions and teaching questions in elementary social studies textbooks. Mismatch of curriculum objectives, text items, and textbook treatment is reported by the EPIE Institute in using its new computerized Integrated Instructional Information Resource to analyze test-text-curriculum items in mathematics and science in a pilot program in three states. EPIE now has a national project under way to code all existing state codes and curriculum guides in mathematics and reading.

In a particularly intriguing study in England, Dixon and Brown (1985) analyzed the questions put to students about literature on the school-end examinations and showed how the emphasis on information and on literal comprehension was limiting and impacting sound instruction in response to literature at lower levels. So provocative is this analysis, so extensive its implications for instruction, that one would like to see similar studies conducted in America relative to the questions put to students in literature, science, and social studies textbooks in relation to tests. One cannot but speculate that the absence of attention to higher-order thinking processes may begin with the teaching apparatus accompanying many textbook programs (Squire 1987).

Studying Text Structure

That the linguistic and rhetorical structures of texts can affect the adequacy of comprehension appears to be demonstrated through a long series of studies on story grammars in teaching and responding to literature. "Considerate" texts promote comprehension; "inconsiderate" texts can impact comprehension negatively (Mandler and Johnson 1977, Mandler 1978, Stein 1978, Brennan, Bridge, and Winograd 1986).

Expository texts also have been found to have structures that can, when properly utilized, facilitate learning (Anderson and Armbruster 1986, Meyer and Rice 1984, Britton and Black 1985, Armbruster 1986, Binkley 1987).

Not only paragraph structure is important to text reading, but also the structural design principles of longer texts (Calfee and Curley 1984, Calfee and Chambliss 1986), which too frequently are neglected in the classroom (Mason and Osborn 1983). Many of the studies of text structure, particularly of expository prose and content area textbooks, indicate that teaching readers about the structure of texts will facilitate reading comprehension (Armbruster 1984, Barnett 1984, Jones, Amiran, and Katims 1984). Schallert and Tierney (1980), however, attempted to relate text structure to the characteristics of readers, a much more uncertain task.

Currently, researchers appear to be testing these assumptions, particularly those associated with basal readers and social studies materials. More clear-cut findings will be required to help teachers in the classroom or to serve as guidelines for educational publishers.

The Selection of Textbooks

The processes used by state agencies and large school districts to select textbooks and other instructional materials have long been railed against but only recently studied systematically.

More than a hundred years ago, the state commissioner of education in New York expressed concern about the variation in both content and quality in available textbooks (Edmonson, 1930), and the issue has been raised periodically over the years (Maxwell 1921, Dodd 1928, Tidwell 1928, Maxwell 1930, Jensen 1931, Burnett 1950, Association of American Publishers and National Education Association 1972, Komoski 1978, English 1980, Keith 1981, Duke 1985).

Much of the concern has focused on state adoptions of textbooks in southern and western states, presently in twenty-one states representing close to 50 percent of the dollar market and a substantial increase in sales during the past twenty-five years as the population has moved south and west. The adoption market thus has been growing in size, even if no state has moved to statewide adoption since Arkansas established secondary school adoptions fifteen years ago. But neither has any state abandoned the process.

A review of studies of adoption procedures, published over the past seventy-five years, will document a gradual liberalization of requirements as almost all states moved from single adoptions, judged inappropriate by critics for meeting the individual needs of children, to multiple listing of five or more texts from which schools could choose those most appropriate for local use. Publishers call such action by states "granting a hunting license." In other words, book representatives still have to sell to local districts, but normally only from those titles that are listed. (In a few adoption states, schools can use a small percentage of textbook funds, say 15 to 20 percent, to purchase nonlisted materials.)

Statewide listing of textbooks on a regular cycle, every five to eight years, provides children in the states involved with fresh materials and reasonable funding for instructional materials on a regular basis, a strength not always perceived by the critics. Publishers particularly have been aware of abuses in "open territory," or nonlisting regions where funding for instructional materials is seldom budgeted on any regular basis, and adoptions can easily be passed over. Many reports of young people using dated social studies or science materials have come from such "open territory" states.

However, the sunshine laws regulating selection of state textbooks provide an open invitation to textbook critics who wish to complain publicly about the content of books being considered. Most of the widely publicized censorship attempts have occurred in states like California and Texas, which provide for open citizen hearings (Jenkinson 1979), although similar objections can emerge in any district.

Another fact about the adoption process, rarely studied by critics until recently, is that procedures followed in large city districts within "open territory" states, like the districts of Chicago, Milwaukee, Baltimore, the Hartford Archdiocese, and others, are remarkably similar to those followed in state adoptions. And the dollars involved in districts as large as Detroit, for example, frequently exceed those involved in states the size of Mississippi.

As public criticism of textbooks in use in the schools began to increase in the 1970s, publishers were wont to point out the enormous variety in American textbooks in level of challenge, quality, and content made available through the American free enterprise system (Squire 1981, Dessauer 1985). But the fact is that as many as ten to fifteen different textbooks are available for selection in each major curricular area. If inferior textbooks have sometimes been selected—and they have—one problem is clearly the processes used in selecting textbooks.

Comments of this kind served to direct attention to the adoption processes, which, to no publisher's surprise, turned out to be varied and complex. Not always were selectors informed about new developments in learning and teaching; on occasion, they were found to lack familiarity with the basic content of the textbooks they were trying to select. Some committees heard presentations from the publishers represented; others did not. Some were trained for the task of selecting instructional materials; others were not. Some had adequate released time to undertake the task; more did not. Farr and colleagues undertook a systematic study of procedures followed in the reading adoption in Indiana, then expanded the research to other states. Almost all adoption procedures that Farr reviewed seemed to lack disciplined, systematic approaches (Farr, Courtland, Harris, Tarr, and Treece 1983, Powell 1983, 1985, Tulley 1983). Wenersbach (1987) reports selection practices in large urban districts to be similar, although she finds schools generally satisfied with their procedures.

Because of the extensive interest in selecting reading programs, most research on textbook selection has been conducted in the reading area by specialists in the teaching of reading. There is no reason to believe that similar practices do not govern adoptions in science, mathematics, social studies, and language arts, but the profession remains open to replication of the selection process studied in other fields. The Indiana findings with respect to reading have been replicated in other states (Winograd and Osborn 1985, Marshall 1987, Winograd 1987), have been summarized and interpreted in various journals (Dessauer 1985, Bernstein 1985), and have even served as the focus for a national conference of the National Association of State Boards of Education (Cody 1986). Subsequent studies, including two of procedures in Texas, report the growing importance of the initial proclamation or call for adoption when it is very specific (Dole 1987), as well as concern with text organization and pedagogical soundness. However, despite this overall concern with pedagogy, few investigators find selectors concerned with the research base of a program, results of publishers' field tests, or market studies. Again and again, researchers find selectors consider textbooks from reputable publishing houses to be of "equal quality." Hence, qualitative discriminations are not always made (Follett 1985, Winograd 1987). But, again, the emphasis in these recent investigations has been almost too exclusively on reading. Given the amount of activity in this area, it is helpful to note that during the past two years, the Center for the Study of Reading at the University of Illinois-Urbana has been at work developing and testing new guidelines for the processes to be used in selecting readers and reports such guidelines are having a healthy effect on improving practice (Osborn 1984a, b, Dole 1987). Similar efforts might well be undertaken in other subjects. In essence, studies suggest that adoptions are most successful when the committee is enthusiastic, has time for reflection, is provided with some staff development, and has good leadership (Dole 1987). However, the research indicates repeatedly that selection committees assume an excellence in pedagogy and direct little concern to examining the quality of instruction in programs being considered. Quite possibly an important service could be provided by those engaged in textbook analysis if more attention were directed to instructional design.

Some Final Observations

In the long run, the only way to secure improvement in textbooks is to take them seriously, to review them critically as one reviews new books or new research of any kind, to hold authors as well as publishers accountable, and to insist that important new research be embedded in the programs. Dora V. Smith once pointed out that quality literature for children began to emerge only as critics began to review each publication with serious purpose. So it will be with textbooks.

As this review indicates, serious study of textbooks in reading, like serious research in reading, has been more extensive than in all other subject fields combined. And not surprisingly, more textbook programs in reading reflect the research (research on instruction and pedagogy as well as research on textbooks) than do published programs in other curricular areas. The reason for this has been demonstrated over and over in this analysis. Teachers of reading care about instructional material, and they often look in materials for those characteristics that reflect the recent research in curriculum and instruction. Not until those who analyze and those who select instructional materials in other curricular areas—social studies, science, and the language arts in particular—impose standards as concrete as those followed in reading are we likely to see greatly strengthened instructional materials in these fields as well.

In the meantime, researchers interested in improving instructional materials in any discipline or curriculum area might well consider some of the studies conducted in reading as models for inquiry elsewhere. A number of suggestions for such research have been advanced in this chapter.

One deterrent to the study of specific textbooks, particularly historical textbooks in various disciplines, is the absence in any central depository of an extensive collection. Few curriculum libraries maintain more than current collections of textbooks (which until recently have seldom been regarded as objects for serious intellectual study). Few educational publishers have even maintained a library of their own first editions of textbooks, and where maintained, they are not readily available. I understand that the Library of Congress may store but has not classified the large number of textbooks submitted for copyright purpose, but in any case, they are not easily accessible. Any student of historical development of texts will find obtaining exemplars depends more on luck and good fortune than on a planned, systematic search.

Also, both the teaching profession and the educational publishing enterprise need more frequent reviews and analyses of the many discrete and isolated studies on textbooks in subject fields if such research is to have consequences. Too many efforts are too isolated, too little known, and too often left to advocates of special pleading to have widespread effect. The Center for the Study of Reading has provided this important service in one curricular area, and the Association of American Publishers has been attempting to provide similar help to publishers by calling meetings of editors with leaders in subject fields each year (e.g., reading in 1983 and 1985, mathematics and science in 1986, writing and thinking in 1987, probably social studies in 1988), but a more permanent vehicle for analysis and synthesis of research on instructional materials must be found.

One final observation: Research on textbooks and on instructional materials also suffers from a lack of sustained interest in such research by individuals extending over a period of many years. One reason that Chall's investigations have been so incisive and so influential is that she has returned again and again to the textbook during the past thirty years. And her work has gained in power and insight with each subsequent investigation. Too many other investigators conduct a single study and then disappear, hardly a way to provide research in any depth. One can hope that some of the recent students of textbook research who seem to have developed a permanent interest, most notably Durkin, Woodward, Armbruster, and Osborn, will continue their present investigations during the years ahead. Valuable insights that will lead to improved instructional material seem more likely to occur when this happens.

References

Alvermann, Donna, O'Keefe, Kathy, and Moore, David W. "The Discussion Practices Recommended in Post-primary Reading Methods Textbooks before and after 1970." Paper presented at the annual meeting of the American Educational Research Association, Washington, DC, 1987.

American Textbook Publishers Institute. *Textbooks in Education*. New York: The Institute, 1949.

Andereck, Mary E., and Dixon, Clifton V., Jr. "Latin America in World Geography Textbooks." Paper presented at the National Council for Geographic Education, October 1983. ERIC ED 240 013.

Anderson, Lorin. "The Environment of Instruction: The Foundation of Seatwork in a Commercially Developed Curriculum." In *Comprehension Instruction: Perspectives and Suggestions*, ed. Gerald G. Duffy, Laura R. Roehler, and Jana Mason. New York: Longman, 1984.

Anderson, Lorin W., and Jones, Beau F. "Designing Instructional Strategies Which Facilitate Learning for Mastery." *Educational Psychology* 16 (Fall 1981): 121–138.

Anderson, Nancy, and Beck, Rochelle. "Central America by the Book: What Children Are Learning." *Social Education* 47 (February 1983): 102–109.

Anderson, Richard C., Hiebert, Elfrieda H, Scott, Judith A., and Wilkinson, Ian A. G. *Becoming a Nation of Readers: Report of the Commission on Reading*. Urbana, IL: National Academy of Education and Center for the Study of Reading, 1985.

Anderson, Thomas H., and Armbruster, Bonnie B. "Readable Textbooks, or, Selecting a Textbook Is Not Like Buying a Pair of Shoes." In *Reading Comprehension: From Research to Practice*, ed. Judith Orasanu. Hillsdale NJ: Erlbaum, 1986.

Anderson, Thomas H., Armbruster, Bonnie B., and Kantor, R. N. "How Clearly Written Are Children's Textbooks? or, Of Bladderworts and Alfa." Reading Education Report No. 16. Urbana IL: Center for the Study of Reading, 1980.

Apple, Michael W. "Making Knowledge Legitimate: Power, Profit, and the Textbook." In *Current Thought on Curriculum*, 1985 ASCD Yearbook. Alexandria VA: Association for Supervision and Curriculum Development, 1985.

Applebee, Arthur N. "Writing Activities in High School Textbooks: An Analysis of Audience and Function." Paper presented at the annual meeting of the American Educational Research Association, Montreal, 1983.

Applebee, Arthur N. *Writing in the Secondary School: English and the Content Areas*. Urbana IL: National Council of Teachers of English, 1987.

Applebee, Arthur N., Langer, Judith, and Mullis, Ina V. S. *Learning to Be Literate in America: Reading, Writing, and Reasoning*. Princeton, NJ: Educational Testing Service, 1987.

Armbruster, Bonnie B. "The Problem of Inconsiderate Text." In *Comprehension Instruction: Perspectives and Suggestions*, ed. Gerald Duffy, Laura Roehler, and Jana Mason. New York: Longman, 1984.

Armbruster, Bonnie B. "Content Area Textbooks: A Research Perspective." In *Reading Education: Foundations for a Literate America*, ed. Jean Osborn, Paul T. Wilson, and Richard C. Anderson. Lexington MA: Lexington Books, 1985.

Armbruster, Bonnie B. "Schema Theory and the Design of Content-area Textbooks." *Educational Psychologist* 21 (Fall 1986): 253–267.

Armbruster, Bonnie B. "Name That Date: Questions in Social Studies Programs." Paper presented at the annual meeting of the American Educational Research Association, Washington DC, 1987.

Armbruster, Bonnie B., and Anderson, Thomas H. *Content Area Textbooks*. Reading Report No. 23. Urbana IL: Center for the Study of Reading, 1981.

Armbruster, Bonnie B., and Gudbrandsen, Beth. "Reading Comprehension Instruction in Social Studies Programs." *Reading Research Quarterly* 21, no. 1 (1986): 36–48.

Arnold-Gerrity, Dorothy. "Sex Stereotyping of Women and Girls in Elementary Textbooks and Its Implication for Future Work Force Participation." Paper presented at the North Central Sociological Association, 1978.

Arnot, Madeleine, and Whitty, Geoff. "From Reproduction to Transformation: Recent Radical Perspectives on the Curriculum from the USA." *British Journal of Sociology of Education* 3, no. 1 (1982): 93–103.

Association of American Publishers (AAP), American Library Association (ALA), and Association for Supervision and Curriculum Development (ASCD). *Limiting What Students Shall Read*. Washington, DC: AAP, 1981.

Association of American Publishers (AAP) and National Education Association (NEA). *Selecting Instructional Materials for Purchase*. Report of a joint committee. Washington, DC: NEA, 1972.

Baker, Robert L., and Schutz, Richard E., eds. *Instructional Product Development*. New York: VanNostrand Reinhold, 1971.

Ball, Edward H. *Republication Learner Verification Report for Language Basics Plus: A Basic Language Arts Program*. New York: Harper & Row, 1979. ERIC ED 178 863.

Barnett, Jerrold E. "Facilitating Retention Through Instruction About Text Structure." *Journal of Reading Behavior* 16, no. 1 (1984): 1–13.

Baskin, Barbara H. "The Dismal Prospect: The Portrayal of Disability in Basal Readers." *Reading Improvement* 18 (Spring 1981): 42–47.

Baumann, James F. "Effect of Rewritten Content Passages on Middle Grade Students' Comprehension of Main Ideas: Making the Inconsiderate Considerate." *Journal of Reading Behavior* 18, no. 1 (1986): 1–21.

Beard, Jacob G. "Comprehensibility of High School Textbooks: Association with Content Area." *Journal of Reading* 11 (December 1967): 229–234.

Beck, Isabel L., and Block, Karen E. "An Analysis of Two Beginning Reading Programs: Some Facts and Some Opinions." In *Theory and Practice of Early Reading*. Vol. 1, ed. Lauren B. Resnick and Phyllis Weaver. Pittsburgh: Learning Research and Development Center, University of Pittsburgh, 1979.

Beck, Isabel L., and McCaslin, Ellen S. "An Analysis of Dimensions That Affect the Development of Code-breaking Activity in Eight Beginning Reading Programs." Pittsburgh: Learning Research and Development Center, University of Pittsburgh, 1978.

Beck, Isabel L., McCaslin, Ellen S., and McKeown, Margaret. "Basal Readers' Purpose for Story Reading: Smoothly Paving the Road or Setting Up a Detour?" *Elementary School Journal* 81 (January 1981): 45–51.

Beck, Isabel L., McKeown, Margaret, and Omanson, Richard C. "Improving the Comprehensibility of Stories: The Effects of Revisions That Improve Coherence." *Reading Research Quarterly* 19 (Spring 1984): 263–277.

Bent, Joanne. "The Readability of College Texts." MA thesis, Kean State College, New Jersey, 1981. ERIC ED 200 925.

Benthal, Herman F. "The Textbook: Past and Future." *Curriculum Review* 17 (February 1978): 5–8.

Berliner, David, and Rosenshine, Barak, eds. *Talks to Teachers*. New York: Random House, 1987.

Bernstein, Harriet. "The New Politics of Textbook Adoption." *Phi Delta Kappan* 66 (March 1985): 463–466.

Bettelheim, Bruno, and Zelan, Karen. *On Learning to Read: The Child's Fascination with Meaning*. New York: Knopf, 1982.

Binkley, Marilyn. "The Impact of Rewriting World History Textbooks for Low-achieving Students." Paper presented at the annual meeting of the American Educational Research Association, Washington, DC, 1987.

Black, Hillel. *The American Textbook*. New York: William Morrow, 1967.

Bloom, Benjamin S. *Human Characteristics and School Learning*. New York: McGraw-Hill, 1976.

Bormuth, John R. "Readability: A New Approach." *Reading Research Quarterly* 1 (Spring 1966): 79–132.

Bracey, Gerald W. "Texts, Tests Don't Match—But Does It Matter?" *Phi Delta Kappan* 68 (January 1987): 397–398.

Braddock, Richard. "The Frequency and Placement of Topic Sentences in Expository Prose." *Research in the Teaching of English* 8 (Winter 1974): 287–302.

Brennan, Allison D., Bridge, Connie A., and Winograd, Peter N. "The Effects of Structural Variation on Children's Recall of Basal Reader Stories." *Reading Research Quarterly* 21, no. 1 (1986): 91–107.

Brezin, Michael J. "Cognitive Monitoring: From Learning Theory to Instructional Applications." *Educational Communication and Technology Journal* 28 (Winter 1980): 227–242.

Britton, Bruce K, and Black, John B., eds. *Understanding Expository Text*. Hillsdale, NJ: Erlbaum, 1985.

Britton, Gwyneth E., and Lumpkin, Margaret C. "For Sale: Subliminal Bias in Textbooks." Report prepared at Oregon State University, Corvallis, OR, 1976. ED 140 279.

Brody, Philip J. "Research on Pictures in Instructional Texts: The Need for a Broadened Perspective." *Educational Communication and Technology Journal* 29 (Summer 1981): 93–100.

Brown, Ann L., Campione, Joseph C., and Day, Jeanne D. "Learning to Learn: On Training Students to Learn from Texts." *Educational Researcher* 10 (February 1981): 14–21.

Bruce, Bertram. "A New Point of View on Children's Stories." In *Learning to Read in American Schools: Basal Readers and Content Texts*, ed. Richard C. Anderson, Jean Osborn, and Robert J. Tierney. Hillsdale NJ: Erlbaum, 1984.

Bryant, Jennings, Brown, Dan, Silberberg, Alan, and Elliot, Scott M. "Humorous Illustrations in Textbooks: Effects on Information Acquisition, Appeal, Persuasibility, and Motivation." Paper presented at Speech Communication Association, New York City, 1980. ERIC ED 196 071.

Burnett, Lewie W. "Textbook Provisions in the Several States." *Journal of Educational Research* 43 (January 1950): 357–366.

Calfee, Robert C., and Chambliss, M. J. "The Structural Design Features of Large Texts." Palo Alto, CA: Stanford University, 1986.

Calfee, Robert C., and Curley, Robert G. "Structures of Prose in the Content Areas." In *Understanding Reading Comprehension*, ed. James Flood. Newark, DE: International Reading Association, 1984.

Carstensen, Leone M. "Language Experiences Found in Teacher Guides for First Grade Reading Textbooks." Ph.D. diss., University of Arizona, 1972. ERIC ED 079 668.

Chall, Jeanne S. *Readability: An Appraisal of Research and Application*. Columbus, OH: Bureau of Educational Research, Ohio State University, 1958.

Chall, Jeanne S. *Learning to Read: The Great Debate. An Update*. New York: McGraw-Hill, 1983.

Chall, Jeanne S., Conard, Sue, and Harris, Susan. *An Analysis of Textbooks in Relation to Declining SAT Scores*. New York: College Entrance Examination Board, 1977.

Chall, Jeanne S., Conard, Sue, and Harris-Sharples, Susan. "Textbooks and Challenge: An Inquiry into Textbook Difficulty, Reading Achievement, and Knowledge Acquisition." Final report to the Spencer Foundation. Cambridge, MA: Harvard University, 1983.

Chall, Jeanne S., Karger, G., and Gregory, J. "Italian Project." Cambridge, MA: Graduate School of Education, Harvard University, 1979.

Chapman, L. J. *Reading Development and Cohesion*. London: Heinemann, 1983.

Cody, C. B. *A Policymaker's Guide to Textbook Selection*. Alexandria, VA: National Association of State Boards of Education, 1986.

Cole, John Y., and Sticht, Thomas G., eds. *Textbook in American Society*. Washington, DC: Library of Congress, 1981.

College Entrance Examination Board. *Degrees of Reading Power*. Readability Report, 1982–83 academic year. New York: College Entrance Examination Board, 1982.

Collins, Allan M., Brown, Ann L., Morgan, Jerry L., and Brewer, William F. *The Analysis of Reading Tasks and Texts*. Technical Report No. 43. Urbana, IL: Center for the Study of Reading, 1977. ERIC ED 145 404.

Conard, Sue J. "The Difficulty of Textbooks for the Elementary Grades: A Survey of Educators' and Publishers' Preferences." Doct. diss., Harvard Graduate School of Education, 1981.

Conners, Robert J. "Textbooks and the Evolution of the Discipline." *College Composition and Communication* 37 (May 1986): 178–194.

Conway, Grace, and Mechler, Geraldine. "A Study of How Basal Readers Reflect Family Living Styles." MA thesis, Kean State College, New Jersey, 1983. ERIC ED 228 630.

Copperman, Paul. *The Literacy Hoax*. New York: William Morrow, 1978.

Crismore, Avon. *The Rhetoric of Social Studies Textbooks: Metadiscourse*. Research Report. Urbana, IL: University of Illinois at Urbana-Champaign, 1983. ERIC ED 239 226.

Cronbach, Lee, Bierstedt, Robert, McMurray, Foster, Schramm, Wilbur, and Spaulding, Willard B. *Text Materials in Modern Education*. Urbana, IL: University of Illinois Press, 1955.

Crowley, S. "The Evolution of Invention in Current Traditional Rhetoric: 1850–1970," *Rhetoric Review* 3, no. 2 (1985): 146–162.

Dale, Edgar, and Chall, Jeanne. *A Formula for Predicting Readability*. Columbus OH: Bureau of Educational Research, Ohio State University, 1948.

Davidson, Jane L., Padak, Nancy G., and Wilkerson, Bonnie. "Reconsidering a Focus for Curriculum Development: Curricular Issues." Paper presented at the annual meeting of the American Educational Research Association, Washington, DC, 1987.

Davis, O. L., Jr., Ponder, Gerald, Burlbaw, Lynn M., Garza-Lubeck, M., and Moss, A. *Looking at History: A Review of Major U.S. History Textbooks*. Washington, DC: People for the American Way, 1985.

Davison, Alice, and Green, Georgia. *Linguistic Complexity and Text Comprehension: A Reexamination of Readability with Alternative Views*. Hillsdale, NJ: Erlbaum, 1987.

Dawkins, John. *Syntax and Readability*. Newark, DE: International Reading Association, 1975.

Dessauer, John P. *Book Publishing: What It Is, What It Does*. New York: Bowker, 1974.

Dessauer, John P. "School Adoptions and Textbook Quality." *Book Research Quarterly* 1 (Summer 1985): 3–81.

DeVecchi, James M. "The Construction of a Logical-Empirical Structure of Knowledge for Differential Calculus Using a Theoretical Framework Based on Learning Hierarchy Theory and Order Theory." *Journal for Research in Mathematics Education* 12 (May 1981): 163–164.

Dick, Walter, and Carey, Lou. *The Systematic Design of Instruction*. Glenview, IL: Scott Foresman, 1985.

Dixon, J., and Brown, J. *Responses to Literature: What is Being Assessed? Parts I and II*. London: School Council Publications, 1985.

Dodd, Clarence T. *State Control of Textbooks*. New York: Teachers College, Columbia University, 1928.

Dole, Janice A. "Improving the Textbook Selection Process: Case Studies of the Textbook Adoption Guidelines Project." Paper presented at the annual meeting of the American Educational Research Association, Washington, DC, 1987.

Donlan, Dan. "Locating Main Ideas in History Textbooks." *Journal of Reading* 24 (November 1980): 135–140.

Dorrell, Jean, and Johnson, Betty. "A Comparative Analysis of Topics Covered in

Twenty College-level Communication Textbooks." *ABCA Bulletin* 45 (September 1982): 11–16.

Doyle, Denis. "The 'Unsacred' Texts." *American Educator* 8 (Summer 1984): 8–13.

Duchastel, Phillippe C. *Research on Illustrations in Instructional Text*. Occasional Paper No. 3. Bryn Mawr, PA: American College, 1980. (a)

Duchastel, Phillippe C. "Research on Illustrations in Text: Issues and Perspectives." *Educational Communication and Technology Journal* 28 (Winter 1980): 283–287. (b)

Duffy, T. M. *Readability Formulas: What Is the Use?* Technical Report No. 23. Pittsburgh: Communication Design Center, Carnegie-Mellon University, 1985.

Duffy, Thomas, and Waller, Robert, eds. *Designing Usable Texts*. Orlando, FL: Academic Press, 1985.

Duke, Charles R. "A Look at Current Statewide Text Adoption Procedures." Paper presented at the spring conference of the National Council of Teachers of English, Houston, 1985. ERIC ED 254 864.

Durkin, Dolores. *What Classroom Observations Reveal About Reading Comprehension Instruction*. Technical Report No. 106. Urbana, IL: Center for the Study of Reading, 1978.

Durkin, Dolores. "Reading Comprehension Instruction in Five Basal Reader Series." *Reading Research Quarterly* 16, no. 4 (1981): 515–544.

Durkin, Dolores. *Is There a Match between What Elementary Teachers Do and What Basal Manuals Recommend?* Technical Report No. 44. Urbana, IL: Center for the Study of Reading, 1983.

Durkin, Dolores. "Do Basal Manuals Teach Reading Comprehension?" In *Learning to Read in American Schools: Basal Readers and Content Texts*, ed. Richard C. Anderson, Jean Osborn, and Robert J. Tierney. Hillsdale, NJ: Erlbaum, 1984.

Durkin, Dolores. "Testing in the Kindergarten," *Reading Teacher* 40 (April 1987): 766–770.

Eberhard, Wallace B. "'News Value' Treatments Are Far from Consistent among Newswriting Texts," *Journalism Educator* 37 (Spring 1982): 9–11.

Edmonds, Ronald. "Effective Schools for the Urban Poor." *Educational Leadership* 37 (October 1979): 15–18.

Edmonson, J. B., ed. *The Textbook in American Education*. Thirtieth Yearbook of the National Society for the Study of Education, Part 2. Bloomington, IL: Public School Publishing, 1931.

Elliott, David L. "Living Document or Historical Artifact? Presentation of the U.S. Constitution in U.S. History Textbooks." Paper presented at the annual meeting of the American Educational Research Association, Washington, DC, 1987.

Elliott, David, Nagel, Kathleen C., and Woodward, Arthur. "Do Textbooks Belong in Elementary Social Studies?" *Educational Leadership* 42 (April 1985): 22–25.

Elson, Ruth M. *Guardians of Tradition: American Schoolbooks of the Nineteenth Century*. Lincoln: University of Nebraska Press, 1972.

English, Raymond. "The Politics of Textbook Adoption." *Phi Delta Kappan* 62 (December 1980): 272–278.

EPIE Institute. *Selecting and Evaluating Beginning Reading Materials.* Product Report No. 62/63. New York: EPIE Institute. 1974.

EPIE Institute. *National Study on the Nature and Quality of Instructional Materials Most Used by Teachers and Learners.* New York: Teachers College, Columbia Univesity, 1976. (a)

EPIE Institute. "Research Findings: NSAIM. Two Years Later." EPIEGRAM 5, no. 5 (1976): 1–3. (b)

EPIE Institute. "Curriculum Alignment Services for Educators: A Capability of EPIE Institute's Integrated Instructional Information Resource." New York: Paper Reporting Service, EPIE Institute, 1987.

European Affairs Division, Library of Congress. *Textbooks: Their Examination and Improvement.* Washington, DC: Library of Congress, 1948.

Farr, Roger, Courtland, M. C., Harris, P., Tarr, J., and Treece, L. *A Case Study of the Indiana State Reading Adoption Process.* Bloomington: Indiana University Press, 1983.

Fetsko, William. "Textbooks and the New Social Studies." *Social Studies* 70 (March 1979): 51–55.

FitzGerald, Frances. *America Revisited: History Schoolbooks in the Twentieth Century.* Boston: Little, Brown, 1979.

Flack, Michael J. *Cultural Diplomacy and Its Presentation in International Affairs Textbooks, 1945–1971.* Pittsburgh: University of Pittsburgh, 1971. ERIC ED 076 454.

Flagg, B. N., Weaver, P. A., Fenton, T., Gelatt, R., and Pray, R. "Children's Use of Pictures in Comprehending Written Text." Paper presented at the annual meeting of the American Educational Research Association, Boston, 1980.

Flesch, Rudolph. *Why Johnny Can't Read.* New York: Harper and Bros., 1957.

Flood, James, and Lapp, Diane. "Types of Texts: The Match Between What Students Read in Basals and What They Encounter in Tests." *Reading Research Quarterly* 21 (Summer 1986): 284–297.

Follett, Robert, "The School Textbook Adoption Process." *Book Research Quarterly* 1, no. 2 (1985): 19–22.

Frase, Lawrence T., and Schwartz, Barry J. "Typographical Cues That Facilitate Comprehension." *Journal of Educational Psychology* 71 (April 1979): 197–206.

Freeman, Donald J., Belli, Gabriella, Porter, Andrew C., Floden, Robert E., Schmidt, William H., and Schwille, John R. "The Influence of Different Styles of Textbook Use on Instructional Validity of Standardized Tests." *Journal of Educational Measurement* 20 (Fall 1983): 259–270. (a)

Freeman, Donald J., Kuhs, Therese M., Porter, Andrew C., Knappen, Lucy B., Floden, Robert E., Schmidt, William H., and Schwille, John R. *The Fourth Grade Mathematics Curriculum as Inferred from Textbooks or Tests.* Research Series No. 82. E. Lansing, MI: Institute for Research on Teaching, Michigan State University, 1983. (b)

Fry, Edward B. "The Readability Graph Validated at Primary Levels." *Reading Teacher* 22 (March 1969): 534–538.

Garcia, Jesus, et al. "Images of Named and Nonwhite Ethnic Groups as Presented in Selected Eighth Grade U.S. History Textbooks." Paper presented at the

Inter-American Congress of Psychology, Miami Beach, 1976. ERIC ED 145 379.

Gentry, Larry A. "An Analysis of the Content of Seven Spelling Series: A Technical Note." Los Alamitos, CA: Southwest Regional Laboratory, 1979.

Gionfriddo, Jeanne J. "The Dumbing Down of Textbooks: An Analysis of Six Textbook Editions during a Twelve Year Span." MA thesis, Kean State College, New Jersey, 1985. ERIC ED 255 894.

Goldstein, Paul. *Changing the American Schoolbook: Law, Politics, and Technology.* Lexington, MA: D. C. Heath, 1978.

Goodykoontz, Bess. "The Relation of Pictures to Reading Comprehension." *Elementary English Review* 13, no. 4 (1936): 125–130.

Graham, George E., Jr. "A Present and Historical Analysis of Basal Reading Series." Doct. diss., University of Virginia, 1978.

Graves, Donald H. "Language Arts Textbooks: A Writing Process Evaluation." *Language Arts* 54 (October 1977): 817–823.

Graves, Michael F., and Slater, Wayne H. "Could Textbooks Be Better Written and Would It Make a Difference?" *American Educator* 10 (Spring 1986): 36–42.

Gray, William S., and Leary, Berniece E. *What Makes a Book Readable?* Chicago: University of Chicago Press, 1935.

Green, Georgia M., and Olsen, M. S. *Interactions of Text and Illustration in Beginning Reading.* Technical Report No. 355. Urbana, IL: Center for the Study of Reading, 1985.

Gutmann, Joseph, Levin, J. R., and Pressley, G. Michael. "Pictures, Partial Pictures, and Young Children's Oral Prose Learning." *Journal of Educational Psychology* 69 (October 1977): 473–480.

Hagerty, Patricia J. "Comparative Analysis of Selected High Frequency Words Found in Commercial Spelling Series and Misspelled in Students' Writing to a Standard Measure of Word Frequency." Boulder: University of Colorado, 1981. ERIC ED 218 608.

Hahn, Carole J., Marker, Gerald W., Switzer, Thomas J., and Turner, Mary J. *Three Studies on Perception and Utilization of New Social Studies Materials.* Boulder, CO: Social Science Education Consortium, 1977. ERIC ED 177 203.

Halbert, Marie G. "An Experimental Study of Children's Understanding of Instructional Materials." *Bulletin of the Bureau of School Service* (University of Kentucky) 15, no. 4 (1943): 7–69.

Hall-Quest, A. L. *The Textbook: How to Use and Judge It.* New York: Macmillan, 1918.

Hanus, Karen S., and Moore, David W. "Reading Comprehension Questions in Secondary Literature Textbooks for Good and Poor Readers." *English Quarterly* 18, no. 4 (1985): 93–103.

Harris, Albert J., and Jacobson, Milton D. *Basic Elementary Reading Vocabularies.* New York: Macmillan, 1972.

Harrison, Colin T. *Readability in the Classroom.* New York: Cambridge University Press, 1980.

Hartley, James. *Designing Instructional Text*, 2d ed. New York: Nicols, 1985.

Hartley, James, and Burnhill, Peter. "Fifty Guidelines for Improving Instructional Text." *Programmed Learning and Educational Technology* 14 (February 1977): 67–75.

Hartley, James, and Trueman, Mark. "The Effects of Changes in Layout and Changes in Wording on Preferences for Instructional Text." *Visible Language* 15, no. 1 (1981): 13–31.

Hawkins, M. L. "Light at the End of the Tunnel, or Are Today's Elementary Social Studies Texts Really Different?" *Education for the Disadvantaged Child* 1, no. 2 (1973): 8–12.

Hefley, James C. *Are Textbooks Harming Your Children?* Milford, MI: Mott Media, 1976.

Heitz, Carolyn Ann. "Vocabulary Load and Control of First Grade Basal Readers Published in the Late 1970s." Doct. diss., University of Iowa, 1979.

Herron, J. Dudley. "High School Chemistry Textbooks: Form and Function—A Symposium: What Research Says and How It Can Be Used." *Journal of Chemical Education* 60 (October 1983): 888–890.

Hiebert, Elfrieda H., and McWhorter, Linda. "The Content of Kindergarten and Readiness Books in Four Basal Reading Programs." Paper presented at the annual meeting of the American Educational Research Association, Washington, DC, 1987.

Hillocks, George, Jr. "Books and Bombs: Ideological Conflict and the Schools—A Case Study of the Kanawha County Book Protest." *School Review* 86 (August 1978): 632–651.

Hirsch, E. D. Jr. *Cultural Literacy: What Every American Needs to Know.* Boston: Houghton Mifflin, 1987.

Hockett, John A., and Neeley, Deta P. "A Comparison of the Vocabularies of Thirty-three Primers." *Elementary School Journal* 37 (November 1936): 190–202.

Holley, C. D., et al. "Utilizing Intact and Embedded Headings as Processing Aids with Nonnarrative Text." *Contemporary Educational Psychology* 6 (July 1981): 227–236.

Hunter, B., Crismore, Avon, and Pearson, P. David. *Visual Displays in Basal Readers and Social Studies Textbooks.* Urbana, IL: Center for the Study of Reading, 1986.

Hynd, Cynthia, and Alvermann, Donna E. "The Role of Refutation Text in Overcoming Difficulty with Science Concepts." *Journal of Reading* 29 (February 1986): 440–446.

Jay, Winifred T. "Sex Stereotyping in Selected Mathematics Textbooks for Grades Two, Four, and Six." Doct. diss., University of Oregon, 1973. ERIC ED 087 627.

Jenkins, Floyd H., et al. *Elementary Basal Readers and Work Mode Bias.* Denton: North Texas State University, 1973. ERIC ED 099 574.

Jenkinson, Edward B. *Censors in the Classroom: The Mind Benders.* Carbondale: Southern Illinois University Press, 1979.

Jenkinson: Edward B. *The Schoolbook Protest Movement: 40 Questions and Answers.* Bloomington, IN: Phi Delta Kappa, 1986.

Jensen, Frank A. *Current Procedure in Selecting Textbooks.* Philadelphia: J.B. Lippincott, 1931.

Johnson, D., with Baumann, James. *The Ginn Word Book for Teachers.* Boston: Ginn, 1983.

Johnson, Linda L., and Otto, Wayne. "Effect of Alterations in Prose Style on the Readability of College Texts." *Journal of Educational Research* 75 (March/April 1982): 222–229.

Johnson, Roger E. "The Reading Level of Elementary Social Studies Textbooks Is Going Down." *Reading Teacher* 30 (May 1977): 901–906.

Jonassen, David H. *The Technology of Text.* Englewood Cliffs, NJ: Educational Technology Publications, 1985.

Jones, Beau F., Amiran, Minda R., and Katims, Michael. "Teaching Cognitive Strategies and Text Structures Within Language Arts Programs." In *Thinking and Learning Skills: Relating Basic Research to Instructional Practice*, Vol. 1., ed. Judith W. Segal, Susan F. Chipman, and Robert Glaser. Hillsdale, NJ: Erlbaum, 1984.

Jones, Ella D. "A Comparative Readability Study of Certain College Textbooks." MA thesis, Kean State College, New Jersey, 1981. ERIC ED 200 924.

Kane, M. B. "Minorities: What the Textbooks Don't Say." *Current* 129 (1971): 13–16.

Kealey, Robert J. "The Image of the Family in Second Grade Readers." *Momentum* 11 (October 1980): 16–19.

Keetz, Mary A. "The Readability of Study Habit Books and College Students' Reading Ability." *Journal of Reading Behavior* 10 (Spring 1978): 97–101.

Keith, S. *Politics of Textbook Selection.* Research report No. 81-AT. Palo Alto: CA: Institute for Research on Educational Finance and Governance, Stanford University, 1981.

Kemp, Jerrold E. *The Instructional Design Process.* New York: Harper & Row, 1985.

Klare, George R. "Assessing Readability." *Reading Research Quarterly* 10, no. 1 (1975): 62–102.

Klare, George R. "Readability." In *Handbook of Reading Research*, ed. P. David Pearson. New York: Longman, 1984.

Koenke, Karl. "Pictures in Reading Materials: What Do We Know About Them?" *Reading Teacher* 40 (May 1987): 902–905.

Komoski, P. Kenneth. "The Realities of Choosing and Using Instructional Materials." *Educational Leadership* 36 (October 1978): 46–50.

Komoski, P. Kenneth. "Instructional Materials Will Not Improve Until We Change the System." *Educational Leadership* 42 (April 1985): 31–37.

Koops, John B. "Recent Practices in Teaching Writing: A Critical Examination of Junior and Senior High School Composition Textbooks." Ph.D. diss., University of Michigan, 1975. ERIC ED 114 863.

Krug, Mark. "Freedom and Racial Equality: A Study of 'Revised' High School History Texts." *School Review* 78 (May 1970): 297–354.

Kuhs, Therese M., and Freeman, Donald J. "The Potential Influence of Textbooks on Teachers' Selection of Content for Elementary School Mathematics." Research Series No. 48. E. Lansing, MI: Institute for Research on Teaching, 1979.

Kurzman, Maurice. "The Reading Ability of College Freshmen Compared to the Readability of Their Textbooks." *Reading Improvement* 11 (Fall 1974): 13–25.

Lantaff, Roger E. "The Effects of Prose Structure on the Recall of Fifth Graders and College Students." Paper presented at the annual meeting of the National Reading Conference, St. Petersburg Beach, 1978. ERIC ED 165 101.

Last, Ellen. "The Texas Textbook Protestors Define Literature and Education." Doct. diss., University of Wisconsin, 1982. ERIC ED 257 071.

Legenza, Alice, and Knafle, June D. "The Effective Components of Children's Pictures." Paper presented at the National Reading Conference, St. Petersburg Beach, 1978. ERIC ED 165 134.

Leviton, Laura C., and Cook, Thomas D. "Evaluation Findings in Education and Social Work Textbooks." *Evaluation Review* 7 (August 1983): 497–518.

Luker, William A., and Jenkins, Floyd H. "Work Mode Bias in Elementary Text Materials." *Journal of Industrial Teacher Education* 11 (February 1973): 16–26.

Lynch, James J., and Evans, Bertrand. *High School English Textbooks: A Critical Examination.* Boston: Little, Brown, 1963.

Mandler, Jean M. "A Code in the Node: The Use of a Story Schema in Retrieval." *Discourse Processes* 1 (March 1978): 14–35.

Mandler, Jean M., and Johnson, Nancy S. "Remembrance of Things Parsed: Story Structure and Recall." *Cognitive Psychology* 9 (January 1977): 111–115.

Marshall, John D. "State-level Textbook Decision Making: The Way Things Were in Texas." Paper presented at the annual meeting of the American Educational Research Association, Washington, DC, 1987.

Mason, Jona, and Osborn, Jean. "When Do Children Begin 'Reading to Learn'?" In *A Survey of Practices in Grades Two to Five*, Technical Report No. 261. Urbana, IL: Center for the Study of Reading, 1983. ERIC ED 220 805.

Mavrogenes, Nancy. "William S. Gray: An Intellectual Biography." Ph.D. diss., University of Chicago, 1985.

Maxwell, Charles R. *The Selection of Textbooks.* Boston: Houghton Mifflin, 1921, 1930.

Mayer, Richard E. *Structural Analysis of Science Prose: Can We Increase Problem Solving Performance?* Technical Report Series in Learning and Cognition, Report No. 81–3. Santa Barbara: University of California, 1981. ERIC ED 205 398.

McCullough, Constance M. *Preparation of Textbooks in the Mother Tongue.* Newark, DE: International Reading Association, 1974.

McGaw, Barry, and Grotelueschen, Arden. *The Direction of the Effect of Questions in Prose Materials.* Urbana: Center for Instructional Research, University of Illinois, 1971. ERIC ED 061 539.

Medway, P. G. "What Counts as English: Selections from Language and Reading in a School Subject at the Twelve-Year-Old Level." Doct. diss., University of Leeds, 1986.

Meyer, Bonnie J.F., and Rice, G. Elizabeth. "The Structure of Text." In *Handbook of Reading Research*, ed. P. David Pearson. New York: Longman, 1984.

Miller, William A. "Reading with and Without Pictures." *Elementary School Journal* 38 (April 1937): 676–682.

Miller, William S. "A Critical Analysis of the Vocabulary of Ten Third Year Readers." Doct. diss., University of Iowa, 1916.

Montare, Alberto, Elman, Elaine, and Cohen, Joanne. "Words and Pictures: A Test of Samuels' Findings." *Journal of Reading Behavior* 9 (Fall 1977): 269–285.

Morris, Judith A., and Johns, Jerry L. "Are 1st Grade Reading Books Easier Than Twenty Years Ago?" *Reading Teacher* 40 (January 1987): 486–487.

National Education Association. *Kanawha County, West Virginia: A Textbook Study of Cultural Conflict*. Washington, DC: National Education Association, 1975.

Negin, Gary A. "Logical Connectives in Industrial Arts Textbooks." *Reading Improvement* 19 (Fall 1982): 170–172.

Olson, Arthur V. "An Analysis of the Vocabulary of Seven Primary Reading Series." *Elementary English* 42 (March 1965): 261–264.

Osborn, Bess, and Bobruk, Toni. "The BASAL: What Does It Demand of the Beginning Reader?" Paper presented at the National Reading Conference, Dallas, 1981. ERIC ED 220 809.

Osborn, Jean. *Evaluating Workbooks*. Reading Education Report No. 52. Urbana, IL: Center for the Study of Reading, 1984. (a)

Osborn, Jean. "The Purposes, Uses, and Contents of Workbooks and Some Guidelines for Publishers." In *Learning to Read in American Schools: Basal Readers and Content Texts*, ed. Richard C. Anderson, Jean Osborn, and Robert L. Tierney. Hillsdale, NJ: Erlbaum, 1984. (b)

Osborn, Jean, Jones, Beau F., and Stein, Marcy. "The Case for Improving Textbooks." *Educational Leadership* 42 (April 1985): 9–16.

Padak, Nancy. "A Comparative Analysis of the Teachers' Roles in Two Junior High Literature Lessons." Paper presented at the annual meeting of the American Educational Research Association, Washington, DC, 1987.

Palincsar, Annemarie S. "Collaborating for Collaborative Learning of Text Comprehension." Paper presented at the annual meeting of the American Educational Research Association, Washington, DC, 1987.

Pauling, Linus. "Throwing the Book at Elementary Chemistry." *Science Teacher* 50 (September 1983): 25–29.

Peiser, Andrew C. "Populism in High School Textbooks." *Social Education* 37 (April 1973): 302–309.

Pelletti, John C. "The Effect of Graphic Roles in Elementary Social Studies Texts on Cognitive Achievement." *Theory and Research in Social Education* 2 (December 1974): 79–93.

Pieroneki, Florence T. "Do Basal Readers Reflect the Interests of Intermediate Students?" *Reading Teacher* 33 (January 1980): 408–412.

Poulos, Nicholis, "Negro Attitudes Toward Textbook Illustrations." *Journal of Negro Education* 38 (Spring 1969): 177–181.

Powell, Deborah A. "An Analysis of Decision Making in Local School District Textbook Adoptions." Doct. diss., Indiana University, 1983.

Powell, Deborah A. "Selection of Reading Textbooks at the District Level: Is This a Rational Process?" *Book Research Quarterly* 1 (Fall 1985): 23–35.

Quillen, I. James. *Textbook Improvement and International Understanding*. Washington, DC: American Council on Education, 1948.

Reid, James M. *An Adventure in Textbooks*. New York: Bowker, 1969.

Render, Barry, Stair, Ralph M., Jr., Stearns, G. Kent, and Villere, Maurice. "Choosing Business Data Processing Textbooks: A Look at Readability." *Journal of Educational Data Processing* 12, no. 3 (1975): 30–35.

Rogers, Margaret A. "A Different Look at Word Problems." *Mathematics Teacher* 68 (April 1975): 285–288.

Rose, Mike. "Sophisticated, Ineffective Books: The Dismantling of Process in Composition Texts." *College Composition and Communication* 32 (February 1981): 65–74.

Rowls, Michael D., and Hess, Robert K. "A Comparative Study of the Readability of Grade Seven Through Twelve Language Arts Textbooks." *Clearing House* 57 (January 1984): 201–204.

Rubin, Andee. *Conceptual Readability: New Ways to Look at Text*. Reading Education Report No. 31. Urbana, IL: Center for the Study of Reading, 1981. ERIC ED 208 370.

Rugg, Harold O. *That Men May Understand*. New York: Doubleday, Doran, 1941.

Sadker, Myrna P., Sadker, David M., and Garies, Ruth S. "Sex Bias in Reading and Language Arts Teacher Education Texts." *Reading Teacher* 33 (February 1980): 530–537.

Samuels, S. Jay. "Effects of Pictures on Learning to Read, Comprehension, and Attitudes." *Review of Educational Research* 40 (June 1970): 397–407.

Schallert, Diane. "The Role of Illustrations in Reading Comprehension." In *Theoretical Issues in Reading Comprehension*, ed. Rand Spiro, William F. Brewer, and Bertram C. Bruce. Hillsdale, NJ: Erlbaum, 1980.

Schallert, Diane, and Gleiman, G. M. *Some Reasons Why Teachers Are Easier to Understand Than Textbooks*. Reading Education Report No. 9. Urbana, IL: Center for the Study of Reading, 1979.

Schallert, Diane L., and Tierney, Robert J. "Learning from Expository Text: The Interaction of Text Structure with Reader Characteristics." Austin: University of Texas, 1980.

Schmidt, William H., Caul, Jacqueline, Byers, Joe L., and Buchmann, Margret. "Content of Basal Text Selections: Implications for Comprehension Instruction." In *Comprehension Instruction: Perspectives and Suggestions*, ed. Gerald G. Duffy, Laura R. Roehler, and Jona Mason. New York: Longman, 1984.

Schwartz, Lita L., and Isser, Natalie. "Attitudes Toward the Jewish Minority in Public Education." *Jewish Education* 45 (Summer/Fall 1977): 33–39.

Schwartz, Roswitha, and Allington, Richard L. "A Comparison of American and West German Basal Texts." *Reading Teacher* 31 (December 1977): 280–282.

Schwille, John, Porter, Andrew C., Belli, Gabriella, Floden, Robert E., Freeman, Donald, Knappen, Lucy B., Kuhs, Therese, and Schmidt, William. "Teachers as Policy Brokers in the Content of Elementary Mathematics." In *Handbook of Teaching and Policy*, ed. Lee Shulman and Gary Sykes. New York: Longman, 1983.

Schwille, John, Porter, Andrew C., and Gant, Michael. "Content Decision Making and the Politics of Education." *Educational Administration Quarterly* 16 (Spring 1980): 21–40.

Selke, Erich. "A Comparative Study of the Vocabularies of Twelve Beginning Books in Reading." *Journal of Educational Research* 22 (December 1930): 369–374.

Seminoff, N. W. "Characteristics of Written Questions in Selected American History Textbooks: An Investigation." Paper presented at the National Council for the Social Studies, 1981.

Shannon, Patrick. "The Use of Commercial Reading Materials in American Elementary Schools." *Reading Research Quarterly* 19 (Fall 1983): 68–85.

Shapiro, Sheila. "An Analysis of Poetry Teaching Procedures in Sixth-Grade Basal Manuals." *Reading Research Quarterly* 20 (Spring 1985): 368–381.

Shebilski, Wayne L., and Rotondo, John A. "Typographical and Spatial Clues That Facilitate Learning from Textbooks." *Visible Language* 15, no. 1 (1981): 41–54.

Shymansky, James A. "Issues in the Analysis of Science Textbooks and the CASST Project." Paper presented at the annual meeting of the American Educational Research Association, Washington, DC, 1987.

Smith, B. D. "Do Pictures Make a Difference in College Textbooks?" *Reading Horizons* 26, no. 4 (1986): 270–277.

Smith, Nila B. *American Reading Instruction.* Newark, DE: International Reading Association, 1986.

Soltis, Judith M. "American Grammar Texts (1850–1984): Their Role in the Explicit, Operative, and Implicit Curricula of Schools." Paper presented at the annual meeting of the American Educational Research Association, Washington, DC, 1987.

Sorenson, Nancy L. "Phonics Generalizations in Five Current Basal Readers." Cheney, WA: Author, 1982. ERIC ED 261 362.

Southwest Regional Laboratory. *Communication Skills Program.* Lexington, MA: Ginn, 1976.

Spencer, Herbert. *The Visible Word.* New York: Hastings House, 1968.

Squire, James R. "Publishers, Social Pressures, and Textbooks." In *The Textbook in American Society,* ed. John Cole and Thomas Sticht. Washington, DC: Library of Congress, 1981.

Squire, James R., ed. "The State of Assessment in Reading." Special issue of *Reading Teacher* 40 (April 1987): 724–791.

Stein, Nancy L. *How Children Understand Stories: A Developmental Analysis.* Report No. 69. Urbana, IL: Center for the Study of Reading, 1978.

Stetson, E. G., and Boutin, F. J. "Evaluation of Twelve Elementary Spelling Programs Using the Spelling Program Effectiveness Scale (SPERS)." Paper presented at the National Reading Conference, 1982.

Steward, M. D. *Prejudice in Textbooks.* Washington, DC: American Council on Education, 1950.

Stewart, Donald C. "Composition Textbooks and the Assault on Tradition." *College Composition and Communication* 29 (May 1978): 171–175.

Sticht, Thomas G., and Zapf, D. W., eds. *Reading and Readability Research in the Armed Services.* Alexandria, VA: Human Resources Research Organization, 1976.

Stigler, James W., Fuson, Karen C., Ham, Mark, and Kim, Myong Sook. "An Analysis of Addition and Subtraction Word Problems in American and Soviet Elementary Mathematics Books." *Cognition and Instruction* 3, no. 3 (1986): 153–171.

Stigler, James W., and Perry, M. "Cross-Cultural Studies of Mathematics Teaching and Learning: Recent Findings and New Directions." Paper prepared for NSR-NCTM Research Agenda Conference on Effective Mathematics Teaching, Columbia, MO, 1987.

Stone, Clarence R. "The Vocabularies of Twenty Preprimers." *Elementary School Journal* 41 (February 1941): 423–429.

Strickland, Ruth G. "The Contribution of Structural Linguistics to the Teaching of Reading, Writing, and Grammar in the Elementary School." *Bulletin of the School of Education* 40, no. 1. Bloomington, IN: Indiana University, 1964.

Taylor, Wilson L. "'Cloze Procedures': A New Tool for Measuring Readability." *Journalism Quarterly* 30 (Fall 1953): 415–433.

Thomas, James L. "The Use of Pictorial Illustrations in Instruction: Current Findings and Implications for Further Research." Research Report, 1976. ERIC ED 160 108.

Thompson, Janet R. "An Evaluative Comparison of Language Arts Achievement Subtests and Language Arts Textbooks." Research project. Orlando, FL: University of Central Florida, 1982.

Thompson, P. J. "A Model of the Textbook in the Ecology of Education." Paper presented at the annual meeting of the American Educational Research Association, New York City, 1982.

Tidwell, Clyde Jesse. *State Control of Textbooks.* New York: Columbia University Press, 1928.

Tinker, Miles A. *Legibility of Print.* Ames: Iowa State University Press, 1963.

Townsend, E. J. "The Text-book Question." *Education* 11 (May 1891): 556–565.

Tulley, Michael A. "A Descriptive Study of the Intentionality of Selected State-level Textbook Adoption Policies." Doct. diss., Indiana University, 1983.

Tyson-Bernstein, Harriet, and Woodward, Arthur. "The Great Textbook Machine and Prospects for Reform." *Social Education* 50 (January 1986): 41–45.

UNESCO. *The Educational Administrator and Instructional Materials.* Paris: UNESCO, 1984.

Venezky, Richard L., Kaestle, Carl F., and Sum, A. M. *The Subtle Danger.* Princeton, NJ: Educational Testing Service, 1987.

Walker, Benjamin F. *Curriculum Evolution as Portrayed Through Old Textbooks.* Terre Haute: School of Education, Indiana State University, 1976. ERIC ED 126 015.

Waller, Robert. *Typography for Graphic Communication and Typographic Access Structures for Educational Texts and Graphic Aspects of Complex Texts.* Bucks, Eng.: Institute of Educational Technology, Open University, 1980. ERIC ED 221 152.

Weintraub, Samuel. "The Effect of Pictures on the Comprehension of a Second Grade Basal Reader." Doct. diss., University of Illinois, 1960.

Wendt, Dirk. "An Experimental Approach to the Improvement of the Typographic Design of Textbooks." *Visible Language* 13, no. 2 (1979): 108–133.

Wendt, Dirk. "Improving the Legibility of Textbooks: Effects of Working and

Typographic Design." *Visible Language* 16, no. 1 (1982): 88–93.

Wenersbach, Ruth. "Textbook Selection Practices in Urban School Districts." Doct. diss., University of Cincinnati, 1987.

Williams, Joanne. "A Study to Determine the Reading Levels of the Math Texts in Grades 1 through 6 Published by Holt, Rinehart and Winston, Scott Foresman, and Field Education Publishers." MA thesis, Kean College of New Jersey, 1979. ERIC ED 169 504.

Willis, P. J. "Mathematics Textbooks." *Mathematics in School* 3, nos. 1 and 3 (1974): 2–4, 7–9.

Willows, Dale M. "A Picture Is Not Always Worth a Thousand Words: Pictures as Distractors in Reading." *Journal of Educational Research* 70 (April 1978): 255–262. (a)

Willows, Dale M. "Individual Differences in Distraction by Pictures in a Reading Situation." *Journal of Educational Psychology* 70 (October 1978): 837–847. (b)

Willows, Dale M. "Effects of Picture Salience on Reading Comprehension of Illustrated and Nonillustrated Aspects of Texts." Paper presented at the annual meeting of the American Educational Research Association, Boston, 1980.

Wilson, Howard E. *Intergroup Relations in Teaching Material.* Washington, DC: American Council on Education, 1948.

Wilson, John T. "The Effects of Individual Differences on Learning from Written Materials: The Control of Inspection Behavior by Test-like Events." Ph.D. diss., University of Florida, 1973.

Winograd, Peter. "Adopting Textbooks in Kentucky: A Retrospective View." Paper presented at the annual meeting of the American Educational Research Association, Washington, DC, 1987.

Winograd, Peter, and Osborn, Jean. "How Adoption of Reading Textbooks Works in Kentucky: Some Problems and Some Solutions." *Book Research Quarterly* 1 (Fall 1985): 3–18.

Woodward, Arthur. "Are We Getting Our Money's Worth from Textbooks? Comments on an Imperfect Instructional Tool and What to Look For." Paper presented at the Textbook Reform Conference of National State Boards of Education and the Council of Chief State School Officers, Washington, DC, 1985. (a)

Woodward, Arthur. "Taking Teaching Out of Teaching and Reading Out of Learning to Read: A Historical Study of Reading Textbook Teachers Guides, 1920–1980." Paper presented at the annual meeting of the American Educational Research Association, Chicago, 1985. (b)

Woodward, Arthur. "Photographs in Textbooks: More Than Pretty Pictures?" Paper presented at the annual meeting of the American Educational Research Association, San Francisco, 1986.

Woodward, Arthur. "From Professional Teacher to Activities Manager: The Changing Role of the Teacher in Reading Teachers' Guides, 1930–1986." Paper presented at the annual meeting of the American Educational Research Association, Washington, DC, 1987. (a)

Woodward, Arthur. "Old Wine in New Bottles: An Analysis of Changes in Social Studies Textbooks from Old to New Edition." Paper presented at the annual meeting of the American Educational Research Association, Washington, DC, 1987. (b)

Woodward, Arthur, and Elliott, David L. "Evolution, Creationism, and Textbooks: A Study of Publishers' Perceptions of Their Market." Paper presented at the annual meeting of the American Educational Research Association, New Orleans, 1984.

Woodward, Arthur, Elliott, David L., and Nagel, Kathleen C. "Beyond Textbooks in Elementary Social Studies." *Social Education* 50 (January 1986): 50–53.

Wrightstone, J. Wayne, and Lazar, May. *A Study of Preprimers through Third Grade Readers in Eleven Basic Reading Series.* New York: Bureau of Educational Research, Board of Education of the City of New York, 1957.

Zahn, K. G. "A Design for Class Testing Mathematics Textbook Materials." *Two-Year College Mathematics Journal* 3 (February 1972): 29–32.

Zimet, Sara G. *What Children Read in School.* New York: Grune and Stratton, 1972.

Zimet, Sara G., Wiberg, J. Lawrence, and Blom, Gaston E. "Attitudes and Values in Primers from the United States and Twelve Other Countries." *Journal of Social Psychology* 84 (August 1972): 167–174.

6

Utilization of Research by Practitioners in Education

Ralph W. Tyler

Senator William Benton was deeply interested in education. When he reached age forty, he sold his share in a profitable advertising agency to become vice-president for public relations at the University of Chicago without salary. There he joined his Yale classmate, Robert Maynard Hutchins, who was then president of the University of Chicago.

Senator Benton was also thoroughly convinced of the value of research in guiding practice in most fields. He had found research in the field of communication of great value in guiding advertising and was sure it could help improve the effectiveness of education. Hence, he was greatly surprised and deeply concerned when Paul Mort, professor of education at Teachers College, Columbia University, reported the results of the studies he and his students had made that indicated it took fifty years after an innovation in education had been demonstrated to increase the effectiveness of student learning before 80 percent of American schools had adopted the innovation. I heard him say many times, "This is intolerable. We must do something to help schools and colleges adopt an effective innovation more quickly."

Why This Delay?

This concern over the delay in adopting helpful innovations in education has not been limited to William Benton. During the past quarter-century, a great deal of research has been focused on this problem. The most common factor in delaying the adoption of research findings is practitioners' belief that research innovations are not relevant to the problems of practice. The late Stephen Bailey sent out a questionnaire to a probability sample of American school superintendents asking them to list the research findings that they had found helpful in their work. Few of them could name any research that they considered helpful. In discussions with these superintendents, he found that few of them were able to recall the nature and results of any educational research as such, but they were using many principles and concepts that had been identified and validated by research investigations in fields of student learning, group problem solving, educational leadership, school finance, organizational behavior, and so forth. These principles and concepts had become so well accepted by leaders in educational administration that they had become the "administrator's guide." Their origin in research investigations had been forgotten.

Because practitioners do not realize that earlier research has developed and validated concepts and principles of practice, they do not carefully and thoughtfully review current research for increased understanding of educational practice. After a while, however, one or more innovative practitioners learn of research that seems to be relevant to the problems of practice they are facing. These practitioners study the research and seek to test the ideas in their own work. This seems to be the typical slow movement of research findings into the practice of schools and colleges.

Can This Delay Be Reduced?

From time to time in the progress of American education, this delay has been reduced. When educational practitioners recognize serious problems on which they need help, some have sought the assistance of research. Two examples quickly come to mind.

The Eight-Year Study

During the Great Depression of the 1930s, most young people could not find jobs, so they remained in high school. In 1929, the high schools enrolled about 25 percent of the age group. By 1932, nearly 50 percent of the age group was enrolled in high school. Many of the new students did not plan to go to college and found the high school program inappropriate to their interests and often meaningless. Their teachers and principals recognized the lack of interest and motivation on the part of these new students. They, too, believed that the curriculum and instructional procedures should be reexamined and reconstructed.

At that time, many elementary schools had become less formal and more flexible in their offerings. More emphasis was being given to student self-direction in learning and in classroom management. The high schools had not changed, so when students who had experienced the informality and self-direction of progressive elementary schools entered high school, they felt they were being treated as small children rather than as adolescent youth.

The high schools in the 1930s were thus experiencing two pressures: (1) to develop an educational program more appropriate to the new students and (2) to develop an educational program and school procedures that would sustain and encourage student self-direction. But the high schools felt unable to make significant changes because of the state requirements and the requirements that colleges and universities used for high school graduates who sought admission.

The Progressive Education Association took the lead in working out a national demonstration. It appointed a Commission on the Relation of School and College composed of well-known public persons as well as college and high school personnel. This commission proposed that a small number of secondary schools that wished to be a part of the demonstration be selected and given eight years to design and implement an educational program that the schools believed better met the needs of their students and would also prepare them for success in pursuing a college education. During these eight years, the school would not be expected to meet the particular course requirements of state or college authorities. Their students would be admitted on the basis of evidence that they had developed the knowledge and skills for college work. This project would include an evaluation component to provide evidence of (1) what students were learning in the new high school programs, (2) their having developed the knowledge and skill required for college success, (3) how well the students in the new programs who went to college succeeded in their college work, and (4) how well the students in the new programs who did not go to college succeeded in the work place.

All the state departments of education agreed to permit high schools in their states to participate in the project. All but one of the major U.S. colleges and universities also agreed to admit students from the selected schools even if they did not meet the usual entrance requirements. Thirty schools and school systems were selected from many applicants to participate in the project.

The project began operation in September 1933. The participating schools quickly discovered that they needed help in devising, developing, and implementing their programs and in evaluating their progress. They called vehemently for help. The directing committee of the project responded by establishing a large number of research committees. There was a committee on studies of adolescents directed by Carolyn Zachry of Teachers College, Columbia University. Each school was invited to study samples of their students to help understand them as persons and especially as learners. In each summer workshop, a group of teachers was guided by Dr. Zachry to gain competence in studying their students as developing adolescents.

There was an overall committee on the secondary school curriculum under the chairmanship of Elliot Dunlap Smith, then Provost of Carnegie Institute of Technology. This overall committee had research subcommittees. One on language in general education was guided by Ivor Richards, who at Cambridge University was coauthor of *The Meaning of Meaning*. Harvard University brought him to the United States to establish the Orthological Institute there. Another research committee guided by Louise Rosenblatt of Sarah Lawrence College dealt with literature as exploration. The committee on science in general education was guided by Robert Havighurst, a physical chemist and a dedicated teacher. The committee on mathematics in general education was guided by Maurice Hartung, a mathematician at the University of

Wisconsin. The committee on social studies in general education was guided by I. James Quillen, a historian, who later became dean at Stanford. The committee on the arts in general education was chaired by Thomas Munroe, curator at the Cleveland Museum of Art. It was fortunate, too, to include Bruno Bettelheim after he arrived from a Nazi concentration camp. Bettelheim earned a Ph.D. in art as well as one in psychology from the University of Vienna. For research in learning, I was able to draw upon my own work and that of my colleagues at the Bureau of Educational Research at Ohio State University.

With this large body of researchers, practitioners had many opportunities to seek research assistance on problems encountered in the progress of the Eight-Year Study. Beginning in 1936 and extending through 1941, summer workshops were held in which teacher and researcher could work together on problems of common interest. The first workshop in 1936 was held on the campus of Ohio State University, but the demand for attendance was so great that, thereafter, we leased small college campuses, where the researchers and practitioners could work and live together for six weeks. We leased the campuses of Sarah Lawrence College, in Bronxville, New York, Colorado Women's College in Denver, and Mills College in Oakland, California. When I moved to Chicago, I arranged for a special dormitory on the campus of the University of Chicago for workshops there in 1939, 1940, and 1941.

The Eight-Year Study demonstrated quite clearly that when practitioners recognize serious problems on which they need help, they seek research assistance and quickly apply relevant findings.

Education of Disadvantaged Children

One other illustration is a more recent example of the use of research without long delay. In 1964, President Lyndon Johnson established a task force on education under the chairmanship of John Gardner. I was a member of that task force. President Johnson asked us to identify serious problems in education that we thought should be given attention by the federal government. Our survey of the situation at that time clearly indicated that children from homes of poverty were having great difficulty learning what schools are expected to teach. The educational achievement of children in

inner-city schools and in schools enrolling sharecroppers and mi-
grant farm workers was far lower than that of children from homes
of middle income. In our task force report, we referred to these
students as disadvantaged children and recommended that schools
enrolling a considerable concentration of these children be given
federal funds to add to the resources then being used in their
education.

Title I of the Elementary and Secondary School Education Act
of 1965 authorized an appropriation of about $1 billion to be
allocated by the states as supplementary resources for schools
enrolling a concentration of disadvantaged children. The identification of this serious problem and the need for knowledge to deal
with it led many concerned practitioners to search the research
literature and to stimulate more research on ways of increasing the
learning of disadvantaged children. In the first three years after the
1965 ESEA enactment, there was little improvement in the
achievement of these children, but by 1969, there was evidence of
significant improvement. And the more recent reports of the National Assessment of Educational Progress show that this group of
students is making more progress than other students, although
their achievement is still low. The volume of research findings on
their preschool education, like Head Start, and on their elementary
education, like Follow Through, is impressive. When practitioners
recognize a problem about which they have little understanding,
they stimulate research as well as seeking findings from previous
studies.

Obstacles to Research Utilization

These illustrations are in some respects atypical. The Eight-Year
Study involved an amazing collection of practitioners and researchers. The education of disadvantaged children is widely seen
as a serious problem impeding the nation's effort to become a
literate society. There are many other less-publicized situations in
which research could help practitioners where immediate utilization does not take place. What are the obstacles?

Perhaps the greatest impediment to researchers and practitioners working together is the lack of a tradition for doing so. Colleges
and universities provide the vast majority of research positions in
the field of education. The tradition in these institutions is to look

to other colleges and universities for ideas to guide their research efforts. The land-grant institutions were established to provide knowledge to guide farmers and engineers, but schools and colleges of education have not followed their example. Nor has there been a tradition among practitioners to seek research assistance as they encounter problems. Instead, new practices have been stimulated largely by movements—the Herbartian Movement, the Montessori Movement, and the like—rather than by an analysis and investigation of particular problems. We have embraced solutions without finding out the problems needing to be solved.

Part of the 1965 ESEA authorized the establishment of educational laboratories. I wrote this section as part of the task force report. Whereas the R and D centers were supposed to focus on research, the laboratories were to focus on the schools and their problems, seeking to bring research to bear upon practitioners' problems. However, most of the education laboratories became R and D centers focusing on research rather than on the problems of practitioners. The education public did not perceive the possibility of an institution based on practitioners' problems. Researchers are accustomed to looking to the university for guidance and rewards. Practitioners are accustomed to looking to school and community leaders for guidance and rewards. It is therefore difficult to get them together and establish a tradition of working together.

Educational Partnership

The importance of such joint efforts, however, is now being increasingly recognized. John Goodlad is giving national leadership to the concept of partnership of schools and universities, and a number of them have been formed. I am participating in one in western Massachusetts called the Coalition for School Improvement. It involves the University of Massachusetts and eleven schools in the area. It has identified several serious educational problems on which practitioners and university personnel are working jointly. I think educational partnerships may help eliminate the situation that Senator Benton called "intolerable." The partnerships seem likely to reduce greatly the time between the findings of helpful research and their utilization by practitioners.

7

Coping with Curriculum

John I. Goodlad

The late Robert Benchley once wrote a book entitled *My Ten Years in a Quandary*. I have been four months—not years, fortunately—in a quandary about what to say in this chapter. Write about whatever you wish, I was instructed, so long as it is relevant to the field of curriculum. Herein lies the quandary: How does one deal with such a dismal field and meet even modest expectations to be interesting?

Several years ago Dwayne Huebner solemnly declared the field moribund and promptly joined a school of theology. In the play *The Prime of Miss Jean Brodie*, our heroine regales the monster standing between herself and her pupils: "Curriculum, curriculum!" she cries out in anger and frustration.

A way out of the quandary might be through satire or parody, but such is beyond my capabilities. My hope, then, is to reach you in some personal way. By invoking some of my jousts with curriculum, I may prompt you to revisit and rethink some of your curricular experiences. I preface everything with a quote from Jerome Bruner: "A curriculum is more for teachers than it is for

179

pupils. If it cannot change, move, perturb, inform teachers, it will have no effect on those whom they teach."[1]

I do not know why these words bring back a dream, but they do. I was very young, perhaps seven or eight; it was summer, and the moon was full. The moon was full in my dream as well, and so it was difficult to determine which was dream and which was not; the whole was in glorious color. (I have been told that dreams are only in black and white, but clearly this one was not.) There were six great horses, more magnificent than the Budweiser sextet, pulling a glorious chariot. The whole stopped in the field, just a few hundred feet from my bedroom window, gleaming and shining brilliantly in the moonlight. I was sitting in the carriage, but I was also watching myself sitting in the carriage, achieving what had eluded and so frustrated F. Scott Fitzgerald: the ability to be dancing in the ball and simultaneously watching himself dancing in the ball. But it was, of course, a dream.

In retrospect, the dream illuminates for me much of what is wrong with both curriculum planning and the field of curriculum. We busy ourselves with objectives, for example, but do not get around to creating the curriculum carriages for our students to ride in. And we certainly do not do much, if anything, to foster the magnificent act of self-transcendence through which students sit in a carriage and simultaneously watch themselves being borne along in life's parade. By contrast, we usually are content to be curricular architects who construct complex scaffolding but never quite get to creating a house.

Coping with the Activity Curriculum

"The wooden canoe caper" occurred when I was eighteen years old and in normal school preparing to teach. The class was about methods of teaching, as best I can recall. We were learning how to teach the elementary school unit on Indians of the Northwest. They dug out their canoes from a cedar log, we learned, in contrast to Indians in Eastern Canada, who constructed them of birchbark.

I was far enough along in my year of preparation to be getting bored and to be wondering whether I really wanted to teach. My career might have gone in any one of a number of directions at this point. Our instructor was quite taken by what I now realize to be "the activity curriculum." We were about to do, not merely listen; and for this purpose, were moved to a kind of shop room where there were wood and chisels for model canoe construction.

We struggled with our chisels and blocks of wood for several class sessions. The absence of our instructor for a period of time provided me with the opportunity I needed. I knew that Indian tribes of the Northwest eased their task by first burning out the log and then scraping away the softened, charred core. This I set out to do on the shop's concrete floor. By the time our instructor returned, I had suffocated the fire but had almost suffocated my classmates in the process.

My teaching career was over before it began, I knew, and I faced in my mind the unhappy prospect of joining my uncle in the real estate business. But no, I was commended for my very active commitment to the activity curriculum!

I pass over the question of whether the instructor was in command of either the subject matter or the activity method and turn to another. When must the teacher's attention shift from the course to be run to the runner? Shift it must, sooner or later. Those curricular planning processes having to do with setting goals, selecting means for achieving these goals, organizing learning activities, and evaluating the whole are for curriculum makers. They offer some hope of something to be experienced by students, but the two certainly are not the same thing. Attention must shift from this curriculum baggage to the nature and quality of the students' encounters with the subject matter—to the chariots, if you will. We might have paddled our canoes, figuratively speaking, right into an Indian village and then observed ourselves interacting with the tribe and its culture. Instead, we had a classroom caper, with the culminating activity going up in smoke. For the uninitiated, it is important to know that the formula for the activity curriculum (what would we do without formulas?) called for a culminating activity.

Coping with Syllabi: The Syllabi Soliloquy

Several months after the wooden canoe caper and now, presumably, prepared to teach, I found myself in circumstances for which I was grossly ill prepared: teaching thirty-three children in an eight-grade, one-room school. Here I experienced the syllabi soliloquy. What I learned from it is that some curriculums are for scarcely anybody.

My classroom bibles were three fat syllabi: a blue one for the first three grades, a yellow one for the next two, and a green one for the final two. They covered seven subjects for all eight grades—potentially fifty-six lessons a day. And I took all this literally; fifty-six periods a day I taught.

But my class lacked the necessary materials. So each afternoon and evening, with the children long gone, I covered the chalkboard (blackboard in those days) with lessons and instructions for the next school day. I learned to leave a space two feet long and ten inches high for the series of spelling lessons to be taught. This I did for six weeks. At the end of six weeks, I took the train to my mother's home, as I often did on weekends. By now, fatigue was deep in my bones and frustration close to the surface. The door I kicked probably still bears the mark. "Curriculum, curriculum!" I cried out with Miss Jean Brodie.

The shift of attention from the course to be run to the runners began the following week. I found myself accepting, indeed encouraging, what I had tried so hard for six weeks to suppress. Because my predecessor had maintained strict grade standards over his several years of tenure in the school, the eighth-grade group was large, overage, and bored with the social studies lessons so many had "covered" before. But the subject matter was much fresher to the younger students in the lower grades, who had difficulty keeping out of the discussions. "Do your seat work," I would command, to little avail.

Suddenly, I found myself listening to what those younger intruders had to say. There was nothing forbidding to nine-year-olds in the eighth-grade subject matter. Their comments were often insightful, more so than those of their older classmates. Soon it became apparent to me that those sacred grade levels, sharply defined by curricular content in the syllabi, were largely fiction. Some readers will recognize here the sources of a book, *The Nongraded Elementary School*, recently reprinted.[2]

There are sobering lessons in this syllabi soliloquy. The first has to do with our misplaced confidence in curriculum engineering and the awesome consequences of this confidence. On the basis of hardly any evidence, we have built a racetrack, marked off with a common beginning point for all, with strides measured off in equal lengths for all, and even places marked for each foot to fall. I said "hardly any evidence." I should have said, "In the face of contrary evidence."

The second lesson poses a paradox. There is much talk these days of teacher professionalism and empowerment, clearly promoting a vision of much better prepared teachers free to exercise their best judgment in a changing panoply of circumstances. Yet, in many states, there is a clear march toward much more specific demarcation of the curriculum into specific objectives, grade-level curriculums and accompanying promotion standards, and tests geared to the prescribed content. This march calls not for highly prepared professionals but for carefully programmed robots and the ultimate technocratization of the curriculum. In the meantime, truly professional teachers must decide for themselves how big a dissenting risk they will take to prevent the curriculum from getting between them and their students.

Coping with Definitions

My most dismal encounters with curriculum have had to do with definitions, mostly because decades of definitional activity have done so little to make the waters defined less murky. These waters become especially murky when the intent is to define curriculum as a field of study. It seems reasonable to conclude that they will remain murky until there is agreement on what a curriculum is. Here the arguments often come down on two extremes: whether the curriculum is a course of studies (a racecourse) or all the experiences of the students (a position inseparable from life itself).

Reflection leads one to wonder about reasons for all this definitional fuss. Curriculum is not whatever one wishes it to be, nor is it just one thing. Rather obviously, it seems to me, there are quite different phenomena deserving the label "curriculum." State departments of education lay out goals and course requirements for the schools. These are curriculums of intentions, sometimes referred to as "formal curriculums." There are other curriculums of intentions, such as those laid out for students by subject specialists. Every high school presents its curriculum of offerings for students—an institutional curriculum. Teachers bring an instructional curriculum into the classroom. And students certainly experience a curriculum, appropriately called the "experiential curriculum."[3] The study of all of these defines curriculum as a field of study.

From this kind of reflection on what a curriculum is and, therefore, on what the study of curriculum is, I have learned, slowly and tediously, a modest lesson. There are quite different species of curriculums, each legitimate, each separate. Any effort to reduce one into any of the others is doomed to failure. One cannot *reduce* an institutional curriculum into an instructional curriculum. One can endeavor, however, to *interpret* the intent and meaning of the former when trying to create the latter.

The frequency and folly of efforts to reduce one of these distinct and separate curriculums into one of the others defy comprehensive documentation. Reduction of a formal state-approved curriculum into, for example, an institutional one assumes that, at a minimum, the former is well conceived in the first place and takes into account, for example, the vagaries of the settings and students for whom it is intended. Worse, such procedure cuts the ground from under teachers, who then perform not as professionals but as robots or automatons following inflexible curricular specifications. For teachers to become professionals, they must be free and encouraged to use their own best judgment.

It is appropriate for state and district guides to include broad goals and domains of knowledge to be encountered. It is even helpful to include *examples* of how concepts such as ecosystems and adaptation might be developed. But the danger, always, is that teachers will follow the examples as if they were prescribed and fail to take advantage of the more interesting and motivating curricular carriages that might be substituted.

In studying curriculum reform projects of the 1960s, I came across an elementary school science project emphasizing the scientific process and visited a classroom to see it in action.[4] The curriculum guide called for a unit on crabs. I arrived at the classroom a little early. Several children were clustered around a large turtle brought to school that morning by a classmate. But my arrival was the signal for crabs. The turtle was put back into its box by the disappointed children, who then focused as best they could on the far more familiar crabs. The turtle might have served just as well as the organizing center for learning about ecosystems and adaptation. But the curriculum guide was interpreted as a mandate, not a guide to be adapted by teachers for the particular circumstances of their classrooms. The curriculum became a course to be run rather than an opportunity for self-transcendence.

Until relatively recently, most states were content to set forth a dozen or so major goals for schooling, each somewhat further defined by subgoals or statements designed to clarify meanings. Each goal usually includes a behavioral area, such as problem solving, creativity, inquiry, and the like, and content, such as other cultures, earlier times, scientific phenomena, the arts, literature, and so forth. These whole behaviors and whole phenomena should remain whole. The teacher should be left free to *interpret* what inquiry might mean for a class of nine-year-olds and to create organizing centers (chariots) embracing his or her knowledge of the subject matter at hand, the specific students to be involved, and the learning process. The teacher may decide to set behavioral objectives for certain lessons, but these are instructional tools, no more—means, not ends reduced from some larger end.

This learning—that the instructional curriculum (one of several) represents a series of *original* decisions integrating the teacher's interpretation of an intended curriculum, subject matter, and the circumstances of the class and not merely a *reduction* of others' intentions—has slowly released me from the tyranny of much curriculum thought. It has also caused me to be sharply skeptical of so much that passes today as rational because it is so neatly linear.

Coping with Objectives

The educational panacea of the 1970s, extended into the present, has been the addition of behavioral objectives to the mandated prescription, sometimes as a substitute for an assumed reduction of broad goals for schooling. State after state prescribed proficiencies for students or competencies for teachers or both. The questioning of this solemnly right, "scientific" process put me out of the club. In earlier times, a period of repentance in the stocks would have been prescribed.

What puzzles me in seeking to cope with curriculum is the array of wonderful encounters with students I have had without benefit of behavioral objectives. Pedagogically speaking, it appears that I went goalless for years. Or, perhaps, I was goalfull all along, like Alice's sudden discovery that she had been speaking prose all her life.

At any rate, whether goalless or goalfull, I gave not a thought to defining objectives over eight years of teaching school at all grade levels. Then, as a student at the University of Chicago, I found myself in my first curriculum course. It was taught by none other than Ralph Tyler, he who has been accused (I choose the word carefully) of being "the father of behavioral objectives." Ironically, although he taught us the importance of and a process for setting curricular objectives, I was not aware of any set for his course. Perhaps he had some in mind but obligingly spared us their enumeration.

Applauding or condemning the so-called "Tyler curriculum rationale" is not on my agenda, except to say that I have found it very useful over the years. But I must digress for a moment to clear Ralph, if I can, from charges of parenthood regarding behavioral objectives. First, if there is a twentieth-century father, it must be Bobbitt, who so overstuffed himself with the virtues of precisely defined objectives that he ultimately became sick of them and recanted.[5] Or, in keeping with the ahistorical character of much discourse in the curriculum field, perhaps we should go back only to Mager or Popham.[6] So far as I know, Mager has not recanted, but the effervescent Jim Popham (who managed or perhaps felt it necessary to maintain his sense of humor in the face of the moribund character of the field) had some second thoughts. Early on, his sports car bore the bumper sticker "Stamp out *all* nonbehavioral objectives." Later, he changed it to "Stamp out *some* behavioral objectives."

For six years, I managed to repress the contents of Tyler's monograph, *Basic Principles of Curriculum and Instruction*.[7] Since then, I have gone to it many times, usually to refresh my impression regarding what he does not say about behavioral objectives. I find not a trace of the process of infinite reductionism Bobbitt at first expressed and so many of today's believers exhort. Tyler has two rather different and very important things to say about goals. First, a good educational objective states the behavior to be elicited in the student and the content or subject matter in which it is to be developed. Second, he proposes not hundreds of behavioral objectives for each segment of the curriculum, but a dozen or so broad goals to which each subject of the curriculum is to make a contribution. Faculty members of the English department in a secondary school, Tyler proposes, would discuss how their teaching might contribute not just to the understanding of their field but to all the academic, social, vocational, and personal goals set for the schools.

A vision of what schools are for and how teachers might use their subjects in pursuit of such a vision tends to slip away when behavioral objectives become ends rather than sometimes useful means. For the past quarter-century or so, I have watched behavioral objectives and their offspring—competencies, proficiencies, and behavioral outcomes—cover the curricular landscape like kudzu. Yet I cannot recall any significant undertaking in my life for which I reduced whatever may have been my intent into even a half-dozen carefully crafted behavioral objectives. Reducing general intentions to specifics can be useful—if one has carefully pondered these intentions. But the results can be mischievous when precision is equated with virtue, truth, or beauty.

Coping with the Racecourse

Some of the blame for what we have had to cope with in the curriculum field must go to interpreters of its Latin roots. Looking for the root of "curriculum," they came upon "currere"—to run, as with a current. Running was then connected with a racecourse, and the damage was done. Dictionary definitions usually begin with this derivation and then run on to define curriculum as "the whole body of courses offered by an educational institution." Something as lifeless as a racecourse becomes the metaphor for virtually the whole schooling enterprise! No wonder, then, that we define what is to take place on the racetrack in behavioral terms and mark off the races to be run—the hundred meter, the thousand meter, and so on.

What a shame that we failed to pick up on another root derivation of curriculum—namely, "curricle," also from the Latin but referring to a two-wheeled chaise usually drawn by two horses. Our attention shifts from the rather uninteresting smoothness of the racecourse, the length of the race, the perspiring runners, and the time taken by the winner. We focus instead on a small chariot of infinite potential. It could be green, yellow, or orange; it could be of plainly functional or intricate design; it could be made of wood or metal. Best of all, it could carry us right off the racetrack to places unimagined, quickly or languidly, and we could choose to pause beside this stream or those trees.

Buried near the middle of Tyler's little monograph, scarcely noticed even by careful readers, is the very essence of what a curriculum must be about if it is to have any effect on students. Tyler named this essence "the organizing center." Organizing centers are connected to one another by the organizing element, providing continuity somewhat in the way the ankle bone is connected to the shin bone and the shin bone is connected to the knee bone.

Interestingly, both the organizing element and the organizing center exist independent of any intended behavioral use of them. But they become alive and meaningful when motivating intentions for them are conjured up and acted upon.

It was a colleague of Tyler's who pushed more deeply into the concept of the organizing center. While at the University of Chicago, Virgil Herrick co-edited with Tyler the papers of a conference on curriculum theory in which the organizing center received some attention.[8] Later, at the University of Wisconsin, Herrick's work with teachers opened up the possibility that the organizing center is the point at which all other curriculum planning makes or fails to make its impact on pupils. In interpreting and editing Herrick's writing on the subject, MacDonald, Anderson, and May had this to say:

> Perhaps the most crucial and central concept related to the teaching operations is the idea of the organizing center. As "the point where all the important aspects of the teaching act can be related and given focus," its effect on the quality of instruction cannot be denied.[9]

The organizing center is the poem, the novel, the film, the episode, or the anecdote used by the teacher to draw students into the discipline, the wonders, the nuances of the human conversation.[10] For Herrick, organizing centers were the ideas, materials, collections, exhibits, places, and people used by teachers to assure for students meaningful encounters with the organized experience of the human race. He insisted that the center of attention chosen have significance in its own right, hold promise for students' intrinsic interests, be accessible to students, have breadth and scope, have capacity for tying together related ideas, and encourage students to run on with concepts or activities beyond the immediacy of the organizing center selected.

The organizing center is the chariot of infinite potential. Herrick's qualifiers lack precision, and, in a way, this is their virtue. They convey a sense of richness so lacking in the reduction of goals to objectives, the prospect of attracting the array of interests inherent in a class, and possibilities for branching out into an infinite variety of learnings. Whereas the reductionist approach to curriculum in recent years has reduced much classroom activity to sterile mechanics, emphasis on the organizing center massages our best visions of what education should and could be. Best of all, the organizing center, creatively planned and presented, connects students with these visions. It is the chariot in which ride our hopes for the future of education in schools.

Buried in the foregoing are a few simple lessons rather painfully gleaned through several decades of coping with curriculum. The major one goes back to where I began: A curriculum is for teachers. For students, we are advised to conjure up chariots.

Notes

1. Jerome Bruner, *The Process of Education* (Cambridge, MA: Harvard University Press, 1977), p. xv.

2. John I. Goodlad and Robert H. Anderson, *The Nongraded Elementary School* (New York: Harcourt Brace and World, 1959, rev., 1963). Reprinted with a new introduction (New York: Teachers College Press, 1987).

3. John I. Goodlad, M. Frances Klein, and Kenneth A. Tye, "The Domains of Curriculum and Their Study," in John I. Goodlad and Associates, *Curriculum Inquiry* (New York: McGraw-Hill, 1979), pp. 43–76.

4. John I. Goodlad, *School Curriculum Reform in the United States* (New York: Fund for the Advancement of Education, 1964).

5. Franklin Bobbitt, *How to Make a Curriculum* (Cambridge, MA: Riverside Press, 1924).

6. Robert F. Mager, *Preparing Objectives for Programmed Instruction* (San Francisco: Fearon, 1962); W. James Popham, Elliot Eisner, Howard J. Sullivan, and Louise L. Tyler, *Instructional Objectives* (Chicago: Rand McNally, 1969).

7. Ralph W. Tyler, *Basic Principles of Curriculum and Instruction* (Chicago: University of Chicago Press, 1949).

8. Virgil C. Herrick and Ralph W. Tyler, eds., *Toward Improved Curriculum Theory* (Chicago: University of Chicago Press, 1950).

9. James B. MacDonald, Dan W. Anderson, and Frank B. May, eds., *Strategies of Curriculum Development, Selected Writings of the Late Virgil E. Herrick* (Columbus, OH: Charles E. Merrill, 1965), p. 107.

10. For further discussion of this human conversation, see Donna H. Kerr, "Authority and Responsibility in Public Schooling," in *The Ecology of School Renewal*, ed. John I. Goodlad, Eighty-sixth Yearbook of the National Society for the Study of Education, Part 1 (Chicago: University of Chicago Press, 1987), pp. 20–40.

8

Research and Practitioners: A Panel Discussion

Gordon Ambach, Marilyn Rauth, and P. Michael Timpane

The final session of the conference brought together three distinguished educators who have a broad understanding of how educational research relates to educational practice. Yet each of the panelists views that relationship from a different perspective.

Gordon Ambach is retiring in June 1988 as commissioner of education for the state of New York after ten years in that post. He is leaving to become executive director of the Council of Chief State School Officers, which includes all of the state school officers in the country.

Marilyn Rauth is assistant to Albert Shanker, president of the American Federation of Teachers. She has been director of the Educational Issues Department of the AFT since 1977 and has worked for the AFT since 1970. Before that, she was a middle school and high school English teacher in Pennsylvania and New Jersey.

P. Michael Timpane is currently president of Teachers College, Columbia University. He has held a variety of administrative and research positions in both federal and private agencies, including

191

the directorship of the National Institute of Education from 1979 to 1981.

This chapter is a transcript of the remarks of these three educators at the concluding session of the conference.

GORDON AMBACH: After yesterday's splendid array of presentations, I cannot help but begin by recalling a story that some of my colleagues here have heard but that I intend to tell anyway. The late Adlai Stevenson had been giving a speech as part of a panel that included other speakers. He was approached when he finished by someone who said, "Oh, Mr. Stevenson, I did think that was quite a speech. I thought it was absolutely superfluous." Stevenson was taken aback a bit, but he quickly responded by saying, "Thank you very much. I intend to have it published posthumously." But that didn't end the exchange. Back came the response, "Oh, what good news. The sooner the better."

I speak for my colleagues in hoping that this panel on research and practitioners is not superfluous given yesterday's fine presentations. This morning's session is, after all, a three-hour one. I think of the sign over an auto repair shop that says, "Come in: We tire, shock, and exhaust you." Let's hope the three hours don't quite do that.

It is with deep appreciation that I join you this morning to recognize the Benton Center and its value and to say as well how much I commend my great friend and colleague of several years, Charles Benton, and the family who have provided the support for this center. Charles and I go way back in the sense of our families' connection and mutual location in the East. But we were also partners in the White House Conference on Libraries in 1979 and in the National Commission on Information Sciences. We have worked together on nationwide issues concerning communication and libraries for many years.

My focus this morning is on research to help practitioners. I am speaking about a very specific group of practitioners, namely, persons like myself who practice the craft of policymaking. We are practitioners, too. Bear in mind that my own responsibilities in New York are for all schools, both public and nonpublic; for all colleges and universities, both independent and public; for all the libraries and museums; for public television; and for licensed professionals. We also do a few other things along the way! It is a huge operation, an $8.7 billion annual operation. It is one in which, for the making of policy, we must have access to research. But this has to be research upon which we can draw in a timely way.

Most of my business is with members of the state legislature, members of the Congress, with their staff members, with members of governors' offices and with governors, whether of my state or elsewhere. I work with business leaders, with farmers, with community groups. My work focuses at the point of connection between those who are directly involved in education and those who, in one way or another, are involved in deciding how the public treasury will be allocated or public authority is used in the interests of education.

I realize that we are not here to deal particularly with historical perspectives. But some historical perspective will illustrate how the practitioners' needs for research change even though what the researchers do may not change over periods of time. Suppose we were sitting here twenty years ago, in 1967, considering what was going on in education. Schools are bursting at the seams with the baby-boomers. There is a teacher shortage in certain areas. A rather vigorous federal agenda for education is being mounted, illustrated dramatically in the Elementary and Secondary Education Act (particularly Title I). There is a concern for equity issues, reflected in the Civil Rights Act. There is Vietnam. In the schools, we hear the concern for relevance in the curriculum. Relativism is important in what should be taught. Electives are busting out all over. It is not a period of time in which we find a deep concern about testing, about standards, or about a core curriculum. Researchers such as James Coleman and Christopher Jencks had come out with findings to the effect that schools really did not overcome the gaps among children if socioeconomic status was taken into account. Much of the public and many practitioners concluded from this research that "schools make no difference at all."

I am not going to dwell heavily on the history from that time to now. But consider some of the contrasts with that time some twenty years ago. Enrollment now, of course, is declining across the country, although there are exceptions to this in some of the states. Enrollment is certainly still declining in the high schools. The teacher shortage is more severe than twenty years ago. The federal role is still strong in education. But prime time today is being given to standards, to the curriculum, to instruction, to teaching technique. By way of contrast with the latter part of the 1960s, there is a very profound commitment today that schools *do* make a difference and, in fact, that specific things within schools make very important differences. People are now looking at characteristics of effective schools and of effective leadership.

What has changed in the overall enterprise of elementary and secondary education in the last ten years? I want to make a few points to set the stage for what I perceive to be the pivotal research questions from here on out. In school finance over the last ten years, we have had five low years followed by five rather good ones. (Of course, there are some very severe regional differences.) For example, teacher salaries right now are just about back to where they were in real dollars in 1975–76. They had slid very dramatically for about six years, and only now are they recovering. Consequently, teachers have about the same purchasing power in the marketplace as they had some ten years ago.

Remember Title IX? It was initiated roughly ten years ago. Over this last ten-year period, change in equity has been significant for handicapped children and for girls. I don't know how many of you ever looked at some of the numbers to see what difference Title IX has made in terms of various characteristics. But do so; it is quite an exceptional ten-year story. Opportunities have increased in the schools downward to prekindergarten and upward to adults who have no high school diploma. New alternatives in the schools are now fashionable. There are alternatives for students, particularly at the high school level, to complete their high school program. There were relatively fewer alternative school programs ten years ago. Now all kinds of new patterns have developed, in part because of the deep concern about high school completion rates. In turn, this has led to a much closer look inside the schools, at the characteristics of the schools, and at new ways of developing accountability and productivity, to use the economic terms. Over this period of time, we have experienced a much increased role for state authorities in setting the tone or direction for what should happen in education.

Now the driving force in the past *few* years is "school reform," which really consists of many different reforms or activities. These started in most places well before *A Nation at Risk* was ever published and were on their way in many school districts or states well before 1983 and 1984, when we had that proliferation of nationwide reports that presumably led the way to reform. They did not. The reports, rather, describe what was going on across most of the country.

But what drove reform? There were a number of things. One was very intense concern across this country about our economic standing in the world. The latter part of the 1970s was after all a period when we awakened to the fact that the trade balance was shifting, that too many Americans were buying their automobiles from foreign manufacturers, leading to near collapse of the domestic automobile industry. We were going soft, losing a competitive edge. Quickly, the view turned to the schools to see what might be done to increase our competitive edge through education. The business community began to recognize much more the importance of education in the economy. Governors and state legislators were seeing that educational issues formed a very ripe political agenda, and that in the competition from one state to the next, it was extremely important for a governor to be able to take a leadership role. Those of you who may have followed the activities of the Education Commission of the States can get a good indicator of this. If you went to those meetings in the mid 1960s, you might have found an occasional governor or two. They came to open it and they came to close it, period. If you had gone to Education Commission meetings in the last two or three years, you would have found ten to twelve governors there for most of the sessions. This is an interesting indicator of the change. What it is saying to us all is that a new political agenda arose, related to education and to this issue of competition among the states.

I have been invited to go to Utah this summer. To speak to educators? No. To speak to the Annual Conference of the State Budget Directors, and the topic of that conference is "Education as a State Investment for Economic Development." The top issues on their minds are (a) what to invest in education, and whether to invest at the elementary, secondary, or collegiate level, and (b) how to deal with the problem of retraining for their people in business and industry so that they can get the next Japanese plant in their state or manage to keep the plants that are in their state. They advocate not only training manpower and womanpower, but they also want to improve the quality of life in the state, to offer a strong educational and cultural system that will attract people to live there and encourage them to stay.

Now these are the kinds of things that have really driven education reform. These are the things that have driven the search for new resources. These are the things that have driven those who make the decisions as to what should be the expectations for students, for teachers, and for the schools.

What is the agenda coming up when we consider this kind of backdrop? I suggest a number of issues. First, there is the issue of assessment. The points I want to raise are not only on my agenda, but are on the agenda of every chief state school officer right now. How do we account for the great thirst of the American public for a score card on education, a thirst that is not going to go away? What can be done to make sense out of the assessment scorecard? I mean among states, among districts, among schools, but especially the issue of how one fits together things like the National Assessment of Educational Progress with state assessment programs and with local assessment programs. We do not want to find ourselves in the circumstance where we spend so much time running around testing children that they don't have any time to learn anything to be tested on. This is a very real danger. In my view, the next two or three years are pivotal in terms of what is to happen with the whole national assessment program. And believe me, what happens with national assessment will have a profound effect on what happens with the statewide assessment programs, which in turn will have a profound effect on the assessment efforts throughout local school districts and in classrooms for the next few decades to come. Once that database begins to develop, no one is going to want to give it up. This is because the trend lines become most important to the assessment efforts, a very critical issue for our collective attention.

The second point concerns what we can learn from international comparisons. In a sense, I think that for these next several years, and perhaps the next decade, policymakers, whether they are politicians or educators, are going to be especially interested in cross-national comparisons. People have tried to develop comparisons by looking back and forth across our states and across school districts, but by and large, the commonalities are so strong that they tend to outweigh the differences. But this does not necessarily hold if one looks at different national patterns, where schooling is organized differently (for example, in the Japanese schools in terms of how children are grouped or what responsibilities they have) as compared with how we do it. I am not advocating adoption of practices found elsewhere. I am suggesting that there will be a continuing and intense interest in this kind of cross-national comparison of educational practices.

A third issue concerns learning the values of civic responsibility. There have been several speeches, and lots of shots fired here and there, about teaching values, or learning values. In my judgment, some extremely critical issues in this area must be addressed. For example, is there a common core or common set of values of civic responsibility that is the domain of neither the political right nor the political left, but is mainstream in this society? And if there is such a core, how does one go about trying to help children learn it? A related issue, I think, concerns the areas of history and social studies. How do we connect the learning of values with the learning of the *religious history* of this nation, which has by and large been systematically pruned from all the textbooks? There are, I'm pleased to say, several people who are very much concerned about how, in secondary or elementary school material, ways can be found to discuss the religious institutions and history of this country without making such a process the inculcation of a *particular* religion.

The fourth point on the agenda concerns high school completion rates. I prefer speaking of "completion rates" rather than of dropouts. You can talk about dropouts, and people talk about trying to get people to stop children dropping out. But this is not the issue. The issue is how do we provide the means for students to complete the high school program successfully. This issue carries with it many different items for a research agenda. One of these items will be very important over the next several years—the question of how much isolation or separation must be arranged for those children at greatest risk from their regular environment or home background. There is a considerable amount of discussion in various places about an extended school day, an extended school year, residential programs, and so on. But the most serious question pertains to children who are at greatest risk, and it concerns the issue of isolation or removal from all the influences in the regular environment that have a harmful impact on their education. Nowhere do I see nearly enough consideration being given to this matter.

The fifth point for the agenda has to do with teaching. I want to ask two questions here. If collegiality and teacher empowerment are such desired objectives in order to motivate teachers, to encourage them to stay in teaching, and to enable them to become a profession, what strategies are followed in order to attain that collegiality? And, indeed, I would even ask whether collegiality can be legislated or gained by collective bargaining.

The last point I would like to make has to do with a topic not really addressed yesterday—money. It is a topic that I and others must deal with all the time. I am speaking about this in a very large sense, not in the sense of what the agenda has been in the past years. That agenda dealt with school finance by means of equalization. I am referring here, for example, to the *Serrano* and *Levittown* decisions, which resulted in a big agenda several years ago. But the agenda that I think has moved up and has almost washed right over us (I say "us" as educators) in the course of the last year or two concerns tax policy. The Congress of the United States came very close to eliminating deductions for state and local taxes on federal income tax returns. They took away deductions for sales taxes.

Do you realize what complete removal of deductibility would have meant for the future of school systems and public financing of education at the local and state levels in this country? Imagine what it would have meant when the next school budget came along with an increase of 10 percent in taxes—that could no longer be deducted in preparing federal income tax returns. This would have had an absolutely incredible impact. And yet I dare say that, in the educational community and in the research community (with the exception of a few economists who happen to be interested in this kind of tax policy), there was very little going on, and almost nothing of tax reform was understood. In the last two years, this issue has probably become the most critical financial issue we have faced in education. And it is not over. As long as the federal deficit continues, and the trade deficit continues, the Congress is going to have to look for sources of revenue. And it is not very hard to change the law by removing deductibility and thus capturing $40 to $50 billion of new resources at the federal level.

This part of the research agenda, having to do with finances for the future, is one in which all of us who deal with the expenditure side must learn also to pay attention to the revenue side. We must pay attention to the entire issue of what happens at the federal, and particularly at the state and local levels, on tax policy and long-term financing of public services, particularly of educational services.

You asked me to tell you something about what a practitioner needs from the research agenda. A great deal! Thank you kindly for this opportunity.

MARILYN RAUTH: Before I begin my discussion of teachers and research, I want to explain why the recent Carnegie report, *A Nation Prepared*, is so important to the American Federation of Teachers. This morning's newspaper reported that the Carnegie project is simply a power grab on the part of the AFT and the NEA. Perhaps it is a power grab, but the real issue is a power grab for what? Albert Shanker and the AFT believe very strongly that programmatic changes in the schools simply will not result in dramatic increases in student achievement, no matter how good some of those changes might be. Only the total restructuring of schools will keep us from falling prey to vouchers and tuition tax credits. We believe that firmly. Without total restructuring, all is lost for public education. If you talk about the power to change schools radically, to provide quality instruction, to change curriculums, then yes, it is a power grab.

We do not see the Carnegie report as a perfect document reflecting exactly what schools ought to be, but rather as the equivalent of the Flexner report on medical education in the early 1900s, having the same capability for professionalizing teaching and for upgrading education that was manifested by the concern of the Flexner report for medical education. That is why we are promoting the Carnegie report and supporting the people who are trying to make the National Board for Professional Teaching Standards work. That is why we are advocating rigorous induction to teaching, as well as new constructs and conceptualizations of teaching in the schools. So we have dreams, but we have no delusions that these changes will happen overnight. It will be a long, hard road, but there are school systems in which the union, the administration, and the universities are already collaborating to make dramatic changes, trying new approaches without knowing the ultimate answers and trying to make sure that students in our schools with whom we have been least successful (and the number of them is growing rapidly) do not continue to fall through the cracks. It is in this framework that I want to talk about research aims.

Does research have any use for practitioners? I remember a conversation with Mr. Shanker in 1970. I was fresh out of the classroom. Mr. Shanker was saying we must develop a science of teaching. There must be a professional knowledge base to which we can point as something that teachers know that no one else knows. And I said at the time, "Well, you know Al, that sounds terrific. You're right; we really need that, and of course there are things teachers know and do that the layman can have no real idea of. But the fact is that there is no one right way to teach, and therefore you'll never be able to come up with a knowledge base for teaching." He said, "You don't think so, hm? Well, if not, how are you going to defend certification of teachers in the future? Why not have anyone come into the classroom and teach? Do you think that would work?" I said, "Well, no, I really don't think that would work." He said, "Well, you had better go back and look at the research and see if there is anything there."

In the early 1970s, we looked. And frankly, we did not find much that we though would relate to what teachers were actually doing in the classroom. I suspect that at the time we simply did not look in the right places.

We reviewed the situation in 1980, again at Al's urging. We convened a group of eminent researchers—Lee Shulman, Ann Lieberman, and Beatrice Ward. We said that we know nothing about research, and, in fact, we are very skeptical about it. We have seen teaching machines. We have seen the introduction of transformational generative grammar. We have seen new math. (Of course, the mathematicians, not the educational researchers, gave us the new math, but we didn't know that at the time.) These were all seen as part of the terrible things that researchers had foisted upon teachers in classrooms and schools. They offered us panaceas. We were going to be able to reach the kids that we had not reached before, but the research never came through. So we thought it was a waste of time and money.

However, Shulman, Lieberman, and Ward pointed us to research around which there was some real consensus and that seemed to have some validity. It was something in which teachers could be interested. Our second task was to develop a process for getting this research into the field. A two-year grant from the National Institute of Education helped us. Could it be done? We did not know. We had been told, "You're crazy. There's nothing there. There is no research that would be of use to teachers, so you're wasting your time." We had $400,000, and I was being told that we were chasing a pipe dream. With the help of our research colleagues, we initially focused on the classroom management research, trying to get something generic that would provide a hook that would engage the interest of all kinds of teachers at different grade levels and in different subject areas. We started calling it "the hooker," and then we decided that probably was not a good way to refer to this research. Better come up with something else!

The results of this work, however, were really exciting. We brought in three teachers, and we developed a process of building-level dissemination. The first thing we had to do was to convert research jargon into teachers' professional language. We produced "research translations," which were syntheses of research in a form understandable to teachers. Each translation we now have is checked whenever possible by the original researchers to make sure we are not minimizing or misinterpreting their work, that we are putting out a very accurate interpretation of what they found and are not going beyond their findings. The research translations are accompanied by training activities to show how research concepts apply to the classroom. Then we selected outstanding teachers—risk takers, innovators, people to whom other teachers would look for verification and validation of new ideas—and brought them together for extensive training. They would read the research translations before coming to the meetings. They would then sit down together, go through the training activities, select those concepts from the research that they thought would be something new and useful for them to try in the classroom. At this point, they went back to their classrooms to try out the new ideas during the two to three weeks between sessions. Then they came back and discussed success or failure and the all important "whys": Why did this succeed with this group of students, or why did this fail? They discovered that often the failure was not attributable to the research itself. It was attributable to the way they implemented it. At other times, it may have been a problem with the research. What we ultimately wanted to do was get that feedback to the research community.

What is so startling about this process? When we began, and this is still the case at many sites, teachers were meeting on their own time, with no stipends, for two hours after school once every three weeks throughout the entire school year, and then throughout the second year and the third year and the fourth year. These people, who had very negative attitudes toward research when we first began this program, are now enthusiasts. They cannot get enough research.

Let me ask you to consider a question. Do you believe that research will provide discrete steps of the teaching act someday? Think about that for a minute. Do you believe, on the other hand, that research serves as an extraordinary tool to help teachers reflect upon practice, to engage in inquiry about what approaches will be most successful with different students in different situations? Do you believe that research can help teachers become problem solvers?

If you believe that research can provide the steps to the teaching act (and some consultants are out there selling such answers to school systems for a lot of money), then you see the teacher as technician. You see the teacher as someone who simply needs to be told what to do, and who can go into any situation and carry out the orders of a consultant, of a researcher, of an administrator. We do not see that as a good teaching, nor do we believe it can help public education survive.

On the other hand, we have found research a valuable tool to get people to reflect upon practice. This is where teachers begin to get excited about research. When we go into schools, we try to get an agreement from the principals that the teachers who will be working with new ideas, new concepts in their classrooms, will not be evaluated on their implementation of those new ideas. Such an evaluation is, after all, the quickest way to get people to shy away from change. And yet we have principals who occasionally come in to some of our sessions to observe, and they get so excited they go back and announce on the public address system the next morning. "All right. From now on, all of you will do A, B, C, or D." It may be to post your rules for the classroom. It may be something related to student motivation, interactive teaching, cooperative team teaching. Whatever they see, all of a sudden they want everybody to do.

This creates a problem. Principals and others assume that it does not matter that not everybody has bought into this, that not everybody understands it. This mistake is made over and over and over again in the application of research. For those of you who are in the research community, the abuse and misapplication of your findings is a problem with which you need to become much more involved. You often say, "Well, that's not what I meant." But nothing is done about it. Research, however, will not be funded in the future, even though we need it desperately, if something is not done about misapplication of research findings, because that can lead to disaster in classrooms and schools.

Let me give you some examples of what happens. One of my colleagues was in Florida last year, doing a workshop on classroom management using some of the research that we have translated. The purpose of this workshop was simply to raise awareness. (We know that no teacher is going to change practice dramatically by going to a workshop on classroom management. School in-service people do not seem to know that yet, in most cases.) At this workshop, all the teachers were talking and asking about "teacher witness": "What about teacher witness? We're all being evaluated on this, and we don't have any idea what it is." When my colleague questioned this term ("I've never heard of 'teacher witness.' Are you sure it isn't something else?"), a district evaluation form was produced on which the term appeared repeatedly as a criterion. I suppose there are administrators all over that school system who are looking for "teacher witness." You laugh, I presume, because you have already deduced what this was. Of course, it was "teacher with-it-ness," Jacob Kounin's criterion referring to the teacher's knowledge of many different things going on in the classroom simultaneously.

Another example is related, on the instructional side, to what John Goodlad mentioned in his speech at this conference. Barak Rosenshine's "instructional functions" were not meant to be written out for each and every lesson a teacher plans. They were to be guidelines for teachers, showing how to provide either interactive or direct instruction. But we find school systems where teachers have to write these functions for each and every lesson. It is like making a student write multiplication tables they have already learned a hundred times. What sense does that make? It demoralizes teachers, transforming teaching to the level of a menial task that they see as an uninteresting, superfluous activity. This demoralization is one reason for the growing teacher shortage today.

The work of researchers is thus getting mauled in the schools, and researchers should demand some accountability for how their work is being used.

We have found that teachers can use research effectively. Several things happen. First, it increases their sense of efficacy. I remember the teacher who was spending a lot of time at the beginning of the year actually teaching students what the rules and procedures were for that classroom. This man thought he was a bad teacher because he was taking so much time for that purpose. Through exposure to research dealing with ways to manage classrooms at the beginning of the year, this teacher was finally able to say, "Hey, I'm doing something that's effective. I am a good teacher." And that happens repeatedly, no matter what we're working with. It verifies teachers' sense of efficacy and therefore makes them better teachers.

Second, by sharing ideas with each other, teachers are able to learn new approaches. If five things they have tried do not work with a particular student or group of students, they often get other ideas from their colleagues and go back to their situations reinvigorated, renewed, and again are preventing students from falling through the cracks. People get excited about this.

Other things happen. Teachers know what they are doing and how to do it. But they often do not know why. The only "why" they

can give when someone challenges them is, "Well, it works for me."
And you know what happens, given teachers' level of authority,
when they get into the "your-judgment-against-mine" game. They
lose. Now they have research to back them up as well as colleagues'
experience, which they are sharing on a regular basis. If I had time,
I could give you stories about teachers who were able to accomplish
even the slightest things, such as stopping the interruptions on the
public address system or the unannounced visitors from coming
into classrooms, on the basis of time-on-task research. I could also
tell you about teachers who, on the basis of research, were able to
overturn spurious evaluations.

Teachers have found research is a tool. One theme of our
Educational Research and Dissemination Program (ER&D) is that
knowledge is power. And again, we are talking about power in the
sense of helping all children learn to their maximum potential.
That is exciting to me.

There are also some terrific spin-offs of this program. Some
administrators, skeptical at first in some instances, have become so
enthusiastic about the union's and teachers' efforts to share research that they are setting up effective teaching centers. A small
rural school system in central Florida, with limited monies but with
a commitment to staff development, released the local site coordi-
nator for our Educational Research and Dissemination Program
full time, set up an effective teaching center, and released one
hundred twenty teachers for six full days a year for development
and training. The second year, they put through another one
hundred twenty and also, at the clamoring of the first group,
brought that group back to go through additional research. Following this lead, other school systems are institutionalizing the
ER&D Program in similar ways.

Teachers have used our research translations on such topics as
classroom management, group management, interactive teaching,
direct instruction, time on task, teacher feedback and praise,
cooperative group learning, communication in multicultural classrooms, student motivation, peer coaching among students, nonlec-
ture approaches to teaching, student learning styles, adult learning
theory, and dissemination strategies. Those who are helping to link
teachers and research are urging teachers not only to use this
material in their own classrooms, but to share it among colleagues

in their buildings on an ongoing basis. They go back and have formal and informal sessions with other teachers in their own buildings. One group has a "research for lunch bunch" still going strong.

Another translation concerns the aim of involving parents in their children's education. Teachers went to a university to do a translation and, finding that there was hardly any research in that area, are now engaging in their own. Thus, one offshoot of this entire effort is that teachers are going to be more and more involved in pursuing research questions themselves.

We started with the process-product research, which had credibility because researchers went in to observe what "more effective" teachers were actually doing. Out of that evolved an appreciation for theoretical research, good theoretical research such as in the cooperative team learning area. Teachers are consequently more sophisticated with respect to a whole range of research issues.

How do we get these translations? We started with Stanford University. One of the teachers who was then working with research through our ER&D Program was released on sabbatical or administrative leave for an entire year; went to the university, which waived all tuition and fees; and was given a quarter-time graduate research assistant to help in interpreting research. This person took courses, although not for credit because we did not want the teacher to be there as a student. We wanted this teacher to be there as a distinguished visiting practitioner on a peer level with the research faculty. She then did the research translations.

At present, Teachers College (Columbia University), Syracuse University, Brown University, the University of Buffalo, and the State University of New York at Geneseo are involved in our work through the Distinguished Visiting Practitioner Program. We hope that shortly additional funding will be available so that we can move into the content areas. Our first effort will involve teachers in working with researchers to define concepts in elementary mathematics essential to understanding higher mathematical concepts and develop instructional guidelines. We are very excited about this growth.

At the end of 1983, our pilot project in education research and development involved 3 sites. As of this date (May 1987), we have 157 sites and expect to have more than 200 by the end of the summer of 1987. Our locals are beating down the door to get into this program. Teachers are becoming reinvigorated. The Far West Laboratory did a study of the effects in the 14 initial sites and found that teachers indeed were changing practice as a result of their work with the research, that teacher collegiality and morale had increased dramatically, and that teachers were staying in teaching and being propelled into new leadership roles. So we view research as absolutely essential to our dream of seeing schools restructured as truly learning-centered environments that serve children's needs. It is long overdue that we get away from the practice of running schools on the basis of serving the convenience of bus schedules, accepting inappropriate textbooks just because they happen to be on hand, or using tests that really don't match our curriculum or our curricular goals. Schools exist to make sure that quality education is being provided to all students. The responsibility of researchers is not to be content to come up with interesting findings, but to find ways to plug into programs like ours and others, to see that information is disseminated beyond technical research journals. The future of educational research, as well as that of education itself, is endangered if we do not find ways for teachers and researchers to work together.

We have made a discovery that has to be remembered in all staff development. It is not singular to us or exclusive to us. We have found that simply the reading of research translations has little impact on practice in the classroom. It is only after working with research concepts in depth over an extended period of time that teachers assimilate research as an integral part of their practice. As they move from one study to another, they find several things. First, they find that the research they always thought was contradictory is in most cases not that contradictory, in that researchers were looking for very different things. They were looking at very different outcomes, and, therefore, the approaches and conclusions have varied.

Second, teachers find that the interrelationships and connections among different types of research really help them develop their own body of knowledge. One study, one bit of information builds upon another in constructing a background, a context from which to approach teaching and learning. That is extremely valuable.

I would like to leave you with one thought. I told you that we tell teachers not only that knowledge is power but also to dare to dream. Yes, the reform movements have not yet produced much of worth in the large scheme of things. Yes, there are a lot of reasons to be skeptical. But, we all know, that we as teachers, and our schools in general, can do much better than we have been able to do in the past. Existing problems may not be our fault. There may be all sorts of obstacles to equity and excellence in schools. But improvement is not impossible. It is not an imperative that we have to make a choice between equity and excellence. Perhaps it is time to think about totally new constructs in the schools. Do we have to have fifty-minute periods for all students, regardless of what we are teaching in a given day, or could faculty in a school system divide time up differently? Is uniform class size sacred? Or could we devise large-group or small-group instruction, depending upon students' needs?

There are many different questions that could be asked. I caution the researchers at the Benton Center not to engage in work that will be obsolete before it even hits the presses, but to try to do two things. First, seek out those school systems that are moving forward to create truly learning-centered schools serving individual students' needs, and help them get the information they need to do it. Second, I know you cannot study something that does not yet exist. But push people into trying new ideas, new conceptualizations of curriculum and instruction, so that we can move toward a school system that succeeds because it learns from its failures and because it searches continuously for better ways to do its work.

P. MICHAEL TIMPANE: I would like to begin with some historical perspective. The first point to make about educational research is that, in some respects, as a nation, we have not been at it very long, nor have we had very many resources. For many years, that could be an excuse. Perhaps we can now stop using this as an excuse and convert it into an explanation for why we are just arriving at our present state. We got started very late relative to many other enterprises and important public issues, and we spent relatively little of our national treasure on the issue, relative to many other areas. Just to mention areas such as defense, medicine,

science, and agriculture is to make the point that those are enterprises to which we have devoted far more resources for research
and often for far longer than we have for research in education.
Such investment as we made started later and is now ripening, one
might say. Congressman Daniel Flood, chairman of the education
subcommittee of the House Appropriations Committee just when
the National Institute of Education was being founded, summed
this point up as well as anybody ever has when he said to an Office
of Education witness, "Well, since the Russians fired Sputnik, there
has been new horizon research of all sorts and kinds, and it's just
too bad that you fellows come along at the tail end after a generation when research has been the word and the thing. Now you come
limping at the end all steamed up about research after everybody
else is beginning to slack it. It's just a burden you're going to
have." That was good history, and it was good prophecy, in many
respects.

The second historical point is that it is a better part of a
generation since Congressman Flood made that observation. We
have made extraordinary efforts and extraordinary progress pursuing the cause. We have also made some extraordinary mistakes.
One in particular I shall call the "Catch-22" of social science in
education. It goes as follows: Thou shalt build a program according
to the canons of social science. Whether it is in the early juvenile
delinquency programs, or the community action programs, or in
Head Start, or in Follow Through, or in Title I, thou shalt use the
best social science theory available to construct the parameters of
the program. Then thou shalt evaluate them according to the
canons of social science. And by such canons, applied inappropriately and prematurely, most of these programs immediately failed!
They were evaluated according to the methodological canons of
social science, but without attending very much to whether the
theories were very powerful in the first place. Thus, there were two
errors of social science very early on: First, the theoretical and
empirical bases for the suggested interventions were overtouted;
and second, in the early evaluation of such programs, failure was
claimed where neither success nor failure could reasonably be
concluded. These, I think, are major errors that, although more
prominent in the early days, have dogged our enterprise consistently.

But other parts of the history are stories of extraordinary progress. One such story is the remarkable tale of progress Marilyn Rauth has just told. Let me give another example: our progress in understanding how change occurs in schools. If I had to point to one stream of inquiry that has been broader and may have more lasting effects than any of the others, it is that. It has many strands to it. I note three of them, again by way of example.

The first is in our historical understanding of how our schools have been built and what their purposes have been. I was at a session yesterday in New York City in which many of the powers-that-be in the New York educational scene were considering whether or not it is now time finally to review the great decentralization and community control arrangements in the New York City public schools. I was very struck with Sandra Feldman's insistent plea in that meeting. "Don't do a thing until you've read *The Great School Wars*." No one should ever again try to reform the New York City schools, Feldman said, without reading Diane Ravitch's history of previous efforts at school reform in New York City. We have improved our historical understanding of how things change and improve in our schools.

Second, the literature on implementation, on organizational change and development, which has led to the school improvement emphasis so prominent today, is another broad stream of research that has profoundly changed our understanding of the schools in the last ten to fifteen years. Third, research on implementation has illuminated another related phenomenon: how knowledge is utilized, particularly in the policymaking dimensions that Gordon Ambach has emphasized. We have moved from what seems now to have been a prehistoric process of integrating research into policy through successive stages of development, demonstration, and evaluation, to a much more political and sociological perspective. Consider Carol Weiss's phrases about "knowledge creep" and "decision accretion" as the ways in which knowledge and policy actually interact. Knowledge "creeps up" on policy; policymaking is not a decisive event that throws out an old order of things in some particular area and puts in a new one. Rather, it is an accretion of decisions. A given decision is likely to lie on top of thirty other previous decisions. That is a very different view of how knowledge feeds into the policy process than we had twenty or thirty years ago.

We now understand that knowledge goes into the policymaking process politically, adaptively, gradually, and probably marginally.

There are a number of other areas of our research enterprise in which I think our progress has been substantial. I will just name them for the most part. The teaching of reading in early grades is certainly different today in most classrooms in the United States as a result of what we have learned in the last twenty years. The same is true of writing. We have made tremendous strides, much of it made here at the University of Chicago, in understanding teaching in our classrooms. The Carnegie Forum work in which Lee Shulman is engaged should produce a very important focus and payoff to that research over the next three to four years. I believe we have learned a great deal about desegregation through research, and we certainly have learned a very great deal about testing and about program evaluation. There is little relationship between the way we think about evaluating programs today and the way we thought about evaluating them twenty years ago. Today's way is clearly far more sophisticated and appropriate.

Now a little contemporary perspective. There is, I submit, a new market for information being created by the educational reforms. This suggests why I think "political economy" may be an appropriate metaphor to understand change today. Change is happening on both the demand and the supply side, and past failures can now be located on both sides. That is, there was neither much to ask for nor much produced. I think the two previous speakers have emphasized several points concerning a change in demand. The first is that the profession wants it, to a degree. That is different, in order of magnitude, from the case in the past. In my view, the weakest link in the political chain of support for educational research has been the lack of strong demand for it from the profession. That has clearly changed in the teacher organizations, and in all education organizations. Second, the reforms being talked about for the professionalization of teaching describe teachers as decision makers, as Marilyn Rauth has suggested. This implies a need for a strong and expanding knowledge base.

Third, it is clear in the course of the reform so far that the new policymakers in education simply assume that research will be available. The emphasis, for example, on school improvement strategies in state and local reforms is clearly a product of the wisdom, hopefully not just conventional, that these decision makers received time after time as they sought the best model to use in educational reform. The "local school improvement model" is what they heard, rightly or wrongly (rightly, I trust), from every researcher they talked to, and it is no accident, therefore, that that model is embodied in many of the current reform efforts.

These decision makers value research. You can see it in the National Governors' Association report, in the report of the Committee on Economic Development, and certainly in *A Nation Prepared*. You can see it in the fundamental change in attitude toward the National Assessment of Educational Progress to which Gordon Ambach referred. Twenty years ago, when the assessment was founded, it was set up explicitly so that you could not make comparisons among states, let alone localities or schools. Now states want state-level knowledge on a national comparative basis, and they want to know programmatically what other states are doing. The state policy perspective has turned around altogether. The basic political strategy used to be isolationist: "We'll do best if nobody really knows what we're doing." Today the demand is that information, both intra- and interstate, be fully and freely available so that every state can measure the progress of its reforms. This is a fundamental change in the political attitude toward information among education policymakers.

On the supply side, I have already made my first major point— that researchers are producing a knowledge base in many of the areas that I have discussed. The future of the reforms teems with opportunities for additional contributions with respect to tracking, work-related education, curriculum in the early grades, technology, and the arts—to name just a few of the issues where we know additional knowledge will find ready uses.

Another important point, however, is that the researchers are themselves looking more closely at the field. They are not very good at it yet, but are much better than they were, and much more inclined toward it than they were fifteen or twenty years ago. One reason for this is probably a deserved humility about the likelihood of producing national or systemwide results, given existing methodologies. Part of it, though, is a growing conviction, shared with the world of practice, about where change actually occurs and where the significance of new information is likely to be found. Another part of it has to do with new and more powerful observational methodologies that require researchers to be more often in the field. For whatever reasons, it seems to me researchers have taken themselves much closer to the field. A content analysis of the annual meetings of the American Educational Research Association programs would, I am sure, bear out this finding.

What is missing? Well, to carry the market analogy a bit further, what is missing are market institutions for the transactions between supply and demand. Earlier I said there has been neither much supply nor much demand. It is not, then, very surprising that there were no strong institutions to conduct the transactions. But that is precisely what we need now, and we are beginning to see these institutions emerge. The regional laboratories were supposed to be such institutions. And they have tried to carry on part of that responsibility. But any contemporary analysis of the paths of reform and of policy change indicates that the regional laboratories are simply not situated rightly or correctly in the system. They can make a contribution, but they cannot do the job entirely. I suspect that many of the projects such as those that Marilyn Rauth described are much closer to what we need. I believe that the project Lee Shulman is engaged in, creating a national licensure exam, will become such an institution perforce, because of the magnetic pull it will have on all that we know about education and teaching.

Indeed, it is in this light that I would put efforts such as the Holmes group in its call for reform in the preparation of teachers. Apart from the great controversy about graduate versus undergraduate preparation of teachers, important though that is, the Holmes group, in my view, is concerned with constructing a model for the professional preparation of teachers, and that model is quite consonant with what Marilyn Rauth has been talking about and very consonant with what is being talked about in *A Nation Prepared*. They suggest a model in which the teacher does research, uses research, and acts as a professional decision maker in the classroom. Moreover, in the professional development schools, which the Holmes group proposes, we see another aspect of this model emerging. Professional development schools will be concerned not simply with better clinical training for teachers. They will also be concerned that there be research and assistance for the benefit of the school itself, that there be a mutuality to the relationship rather than simply the school doing the college and profession a favor.

But I would not claim that the process of institutional change is more than just begun in the schools of education, where we must grapple with the kinds of training, incentives, and rewards that would encourage faculty to give such matters high priority among their interests and activities.

The product that we seek is in principle extremely challenging. We seek research that does what research is supposed to do in almost any setting—advance theory, method, and measurement. We also seek research that, without giving up anything qualitatively along those dimensions, will also contribute to practice and to policy. That is a tall order—one we have just begun to fill.